Longing

Longing

Jewish Meditations on a Hidden God

JUSTIN DAVID

CASCADE *Books* · Eugene, Oregon

LONGING
Jewish Meditations on a Hidden God

Cascade Books
An Imprint of Wipf and Stock Publishers
199 W. 8th Ave., Suite 3
Eugene, OR 97401

www.wipfandstock.com

PAPERBACK ISBN: 978-1-5326-3135-1
HARDCOVER ISBN: 978-1-5326-3137-5
EBOOK ISBN: 978-1-5326-3136-8

Cataloguing-in-Publication data:

Names: David, Justin

Title: Longing : Jewish meditations on a hidden God / Justin David

Description: Eugene, OR: Cascade Books, 2017 | Includes bibliographical references.

Identifiers: ISBN 978-1-5326-3135-1 (paperback) | ISBN 978-1-5326-3137-5 (hardcover) | ISBN 978-1-5326-3136-8 (ebook)

Subjects: LCSH: Desire—Religious aspects—Judaism | Desire for God | God (Judaism) | Jewish philosophy | Negative theology—Judaism

Classification: BM610 D184 2018 (paperback) | BM610 (ebook)

Manufactured in the U.S.A.   01/02/18

Contents

Acknowledgments

Thank you to everyone at Cascade Books who brought this book to light. Matthew Wimer and Brian Palmer were exceedingly patient and gracious in giving me the time and space to complete this book in the manner that I needed. I am grateful for the expert editing of Dr. Robin Parry, who shepherded my jumble of thoughts to publication, and the meticulous and beautiful typesetting of Ian Creeger.

Many people have supported me along the journey of this book. It is a great privilege to serve as the Rabbi of Congregation B'nai Israel in Northampton, MA. The CBI community has always challenged me to dig deep and find my rabbinic voice. I hope my CBI friends see some of our many conversations in this book. A special debt of gratitude goes to the Tuesday lunchtime study group—fifteen years and still going strong as we walk ever so slowly on our journey through the Hebrew Prophets!

Rabbi Jeremy Kalmanofsky, Rabbi Nancy Flam, and Rabbi Martin Cohen all provided critical feedback and encouragement for an essay that became the template for this book. Your support and friendship bolstered my confidence to speak personally and authentically.

My dear friend Greg Harris, a master writer, teacher, and editor, read the first chapters I had written and was exceedingly generous with his time and attention. Greg's keen literary instincts and deep menschlikeit persuaded me that I had a project worth pursuing.

There are a number of personal stories in this book and I have changed the names of everyone who interacted with me privately. Nevertheless, I would like to thank a number of longtime friends who continue to teach and inspire me. Dr. Lisa and Ze'ev Kainan, Rabbi Sharon and Or Mars, Debbie Perla and Dr. Ezra Kopelowitz, Dan Schifrin and Abby Friedman, Rabbi Batya Glazer, Rabbi Gil Steinlauf, please accept my humble and deep gratitude.

My brother-in-law and sister-in-law, Adam Wolf and Sumana Coop-pan Wolf, and my wife's parents, Ira and Elaine Wolf, are always sources of loving support. I hope this book opens up new conversations in our shared lifetimes together.

My parents, Rabbi Jo David and Sofer Neil Yerman, profoundly re-oriented their lives when they discovered the beauty of Jewish tradition as adults. I would not have the richness of Torah and Judaism had you not pointed the way.

My wife, Judith Wolf, carefully read the entire manuscript through several drafts and greatly improved on my ideas by contributing her characteristic depth and critical insight.

Judy and our sons, Lior Shalom and Ezra Yosef, are my greatest joy.

Tam ve'nishlam Shevach La'El Boreh Olam
Completed, with gratitude for the Oneness who renews all creation.
27 Iyyar, Day 42 of the Omer, 5777
May 23, 2017
Northampton, MA

Introduction

Every Tuesday at 12:15, for the past fifteen years, I have led an adult study group as the Rabbi of a thoughtful and vibrant congregation in a lovely New England college town. The group started out as a way to engage an outspoken lady with a generous heart. Before my tenure officially began, I was helping movers bring boxes into our new house when this magnanimous woman dropped by and noticed the spacious patio facing the backyard. Surveying the space, she volunteered, "this can be where you have a study group. That's what I need." And so, in part to launch myself as a teacher in my new community and in part to win over a formidable personality, I started my downtown study group.

For three years, we studied Talmud, that engaging, sometimes Byzantine, sometimes maddening collection of discussion, interpretation, and argument at the heart of Jewish tradition. Despite the challenges of the text, the group came alive with vigorous discussion week after week. Nevertheless, I felt ambivalent about our trajectory. The conversation was lively, but not necessarily personal. We spent as much time wrestling with the underlying notions of rabbinic tradition—authority, obligation, and community—as we did with the teachings themselves. After a while, I began to sense that we all needed a change. Our conversations were becoming increasingly abstract, and it seemed that we would generate more juice by looking at texts that could both elicit and frame our personal stories. So in the late spring at the end of our third year together, I proposed that we take a break from the Talmud. Instead, I suggested that we make our way through the Hebrew prophets, beginning at the Book of Joshua, where the Torah leaves off its narrative, and continuing through the famous stories of the Judges that would include Gideon, Jephthah, Samson, and Delilah, and onto the stories the first kings of Israel: Saul, David, and Solomon. We would learn about the first great prophets after Moses, such as Elijah and Elisha, and eventually the great literary prophets Isaiah, Jeremiah, and

Ezekiel. I stressed that the journey through these stories would take years, but along the way, we would confront the perennial questions of God, the Jewish people, belief, the Jewish future, and many more. But instead of facing these riddles as abstractions, we would see them refracted through the eyes of human beings like ourselves.

A palpable, approving sigh went through the room.

The truth was I needed a change as well, as I began to face the vicissitudes of being a congregational rabbi. I had come to the congregation riding a wave and a buzz. Although young, I was not newly minted, but had three successful years cutting my teeth in a large, urban congregation. I brought a needed dose of warmth and spirituality, with just enough experience to pretend like I knew what I was doing. But after a few years, the glow of being the new rabbi, the "young rabbi," was beginning to wear off. My presence was now taken for granted. I had made some difficult and not necessarily popular decisions. I began to wonder, in a new way, how to find satisfaction in this life to which I had dedicated myself. Intellectually, every rabbi knows that real happiness is not found in praise or approval. But the mind has a way of following the ego, and while I would not admit it to myself at the time, I so much wanted and tried so hard to be the epitome of the "good" rabbi, the "warm and caring" rabbi, the "smart" rabbi. I told myself that I was simply being authentically me, but I was also aware that some kind of unrecognized inner striving was wearing me down. I knew that I had to recover an inner dialogue that was true to me, apart from everyone and everything else, in order to achieve a sense of sanctuary and peace.

As if to mirror the changes taking place—in my relationship to the congregation, to myself, and to the texts we studied—the study group also changed. People left, the numbers diminished. It was hard not to experience this natural ebb and flow as a kind of judgment or abandonment. But in time, new people joined, and the group once again grew to a robust size as it found its own groove. The prophetic stories, initially from the books of Joshua, Judges, and the two Books of Samuel and Kings, energized the group with their epic drama, religious charisma, and their confounding portraits of God. The all-too-human heroes, prophets, and kings elicited fresh questions and insights from the group. Seeing these stories through their eyes, I rediscovered my love for the lives, the struggles, and the questions of the Hebrew prophets. Each week generated vibrant conversation as we wedded our personal questions to the themes of prophetic suffering, justice, and redemption. Over time, the group itself developed a new dynamic. We had succeeded in becoming a true chevra, or study partnership, in which we collectively discovered and often created the multiple meanings in these stories.

Together, we wrestled with the question of what a life of holiness really means or feels like. Most of us could articulate some understanding of the importance of moral living and the rituals that awaken our attention to seemingly insignificant moments. But all too often, our efforts to find language for some kind of transcendent spiritual frame, the ability to articulate "what IT all means," fell short. It is easy to understand why. Often, we rely on culturally shared expressions, which being commonly used, feel clichéd: they may generally describe what we feel or aspire to, but without the bite of our specific experiences. The other problem is that, when talking about such heady subjects as the uniqueness of the Jewish God, God's demands of human beings, or the balance of love and justice in the world, it's easy to trail off to abstractions, losing contact with the immediacy of the concrete circumstances of our lives that give rise to these questions in the first place.

By contrast, the prophets address the "big questions" in real time and in personal terms. Hosea, Isaiah, Jeremiah, take your pick, speak with an emotional urgency that grabs you by the collar as if to say, "You self-satisfied, apathetic, narcissistic human being—*wake up!* Take a look at the suffering and pain of the world, of the sorry state of your own soul, and reconsider everything! Turn to a life without pretense, shun all illusion, and turn toward love. And, as you turn toward love, you will be pulled toward a life in pursuit of executing justice and encountering grandeur, helpless to resist."

These are not merely words of imposing moral and spiritual logic; they express a universal set of experiences, conveyed here in the unique key of Judaism's foundation. The prophets, as spokespeople of God to every human soul, convey a connection to mystery, and, conversely, the mystery of connection. We cannot fully account for why people across all cultures sense, against all reason, a reality that lies beyond our daily experience. Just as mysteriously, despite all we know about human behavior and psychology, we cannot explain the impetus behind the human need to love. The great rabbi, scholar, and philosopher Abraham Joshua Heschel spoke of such deep encounters with nature, human beings, and what appears to lie beyond as "sublime" or "holy." He believed the prophets sensed in these moments not a static and entirely random universe, but a cosmic pathos that links God, all creation, and human beings in a shared emotional life. Over years of reflection on both personal triumphs and some heartache, I have come to realize how I, too, have always yearned to experience and understand that web of relationship in all its grandeur and depth.

Over time, the study group grew into a forum in which I puzzled over my own relationships to God and people, and the transcendent reality through which we are all connected. But something else happened that was a complete surprise to me, and brewed for a while without my ever being aware. In addition to becoming part of my story of looking toward Judaism to puzzle over the big existential questions, the group also became a forum in which I, mostly unconsciously, came to make a new peace with the central traumatic event of my own childhood.

My upbringing was shaped by early abandonment and subsequent attempts to make it better. My parents divorced when I was an infant. My mother, nineteen at the time, went to work while my father, a newly minted PhD, spent long days in his lab. I came to live with my grandparents, who raised me until I left for college, visiting with my mother most weekends except for those when I would go with my father. When I was ten, my father, remarried and with a two-year-old, ceased contacting me. While I have lived for the past thirty-five years as a happy, productive, and outgoing person, as if this trauma didn't happen, I always find myself circling back to its undeniable imprint on every aspect of my life.

My family did not provide Judaism as a salve for the instability around me, though I would later seek a refuge within Jewish life, particularly community and study. My home was culturally Jewish but light on any real sense of ritual or textual tradition. Although my family made sure that I knew about great literature, art, and music, my day-to-day pop culture as a child revolved around sitcoms, pop music, and a little sports. The nouveau riche, suburban town I grew up in was a place that valued material comfort over nurturing souls and minds. I always felt out of place. As someone who worked in my childhood synagogue reflected decades later, "If you weren't beautiful or rich, they didn't want you."

Growing up in such an environment, it was either a miracle or inevitable that I would later be drawn to the inwardness of study and prayer. I was always different—studious, curious, creative, and contemplative. As a child, I somehow knew that all the conventions of Hebrew school, despite themselves, expressed something more grand, something that was unseen yet real.

When I began studying the prophets seriously as a rabbinical student, I recognized their righteous anger from my own experience as a child and teen, when I first began to scorn the shallowness and materialism around me. Looking ahead as an adult, I was inspired more by their affirmations of everything that I aspired to: seeking justice and pursuing the care of the Other, upholding the dignity of the outsider and the oppressed, and dedicating oneself to fundamental and abiding love.

As my relationship with the Tuesday study group deepened, I found myself engaging with two distinct and internal voices in our study together. As a rabbi, I reveled in each chapter of the prophets, uncovering hidden meanings in all the things we rabbis look for: connections to other texts;

reflection of historical context; the poetic use of images, particular Hebrew words and phrases; the *middot*, or inner characteristics of the heroes, kings, prophets, and villains. But I also began to listen to the voice of my childhood self that has never given up on searching out a sense of refuge, security, and abiding love.

On the surface, our format was simple: read, pause, and talk. Usually, I would stop the group at a natural break in the text and the conversation would proceed organically. There was never a shortage of what to talk about. Our group included people who channeled their heartache into grievances against God and the very idea of God. There were psychologists who tried to see the balance of the good and the bad in God's frequently authoritarian brand of love. Others drew on their life experience to tease out themes of resilience, justice, fate, and compassion. Each of our sessions left me with more questions than answers.

But sotto voce, I looked to the group to reassure me that I was asking the right existential questions of myself. It was no accident that the group of learners who had organically formed around me was a generation older than me and included many people who shared my interests in music, literature, and other intellectual and cultural pleasures. In a quiet but meaningful way, the members of the group became my "teachers" on a number of levels. In fact, I recognized that with their anti-authoritarian ways and their unconventional spirit, many of the people in the group would have been wonderful parents for me. And so the study experience drew me deeper into a dialectic between different parts of myself. Week to week, I began each session in the role of "rabbi," with a program of study and methods to get at the text. But driving my curiosity was a personal and ongoing search for love and refuge in Jewish tradition that had been with me since the first time I entered a synagogue as a boy. That yearning fueled my quest for insight and shaped the insights themselves. Often, the momentum of the group combined with the words on the page to elicit thoughts about God, Judaism, and spirituality that I never expected.

One moment stood out from all the others. Our group had been reading for weeks from the end of the First Book of Kings and the beginning of the Second Book of Kings about the prophet Elijah and his disciple Elisha, arguably the stars among the early prophets. They are, perhaps, the greatest prophets not to have books of their own. Elijah is the great wonder worker, and his life has a number of parallels to that prophet beyond all prophets, Moses. Elisha follows Elijah dutifully, attending to him and learning from him as they journey around the land of Israel. These are powerful and dramatic stories in which it seems the fate of the Israelite people is on the line all the time. In the presence of Elijah and Elisha, rain comes to slake drought; kingdoms rise and fall; entire populations are delivered from famine; the dead come back to life. Elijah and Elisha are not only vessels through which God communicates with the Israelites; they appear to be the moral and spiritual foundations upon which the people of their day depend for their very lives.

But then Elijah informs Elisha he is about to leave this world and be taken up to heaven. Elisha continues to follow Elijah across the hills of the Judean desert, across the Jordan River and back. The Bible records no special emotion or pathos around these last days of Elijah with Elisha. They both appear completely stoic.

And then, in an instant, Elijah is taken up to heaven—he doesn't die, but he is nevertheless lost to Elisha forever. At the moment of Elijah's ascent, Elisha cries out, "*Avi, Avi*! My father, my father!"

This is one of the few scenes in the entire Bible in which someone calls out in mourning for a dying parent. Except that Elijah isn't really dying, he is not Elisha's father, and Elisha does not really mourn. In this singularly heart-rending and confounding moment, Elisha's cry of "*Avi, Avi*" expresses fundamental yearnings we all share. It is a moment of simultaneously losing and embracing a father, of feeling as a child being abandoned and as an adult coming into maturity, of gratitude to God for a fatherly mentor while protesting the inevitable loss, of seeking connection in this world to the surrogate father and to his being beyond it. Paradoxically, Elisha's loss and abandonment is also the first moment when he can emerge as himself. With Elijah gone, Elisha must come into his own as a mature prophet, literally taking up his mentor's mantle in order to bring healing to the world.

Because of our long-standing, multi-layered trust, the group gave me the space in which to consider all of these ways in which we all may cry "*Avi, Avi*" simultaneously. And with this space, I began to draw out some of the personal dimensions of this moment in Elisha's life. This kind of protest, from the depths of one's soul, I said, was integral to how we relate to God in Jewish tradition. But with a caveat: "*Avi, Avi*," the longing for a parent, is the kind of protest lodged only by someone who has deeply known the blessings of a loving father. Being on the "inside" of Jewish spirituality, then, seems to require that we have had loving parents in order to teach us the ways of love, longing, and protest Elisha embodies. What happens, then, when our loving parents fail? Where do we go to find surrogates for that love? Can we find them in a spiritual life, in God? In the comfort afforded by study? The communion of prayer? The embrace, however imperfect itself, of community? I spoke generally, but was really wondering about myself. The group was generous and patient with me that day.

This moment of unpacking *"Avi, Avi"* lingered in my mind long after that initial session, and I took the time to consider whether my personal questions reflected larger themes in Jewish thought and Jewish tradition. Expressing both his intimacy with and distance from God, Elisha's cry of *"Avi, Avi"* struck me as embodying the classic conundrum of the Jewish God: God is always close and present, like a parent, but also always remote, like a parent in retreat. More generally, Jewish tradition ponders a God whose absence is as much a compelling quality as its presence. For example, while the Torah describes God as "appearing" to Moses at the burning bush, Moses still has to ask, "What is your name?" as if to remind us that God's unlimited power is bound up with God being mysterious and unknowable. God's answer, *"Ehyeh asher ehyeh,"* literally "I will be that which I will be," is cryptic, and does nothing to silence Moses' reluctance to accept his mission. And even after Moses agrees to lead the people in pursuit of this perplexing and elusive God, Moses continues to yearn for God's proximity.[1]

Later in the Exodus narrative, after the crisis of the Israelites constructing and worshipping a golden calf against God's direct commandment, Moses attributes the people's waywardness to the reality of God's distance. And so, in a scene that is a climactic showdown of wills, Moses demands of God, "Show me your glory," in other words, "fully disclose yourself to me." God responds generously but ambivalently, saying, "I will pass all my goodness before you, but you shall only see my back. For no human being shall see my face and live." As a Jew, to live with God is to accept that we may always yearn and try to draw close only to confront the ultimate hiddenness of God.[2]

Elisha's cry of *"Avi, Avi"* translates this theological problem into human terms, expressed as a fundamental and existential longing. Personally, I believe that many of us harbor a version of Elisha's archetypal cry as an ongoing yearning for one, perhaps the One, who is always present yet elusive. It may be a specific longing for a parent, a child, a mentor, or a lover. It may be a more generalized desire for the independence, resolve, and purpose that comes with feeling secure and loved. It may be inchoate and not directed toward anyone or anything.

I believe that whether we are aware of them or not, we play out these longings on multiple stages: our relationships, our work, our families, and our spiritual lives to name a few. But I also believe we marshal these longings to provide the fuel and direction for our spiritual lives. While many of us are happy to see ourselves more generally "spiritual" than particularly

1. Exodus 34.
2. Exodus 33.

"religious," my experience has shown me that the template of Jewish life—
texts, traditions, rituals, communal engagement—offers fertile ground for
exploration. The biblical and talmudic stories of Jewish tradition set the
stage for us, giving us a God who is the One who is most real and yet most
elusive and hidden. Like all stories and texts in our tradition, engaging with
Elisha's story draws us into a continual dialectic. We may begin by recognizing our yearnings in this story, and so acquire an expanded vocabulary with
which to reflect. As we reflect on the story with our personal questions, we
almost rewrite it, inserting ourselves as actors in the ancient biblical narrative. Engaging in this back and forth again and again over time transforms
our first reading of the story into a journey. That journey may or may not
take us to God, but Jewish tradition is much more interested in us being part
of the story than arriving at its conclusion.

In this book, I invite us to live with the existential challenge inherent
in Elisha's cry of *"Avi, Avi"*: to uncover our longings for closeness against
the inevitability of loss and abandonment, and in doing so to wrestle with
Judaism's notion of a hidden God as a means to develop a sense of spiritual
closeness. I have an open-ended view of what this means. For some of us,
spiritual closeness is found in what Freud called an "oceanic feeling," of being swallowed up in the reality of God. Some of us may find the traditional
Jewish paths to God through ritual, study, and acts of kindness to be suffi-
cient, with or without some kind of numinous experience. The path of social
justice, whether through direct action, advocacy, community organizing, or
some other mechanism, may be the foundation of our spirituality. And at
times, the workings of the rational mind may bring us to the level of insight
we find most authentic, allowing that reason may bring us more often to
confusion rather than certainty. There are certainly innumerable paths to
God that I have not recounted here, and I would not privilege one over the
other. In fact, I would imagine many of us drift among the various modali-
ties I've mentioned above. I certainly have, and my goal in this book is to
welcome us to experiment and explore. But the common factor among all of
the above responses, I believe, is a sense of longing. Which is to say, I believe
we all harbor a desire for something that we wish to have in our lives that we
know may be ultimately unattainable.

Although my experience with an estranged father forms the narrative thread of this book, my own story is only an illustration of a dynamic
between human beings and a hidden God that is as old as Jewish tradition
itself. While a timeless struggle, it is also an urgent and current one. I believe
that a thoughtful, nuanced, yet emotionally resonant discourse about God is
much needed in our time. All too often, I encounter people who are alienated from religion because of all of the violence and oppression done in the

name of God. Others simply are fed up with the social pettiness that can sometimes accompany religious life in community. However, both camps overlook the fact that dissatisfaction often drives spiritual seeking in the first place. Don't the varieties of disillusionment represent a kind of longing? Perhaps by casting our contemporary misgivings on the canvas of Jewish tradition, we can reclaim some of that authentic seeking for ourselves. As a rabbi trained to respect the power of dialogue, I believe that renewed conversations about God, both internal and with each other, can bring us unforeseen gifts both individually and collectively.

This book advances an argument from experience, namely, that living in the lonely space created by a seemingly absent God helps us foster the spiritual closeness we all need. If we have felt the closeness of God, whether directly or by naming an experience as such, we know the impact these moments have on our lives. But there is also much to be learned from those times when we feel alone. I have alluded to how I have arrived at this exploration through reflecting on how my own life was shaped by my father's abandonment. People often assume that because I am a rabbi, I have a deeply personal belief in God, that I believe God is present and interacting with me each day. But that has never been the case. At my core, I cling to an abstract, de-personalized view of God. One day, when having lunch with a mentor, I wondered out loud if I resisted a personal God because I did not have a meaningful experience of a loving father.

Eighteen years later (a "life" in Jewish tradition), I have a little more perspective on this question, having confronted my father, and, perhaps most importantly, experienced deep closeness of my own. I have also invested time and energy in studying the texts of Jewish tradition, allowing them to shape and challenge me. While my own personal belief is closest to that of Moses Maimonides, who claimed that God's lack of form rendered all description meaningless, I am nevertheless drawn to the God of experience who is revealed in moments of awe and intimacy. I do not have any kind of static "belief in God," but rather, I move back and forth across different understandings and experiences day to day as my life changes.

In addition to setting my story and that of Elisha as frames to explore our personal longings, I also look to the mystical trajectory of sixteenth-century Lurianic Kabbalah to give this book a sense of scope and perspective. While this reference may seem esoteric to someone encountering it for the first time, I hope it is an accessible and meaningful way to think of the ongoing dynamism in our world and our spiritual lives. At the risk of oversimplifying, the Lurianic arc is a three-fold pattern of stages: *tzimtzum* (withdrawal), *shevirat ha-kelim* (shattering of the vessels), and *tikkun* (restoration). Originally, these terms describe the stages of creation of the cosmos, but have come to be seen as metaphors in the ongoing evolution of a person's interior life.

Tzimtzum refers to God's initial act of withdrawal into the Divine Self so as to create the negative space in which the universe could exist. As a result, like a balloon filled with too much air, God could not hold all of the divine energy, so God "burst," as it were, and the "shards" of the original divine being became the stuff out of which the universe was created. *Tikkun*, a term that may be more familiar, refers to the process by which each person releases the "light" from the "shards" of creation through acts of kindness and spiritual devotion, thereby restoring the universe and God to its original and unified wholeness. Thus, we have the ubiquitous phrase, "*Tikkun Olam*," a vision of a universe that has been healed through our actions. On a personal level, we may experience variations of all three of these stages: *tztimtzum*, or moments of withdrawal into solitude and isolation, *shevirat ha-kelim*, or breaking the vessels of our assumptions and tired ways of being, yielding ultimately to *tikkun*, a restoration of wholeness and peace. We may experience these as a gradual ebb and flow or suddenly and unpredictably, or we may not have any idea if this framework bears any relationship to our actual experience. But maybe the vocabulary can prove useful in naming episodes from our past or perhaps our future.

In this book, I begin by personalizing the experience of "*tzimtzum*," or withdrawal. When have we experienced a fundamental sense of absence, and how have we, in turn, isolated ourselves? In this sense, our own "*tzimtzum*," may refer not only to God's remoteness, but our acts of alienating ourselves from other people or from the whole enterprise of Judaism and a spiritual life. Of course, it could refer to isolation that is sprung upon us, absolutely no fault of our own. For me, the "shattering of the vessels" encapsulates a period of creative destruction that is a common and perhaps necessary feature of our personal lives and contemporary religious life in general. While I have had many such periods, my first was probably my time in college when I became aware of the trauma of my early life and at the same time was reevaluating my views of God and Judaism. While daunting and painful at times, it can be an enormously creative process of reflection and discovery, as "shattering the vessels" compels us to entertain new modes of understanding and action. That something new, for me and for all of us, is *tikkun*: making peace, moving on, and incorporating a personal sense of Jewish meaning into a life of service to others. For a first-time reader, these ideas might take some getting used to, but it's my belief that all great religious ideas are basically simple. So if I have done my job, Luria's ideas will illumine and not confound.

While this book tells my spiritual story so as to elucidate powerful and sometimes contradictory Jewish ideas, I also hope to issue an invitation to my generation of Jews, Generation X and younger, to consider the depth of Jewish tradition and community as our existential questions take on more weight as we proceed further into middle age. I am concerned that we have not created a compelling collective story, and so are missing an important tool with which to understand ourselves and our lives. Our grandparents' generation lived lives we could only imagine: they fled Europe, the Middle East, and North Africa, scraped through the Depression, fought World War II and helped build (sometimes literally) the State of Israel. Along the way, they also created synagogues, Jewish Community Centers, Hillel, Brandeis University, Jewish camps, basically the entire infrastructure of the American Jewish community.

Our parents' generation, some of whom comprise the alternately adored and reviled Baby Boomers, softened the conformist edges of their parents, and by doing so transformed the existing Jewish infrastructure. Boomers have given us feminism, spirituality, and organizational change. They have placed *Tikkun Olam* at the center of the agenda of American Jews, and their general political liberalism has broadened the conversation about the Jewish people and the role of Israel. They have introduced new rituals, new ways of being Jewish, and generally created more realistic expectations for their communal leaders.

What will be the lasting statement of Generation X and the generations who come after us? Studies show that, unlike our predecessors, the Baby Boom generation, we appear less inclined to reinvent Jewish life than to opt out. Perhaps more importantly, we have yet to define our generational narrative. While many cataclysmic events have occurred in our adulthood (the fall of Communism, genocide in Bosnia, the trauma of 9/11, two wars in Iraq and one in Afghanistan, mass incarceration, the unraveling of a social safety net, globalization, climate change, a new understanding of institutionalized racism, and now an unanticipated presidency), we have not galvanized ourselves to articulate a collective response.

Then again, not having a single, identifiable generational narrative may suggest its own kind of identity. I would assert that one aspect of the Gen X worldview may be to embrace that very feeling of outsider-ness, that sense of dislocation and loneliness, and to draw on that experience as a lens through which to see ourselves amid the depth of Jewish thought and spirituality. As a people, we are, after all, wanderers in the desert.

My interest in Elisha stems from the way in which Jewish tradition looks back to the prophets, those original outsiders, in every generation. In the Hebrew Bible, our prophets came on the scene to stir the people, against the grain, to draw close to God through moral action and reverence for the source of creation. This prophetic perspective thus came to infuse the bulk of the Hebrew Bible and subsequent Jewish tradition as each new historical period sought to recapture the *ruach ha-kodesh*, the spirit of holiness, charisma, and moral authority of the prophets. In turn, the Talmud re-imagines the prophetic role as that of the rabbis, the master teachers of both written and oral Torah. In the Middle Ages, Moses Maimonides asserts that philosophy has claimed the prophetic mantle. The mystics of the Zohar in the thirteenth century see the words of the prophets as encoding the creation of the universe.

In modern history, the prophets have been the touchstone for those seeking to revive the spiritual and moral voice of Jewish tradition. The Reform Movement in America asserted the supremacy of the prophets over rabbinic tradition in order to establish a new kind of Judaism for a new land. At around the same time in late nineteenth-century Palestine, Jewish pioneers followed suit, absorbing the almost seismic resonances of the prophets to imagine an enlightened, just, universalist, and pluralistic Jewish society in the land of its birth. As Hitler launched his plan to conquer Europe and annihilate its Jews, a very young man breaking away from his provincial hasidic household wrote a PhD thesis for the University of Berlin on the psychological and spiritual experience of the prophets. Almost thirty years later, that young man, Abraham Joshua Heschel, was propelled by his prophetic sense of justice to forge a friendship and alliance with Dr. Martin Luther King, thereby establishing the pursuit of social justice as the cornerstone of American Judaism.

As a generation born around the time when Heschel and King met, we have both an opportunity and a responsibility to renew our connection to this potent ground of inspiration and wisdom. It doesn't matter how much we know or don't know, whether we opt in or opt out. We live in a world of violence and generations of broken promises, both here in North America and in Israel. We have not been compelled to serve, or, finding service repugnant, to rebel. We have been left to our own devices to choose our commitments. Since we have the opportunity to choose, I would follow the example of my teenage rabbi by encouraging us to learn about our tradition so as to understand that being on the outside gives us a special way in. And that once we have gotten a taste of the dialectical belonging and independence of thought Judaism asks of us, we will want to drink more deeply from this well.

More specifically, I hope that a consideration of Elisha, and his relationship to a remote God, offers a window onto the possibilities of a contemporary Jewish spiritual and ethical life for us all. Like Elisha, we have inherited narratives from previous generations, and have been left to puzzle whether or not they are our own. This particular and peculiar story speaks to my experience of recovering a sense of purpose and transcendence in a world of abandonment and confusion. We all suffer, and so this book invites us to consider the ways in which suffering provokes both the doubt and the yearning that helps us heal ourselves and this world. As Elisha's moment of crying *"Avi, Avi"* implies, there is no cure for suffering, no assurance that the pain of this world will be magically soothed. We live with paradox, fear, and uncertainty. But walking in the footsteps of Elisha does give us one bit of assurance—that there is "something" there, a "something" worth walking towards, becoming a part of, wrestling with, yelling at, and loving, even if that "something" is usually manifest as absence or veiled in loss.

And so, this book is a *midrash*, an interpolation of a moment in the biblical text as it intersects with human experience, a moment that weaves Jewish ideas, my personal life, and universal experiences. As I share my own experience, I tell my story not as a memoir, but as an illustration of a pursuit as seemingly futile and unattainable as closeness to God, but that nevertheless gives us wisdom and depth along the way. My experience is less important than the common struggles and questions that animate it. Tracing the echoes of Elisha's longing cry of "Avi, Avi" throughout my life, I hope to illumine for others a bit of what I believe we all share: the roots of sadness and disappointment, a yearning for connection, and hope in the prospect of inner resilience and human community. And, as befits Jewish teaching, I hope a reader will come away with more questions than answers.

Part 1

Beginnings

The Loss and Inauguration of Elisha the Prophet

2 Kings 2:1–15

(1) When God was about to take up Elijah to heaven in a whirl-wind, Elijah and Elisha journeyed from Gilgal. (2) Elijah said to Elisha, "Please stay here, for Adonai has sent me to Beit El. Elisha said, "As God lives and as you live, I will not abandon you," and they went down to Beit El. (3) Disciples of the prophets of Beit El went out to Elisha and said to him, "Do you not know that today God will take your master from you?" And he said, "I surely know. Be silent."

(4) Elijah said to him, "Elisha, please stay here, for God has sent me to Jericho." Elisha said, "As God lives and as you live, I will not abandon you," and they arrived at Jericho. (5) Disciples of the prophets approached Elisha in Jericho and they said to him, "Do you not know that today God will take your master from you?" Elisha said, "I surely know. Be silent."

(6) Elijah said to him, "Please stay here, for God has sent me to the Jordan." He said, "As God lives and as you live, I will not abandon you," and they walked on together. (7) Then fifty men from among the Disciples of the prophets followed and stood opposite them from a distance, and the two of them stood by the Jordan. (8) Elijah took his mantle, rolled it up and struck the water, dividing it evenly in two, so that they both crossed over on dry ground. (9) As they were crossing, Elijah said to Elisha, "Ask what I shall do for you before I am taken from you." Elisha said, "May a double portion of your spirit be upon me." (10) He said, "You have asked something difficult. If you see me as I am taken from you, it will be so. And if not, it will not be so." (11) As they were walking and speaking with each other, there was a chariot of fire, and horses of fire. They separated the two of them and raised Elijah to heaven in a whirlwind. (12) Elisha saw it, and he cried out, *"Avi, Avi!* My father, my father! Chariot of Israel and its horsemen!" And then he saw no more. He grabbed his garments and rent them in two strips.

(13) He raised the mantle of Elijah which had fallen from him, and returned and stood on the bank of the Jordan. (14) He took the mantle of Elijah which had fallen from him and struck the water and said, "Where is Adonai, the God of Elijah?!" And even he, as he struck the water, divided it evenly in two and Elisha crossed over. (15) The Disciples of the prophets at Jericho saw him from a distance and said, "The spirit of Elijah has come to rest upon Elisha!" And they came to greet him, and they bowed low to the ground in front of him.

Chapter 1

Pulling Away

The beginning of a spiritual life may be a vague but abiding yearning. For every insight or bit of knowledge we may glean through reflection, meditation, prayer, study, or a meaningful experience, we are intrigued even more by what remains hidden. It may seem absurd, even Kafkaesque, to devote ourselves to a hidden reality that rarely shows its face, but in a spiritual life, concealment is actually its own reward and pleasure. This has been my particular experience in my own spiritual exploration and pursuit of Jewish life, and in sharing these thoughts I am echoing the great Hasidic master from the nineteenth century, Rabbi Nachman of Bratslav.

In his introduction to his definitive work, *Likkutei MoHaRaN*, which means the Gleanings of Our Teacher Rebbe Nachman, he declares, "Behold, for the Holy One has given you a great treasure. Things that reside at the heights of the universe!" Treasure, of course, is often buried, and who among us can find the heights of the universe? Spiritual insights are deep because they are hidden, clothed in a new form, and as such are both understood and obscured: ". . . by way of limitations and ongoing distillation from above to below, from the supernal intelligence to the lower intelligence, until it is cloaked in the garments, the thoughts of our Sages."[1]

And yet, even in their concealed state, spiritual insights may change our lives:

> Each and every teaching (Torah) that was revealed to the "trea-
> sured people," all were filled with wondrous insights for true
> service of the exalted Creator . . . to rouse the slumbering and

1. Nachman of Bratslav, *Likkutei MoHaRaN*, 3.

17

wake those who sleep, . . . to release from prison those who
dwell in darkness, . . . to return them to God in truth and on
a clear path, set out before them, along the path walked by our
ancestors forever.[2]

However, the nature of these discoveries is that, whatever we think we
have grasped, there is always more to know:

Behold, even though these matters are revealed and understood
a bit through the meaning of their words, nevertheless there
is more within them . . . for there is still inwardness in these
matters, locked up and sealed beyond everything. For they are
matters that the Ancient of Days concealed. That require being
concealed and revealed. In order to bring into this world. For
that which is concealed is that which is revealed.[3]

When we seek to know with a knowledge that springs from our sense
of awe and wonder, we can anticipate the delight and surprise of discovery.
But the more profound that discovery, the more we will feel the elusiveness,
the "hiddenness," of that which we seek.

Beresheet—A First, Wondrous Word

I trace my own spiritual life to my teenage years, when the Torah came alive
for me with its first word, "*Beresheet*." Actually, more had come alive for
me already, but that first word, "*Beresheet*," represented the excitement of
knowing and not knowing at the same time. I had just returned from my
first trip to Israel, a six-week tour during which I fell for the country, its
landscape, language, and culture. I felt passionate emotional stirrings—for
connection to the Jewish past and present; for spiritual connection, friendships, and romance—they were all tied in the same bundle. Later, I would
come to name these stirrings as "*hitlahavut*," literally "being on fire," a condition of soul described in the literature of Jewish mysticism, particularly
the Hasidic masters beginning in the eighteenth century. I would return to
this feeling again and again in the years ahead to reinvigorate my spiritual
life, confirm its authenticity, and continue to explore new dimensions of
wonder. But for now, it was simply a newfound feeling of love, enthusiasm,
and curiosity. As a "welcome home" present to help guide me on what they
anticipated would be my new path, my mother and stepfather gave me a
humash, a bound version of the Torah with commentary, knowing I should

2. Ibid.
3. Ibid.

have something to build on after this experience. I opened the cover and, as is the custom, there is the first word, printed in bold and enlarged block letters in Hebrew—*Beresheet*.

At the time, I had no idea what the word meant out of context, but seeing it right there, at the beginning, with the special typography, I immediately understood that this was the word that was translated as "In the beginning." But with my newfound passion and excitement, I invested the word "*Beresheet*" with much more. Given the vastness of what I had experienced over the previous six weeks, I had to believe that vastness was contained in the first word of the Torah that started it all. At the very least, it struck me that where English began the Torah translation with multiple words, the original Hebrew packed it into one. If the Hebrew could condense all of that meaning—not only the extra words but the beginning of the cosmos—into one word, then "*Beresheet*" had to mean something infinitely more than the prosaic "In the beginning." Perhaps the word was ultimately inscrutable, its meaning undone in the attempt to express everything. In a very personal, private way, I had the sense that this one word was calling me on, inviting me to delve deeper into the mysteries of holy teaching, but only through hints and signs. I knew almost no Hebrew, I had no tools to parse the grammar or understand this evocative word in its literary or historical context, but I had an inchoate sense that it was beckoning, showing me everything and hiding everything at the same time.

As an adult, my spiritual life has entailed acquiring and refining the skills to analyze Hebrew text on multiple levels, from the hidden meanings buried in grammatical subtleties to the mystical implications of each letter. And as my learning has deepened, the mystery of spiritual beginnings, contained in the word *Beresheet*, has become both more revealed and more concealed. The dialectic of gathering the tools to know, but ultimately reaching the place of not knowing, was something I encountered the first time I tried to read a traditional commentary, in Hebrew, on this first word of the Torah. I was twenty-two, in a bookstore in the ultra-Orthodox *Meah Sha'arim* section of Jerusalem. This was a time of new beginnings, spiritual and otherwise. I was traveling with my fiancée, Judy, and upon returning home from Jerusalem we would move in together. Having been to Israel before, when I was fifteen, I now felt that something real and palpable was taking root within me—a desire to learn, to draw closer. In my last year or so of college, I felt new stirrings about wanting to become a rabbi, and so I had learned some Hebrew, taken some classes, and read a lot of Jewish books. On this short trip, I made a lifelong friend, an Israeli with profound religious roots, who inspired and challenged me and suggested I check out this one particular bookstore.

In the store, I opened a *Mikra'ot Gedolot*, a traditional commentary covering the entire Hebrew Bible that arranges canonical scholars and traditional text on the same page, as if they are having a dialogue with each other over a millennium. Picking up this book for the first time with the intention of studying it, if only for a moment, I felt as if I were entering this timeless conversation. I'd studied enough Hebrew at this point to understand the first few words of Rashi, the great Rabbi Shlomo ben Yitzchak, who lived in eleventh-century France, whose commentary usually appears on the inside column as a gloss on the words of the Torah. I only needed those first few words to deepen my sense of awe and wonder at the word *Beresheet*.

The Torah Never Means What It Says

A great teacher of mine quipped that "The Torah never means what it says," and any lifelong student of the Torah will admit that is true, albeit sometimes in more modified and pious language. The eleventh-century French scholar Rashi is perhaps the most well-known author who shows how this is the case with each line, word, and sometimes letter of the Torah. While the details about Rashi's life are more bound up in myth than confirmed by evidence, his popular biography says a lot about how Judaism classically views a spiritual life as revering the old while seeking out the new at the same time.

Both of these strains come together in Rashi's opening words to his commentary on the Torah. Reflecting on the meaning of the word "*Beresheet*," Rashi pays tribute to a teacher in writing, "Rabbi Yitzchak says . . . ." One traditional assumption is that this "Rabbi Yitzchak" is Rashi's father, who according to legend was a humble winemaker. As the name Rashi is actually an acronym for "Rabbi Shlomo ben Yitzchak," the tradition may be historically accurate. However, the tradition concerning Rabbi Yitchak may be just a long-repeated assumption. The midrash, which predates Rashi by at least 800 years, quotes a rabbinic sage named Rabbi Yitzchak who advances a rather novel idea about the Torah itself. Rashi then draws upon this Rabbi Yitzchak in his own commentary on the beginning of Genesis.

In this first comment, Rashi learns from "Rabbi Yitzchak" that the Torah did not need to begin with the account of creation, but rather the first actual commandment in the Torah in the book of Exodus: God's instruction to Moses about a new calendar, a new way of sanctifying time, and the Passover sacrifice that would be the Israelites' prelude to liberation from Egypt. It's a great insight, but it is actually found much earlier than Rashi's day in the classic collection of *midrashim*, Rabbinic interpretations of the

Torah, that predates Rashi by about 800 years. As a scholar with an encyclopedic knowledge of the sayings of his rabbinic forbears, it is plausible that Rashi would have known this *midrash* directly from its source. Ultimately, we do not know if Rashi is drawing on an earlier source that he knew or if he is in fact quoting his own father. But it is telling that Jewish tradition favors the theory that Rashi, in his first comment on Genesis, invokes the relationship between parent and child to inaugurate the reader into a deeper understanding of Torah.

At the age of twenty-two in that bookstore in Jerusalem looking at the beginning of the Torah with Rashi's commentary, I was taking a decisive step into this world of wonder and discovery for the first time. On that first word, *Beresheet*, Rashi reflects,

> Rabbi Yitzchak said, "The Torah could have begun with 'This month for you shall mark the beginning of months' (Exodus 12:1), which is the first commandment with which Israel was commanded. And so, what is the reason the Torah begins with the word, '*Beresheet*'?"

As mentioned before, Rashi is delving into the nature of Torah itself. If Torah were merely a book of sacred instructions, it should have begun with the first true commandment in the Torah, addressed to Moses, Aaron, and the people as a whole. This occurs not even in the book of Genesis itself, but in Exodus, as God is preparing to free the people from slavery in Egypt. By orienting Moses and Aaron to the cycle of the moon, they are being directed to a new mode of marking and sanctifying time, and therefore a new stage in their knowledge of themselves, of God, and their destiny in history. But the Torah does not begin here. It begins at the beginning of time itself, and in a manner that invites us to consider our most fundamental, existential questions.

In the bookstore, I didn't read on past this original question, because I couldn't. I needed more Hebrew. I could have found a copy of Rashi in English and read his commentary, but I preferred to wait until I could encounter his words in the original, happy to live with his meaning concealed in the meantime.

Nevertheless, that one question filled me at the time with an urgent sense of curiosity. If I could put my wonder at this statement into words, it would go something like this, "If the Torah did not need to begin with *Beresheet*, the beginning of the universe, what would better capture a sense of beginning—whether for the universe, for humanity, for me? What is a beginning anyway? What is the source, the foundation, of Torah, of all that is worthy of being known? Where does the animating essence of this world come from?" All contained in these first several words of Rashi, these were not purely rational, philosophical, or scientific questions for me. When I read these words from eleventh-century France, I felt, and still feel, as if Rashi is drawing out from some hidden part of me the basic questions I have at the root of my deepest self, stripped away from everything, in complete isolation: "What is my basic foundation? What is there at all?"

A few years later, I had learned enough Hebrew to read and understand Rashi's entire comment in the original Hebrew. And now, more than twenty-five years later, I still find that Rashi's comment on that first word of *Beresheet* contains some of the most basic questions that animate a lifelong sense of wonder.

> This verse calls out, "Explain me!" As our Sages explained, "God created the world for the sake of the Torah, which is called, 'The Beginning (*resheet*) of God's path' (Proverbs 8:22) . . . ." And if you should explain the verse according to its plain meaning, this is how you should explain it: "At the beginning of the creation of heaven and earth, when the earth was unformed and void, and darkness (was on the face of the deep), God said, 'Let there be light.'" For the scripture did not come to teach us the order of creation, to say that these came before these. For if it had come to teach this, it should have been written, "At the very beginning (*barishonah*) God created the heavens . . . ." For there is no *"resheet"* in Scripture that is not joined to the word that follows it. . . . Here, similarly, you should say as if it were, "In the Beginning of God's creation . . . ." And if you should say that (*Beresheet*) came to teach that these were the beginning of all that was creation, and that its interpretation is, "In the Beginning of Everything God created these . . . ," you should be astonished at yourself, for indeed, the waters came first . . . but the Torah had not yet revealed when the waters were created . . . .[4]

I found that the basic insights in Rashi's long *Beresheet* comment are intuitive to anyone who has watched a wound heal, a new leaf appear in springtime, or a new dawn break. Each beginning is part of a chain of ongoing beginnings, and so the word *Beresheet* points us to something, "a" beginning, while denying us the possibility of knowing everything about the beginning of our universe. Drawing on the intricacies of Hebrew grammar, Rashi demonstrates that the first word of the Torah cannot describe any absolute "beginning." If it did, the first word of the Torah would have to be

4. Rashi on Genesis 1:1.

a different word entirely, *"ba-rishonah,"* literally, "at the head," and not the word we have, *"Beresheet."*

Instead, as Rashi shows, the word *Beresheet* is one half of a compound form, referring to a beginning of something and not The Beginning of Everything. The first letter in *Beresheet* is the preposition *"b,"* which means "in" or "at," but most definitely does not take the direct object marker that would mean "the," as in *"the* beginning." Next is *"resheet,"* which means "beginning of . . ." again, without the kind of direct object marker that proclaims "this is the one and only beginning of everything!" Taken together, the word *Beresheet* cannot stand by itself to provide the definitive moment in time when everything comes into being. Instead, it introduces some kind of "beginning of" something, but not the first and certainly not the last. In contemporary, critical editions, *Beresheet* is usually translated as "When God began to create the heavens and the earth . . . ."

By debunking our expectation of reading "In the beginning," Rashi implies that creation is a *process*, and not something that starts or ends at a specific point. And so, to the extent that *"Beresheet"* alludes to any kind of "beginning," it is but one beginning amid a series of beginnings. In this vein, a famous *midrash* teaches that before our universe was created, countless others were created and destroyed.

In keeping with Rabbi Nachman of Bratslav's teaching, all that is revealed actually conceals something else. While we may all be tempted to see in *Beresheet* an orderly recounting of the creation of the world, the elegance of this first chapter of Genesis conceals other elements central to creation. Rashi points out that their bias toward order should produce an "astonishing" question, namely, why is there water in the first verse before the Torah tells us that God created it? While interesting from the point of view of the text, Rashi's insight is actually a deeper challenge. In illuminating our bias to perceive the apparent order of the world, Rashi's comment suggests that there is always something missing in our understanding, something more to be known, however much we believe is revealed.

So our beginning is, as our tradition imagines it in so many forms, the middle of a process, part of an unfolding of countless worlds both known and unknown.

What is true with the cosmos in this regard is true with respect to human beings, and Torah study invites us to consider ever-deepening questions about ourselves, the universe, God, and the unknown. In this vein, I believe that each of us has a personal, spiritual *Beresheet*, a point of contact with our own experience that reveals and conceals, giving us a glimpse of who we are while challenging us with questions about who we can become.

My Spiritual Beginning

I discovered the word *"Beresheet"* as well as my own personal *"Beresheet"* at the same time in my life. I was almost sixteen and it was a time of teenage discoveries as I delighted in new passions, deepening friendships, and an emerging sense of purpose. But for all my wonder and joy, I knew that, in order to emerge into this newly mature and unknown self, I had to confront a specter of loneliness in my life.

My parents divorced when I was an infant, my mother all of nineteen with just a semester of college behind her, and my father a new PhD with responsibilities to his work and his lab. To live close to work, and to give her a sense of her own life, my mother took an apartment in New York City while I lived with my grandparents on Long Island. My mother had custody, so I saw her more often than my father as she visited with me most weekends, but I also visited with my father. I adjusted well as a boy—I got good grades in school, I had friends—enough to keep sadness and pain at bay most of the time. By the time I was a teenager, I embraced my difference as something positive, a feature of prized non-conformity that helped me see the world differently. I liked seeing the world differently—through the prisms of art, music, and literature, big questions and challenging ideas.

For reasons that were never made clear to me at the time, my father cut off all contact with me when I was ten years old after spending a winter vacation together. I knew there was a custody battle going on, and that my father was petitioning to have me live with him, even though I was content to stay with my grandparents. There was behind-the-scenes animosity between my father and mother, but my father and I enjoyed only warm and loving moments. I never expected to be cut off so abruptly.

There was nothing in my early life to suggest that my father would have abandoned me. From my earliest memories, he was gentle, decent, and kind. If anything, our relationship blossomed during the three years before my father's absence. I was eight when he and my stepmother, Lauren, had Max. For both my father and me, Max's birth represented a fresh chance to capture a renewed sense of wholeness. As an only child of divorced parents, I had always yearned for a sibling, never believing it was possible. During the pregnancy, I remember expressing to my father how I was looking forward to being a "half brother." My father, in his gentle and instructive way, corrected me: I would be a "brother," not just a "half." I believe that, as much as I wanted to be a brother, my father wanted me to be one even more.

When my father introduced me to Max as a newborn, the three of us were alone. We were silent, and my father was beaming, basking in the miracle of new life and also in the wordless transformation of a father and his two sons into a family. As a father myself, I have known countless moments like this, filled with joy and great humor. If anything, they can become so pedestrian that it is easy to overlook them. But this was my father's first moment of happiness with his two sons. It must have been precious to him. It was a feeling that now, I would call holy: intensely quiet, intimate, supremely happy, and timeless.

In the years after Max was born, there were more frequent visits, now augmented by sleepovers, a month of a summer. My father, Lauren, Max, and I shared many happy moments, and I can honestly say that I came to love my father. I felt his love as well, through his attention, the wholesome outings he planned, the way he read to me at night and shared his quirky sense of humor.

Things were so good that my father filed for primary custody, and he had every reason to do so. While I will never know for sure, I sense that my father felt as if he was finally coming into his own. For years, my father abided by a custody arrangement that was a fabrication—while my mother was my guardian, I lived with my grandparents. My father claimed, truthfully, that my mother actually resided at her apartment in Manhattan and visited me on Long Island on weekends. She was acting like the non-custodial parent while he, in fact, lived a life in a stable, intact nuclear family. As a father now, I can only admire his effort. He took a stand to give his son the nurturing and the constancy he thought I lacked. On paper, he should have won the custody suit. Except, I had no desire to go live with my father. According to the protocol at the time, my wishes meant a lot to the family-court judge. Reading through the official testimony almost thirty years later, I saw confirmation of what I knew long ago. The judge believed that, as a "well adjusted" boy of ten, I could advocate for my best interests. My father lost. I was relieved. Looking back, I can only imagine how demoralized and angry he was.

Shortly after my father's suit was dismissed, I stayed with my father, Lauren, and Max over a ten-day vacation. It was uneventful, which means that it was warm and loving. But afterwards I simply didn't hear from my father. A week turned into a month, six months, a year, multiple years. My father never gave me an explanation, never declared that our relationship was over. In the first year, he sent me a few letters, but I never looked at them. I was afraid of what might be inside. Day to day, my life went on, and I was happy in school, with friends, and with my daily routine. As long as I didn't have to face my father and his discontent, my world would continue undisturbed.

Those letters are lost, and to this day I don't know what was inside them. Then, as now, I imagined that they express the sense of loss and disappointment that my father experienced. Thirty-five years removed from the experience, I can understand and empathize with my father's feelings, or at least what I imagine them to be. But at ten, they were simply frightful, and so I found it easier to avoid reading those letters. I suppose that, as my father withdrew from me, I withdrew from him. As I later came to embrace the mystical idea that God's first act in creation was to "withdraw into God's self," I wonder if my own willing estrangement at ten years old was the real beginning of my spiritual life.

Turning my back, living my life without any reaching back, was a means to sustain the blow of my father showing he didn't love me anymore, or so I thought. I convinced myself that it was a relief not to have him—to be unburdened by the expectation of loving him. I found, without any surprise, that I could move on, finding success as a good student, a passable athlete, a hard working and all around good kid. As the years went on, I lived happily. I thrived in every way as a teen. Although there were moments when my father's absence felt like an aching, lingering darkness, I rarely felt acutely sad. And yet, from time to time I knew, consciously, that I was confronting an impossible choice: distance myself from my father in order to live my own life, or face him, for no other reason than a son is not supposed to let go of his father.

Confronting My Father, Facing the Truth

Shortly before I was sixteen, after that summer in Israel, I acted on these contradictory impulses of anger and love by calling my father and inviting him to dinner. In my own mind, our years of separation had made me powerful. If anything, I felt that my own emotional withdrawal from my father made me more independent, and therefore stronger than I otherwise would have been. Convinced of my own invincibility, our meeting was to be an exercise of power. I knew and was proud of my own inner strength. I was a musician, rooted in the exploration and insights of the soul. Feeling my own depth of personhood, I drew my strength from the intuitive self-knowledge that I had a mind and heart that could feel deeply. My body, too, was surging, its own reminder of burgeoning power. In my mind at the time, my father was ancillary to my well being. When we met, I would demand to know where my father had been all these years and what he had been thinking. And whatever his response, I would claim the ultimate victory in the conviction that my life of resilience and purpose was the counterpoint to his weakness.

But when I spoke with my father on the phone to set up our meeting, his familiar qualities of gentleness and intelligence disarmed me. I experienced him as kind and charming. As these were qualities I aspired to myself, I felt an intuitive and immediate love for my father, against my will. Upon seeing him for the first time in more than five years, he looked older, but vigorous, the combination of the two qualities evoking from me deference and respect. We embraced and then settled easily into dinner amid a flowing series of lovely conversations. It was as if we were old college buddies reuniting for an annual get together, only that we had missed a few.

As our evening unfolded, I wanted to stay in that place of pleasant and meaningful conversation, relating to my father as I would an older friend, a trusted teacher, a mentor. Just as I had avoided reading the letters he sent me, now too it felt better to be with the man whom I had come to know and love over time, rather than engage the one whose distance was a sad mystery. But of course, I also knew that to keep talking in this way would be a lie. Worse than that, if I ended the evening without confronting my father, all my supposed strength, my entire cultivated being, would have been exposed as nothing.

When the plates were cleared, I steeled myself to confront him over his absence from my life. I do not recall feeling angry, even though I had prepared myself by recalling every justification to do battle. Despite my feeling invincible in the days and weeks leading up to this moment, I felt a pervasive, disembodied fear. I could feel the question, the breath, the words lodged in my throat as I mustered the will to express them. Straining against a heart pounding in simultaneous fear and triumph, trying more than anything to speak in a clear and direct voice, I asked, "Why haven't you contacted me all these years?"

Did my father know this question was coming? He must have. Almost without hesitation, he answered, "Well, your mother and grandmother didn't want me to see you and didn't let me."

I was prepared for this answer and knew that it was part of my father's sacred myth. Years earlier, my mother and grandmother had warned me that my father blamed them as a justification for his absence, but that I was free to see him anytime. And so, equally spontaneously, in a probing but not angry tone, I replied, "You know that's not true."

At this point I remember my father taking an awkward pause and responding, "Being in contact with you became too much of an emotional strain on me and my family."

Confronted with the truth, there was simply nothing I could say. I was decidedly unmoved, which did not surprise me in the moment, but I was puzzled in the weeks and months ahead. Set for battle and the inevitability of triumph, I was unprepared to simply accept the truth. It was a truth I had known for years. I knew that there was nothing I or anyone else had done to completely bar my father from my life, so his weakness and lack of resolve was the only possible explanation. As long as I didn't have to face my father directly, this conclusion gave me the comfort of righteous indignation, a buffer against the familiar sensations of fear and loneliness that were a part of my life.

After hearing my father's revelation, my task would now be deeper, more demanding and lifelong. Confronted with the truth, I could no longer hide from my own feelings and the threat they posed to my emerging sense of self. At sixteen, I knew what I wanted out of life: to find love, to stay absolutely committed to someone over the course of my life, to be an abiding father to my children, and way behind all of this, finding work that mattered to someone other than myself. All of this was predicated on believing that I had this love to give. But having met my father and hearing his answer to my question, I could only wonder why he would ever leave me.

Loneliness and Comfort—Wrestling with Beings Human and Divine

I share my story because I have come to believe that a life in pursuit of questions about God, spirituality, community, and belonging in Judaism entails a confrontation with loss and existential loneliness. It is simply something I have learned from experience that feels authentic. In seventeen years of being a congregational rabbi, and more importantly, in almost thirty years of living Jewish life as an adult, I have found that everyone has a story of loss and sadness that animates their seeking a connection, whether through ritual, spiritual exploration, or communal life. Even in the midst of the joy and comfort of celebration, the prospect of being alone provides necessary fuel for the spiritual life.

Over time, I have come to see how the experience of living with my father's abandonment was among the *Beresheet* moments that galvanized and awakened my mind to a lifelong spiritual yearning. Even in my father's absence, I never stopped feeling connected to him. While I never fully desired a renewed relationship with my father, I sought out experiences of love that would give me the kind of foundation for my life as if he had always been there.

Without question, my father's actions hurt me deeply. But they also initiated me into an existential struggle that is as old as the Torah itself: reaching out from the void of loneliness toward communion with someone or something that initially seems absent. Even in the broadest of strokes, the lives of our biblical patriarchs and matriarchs illustrate how a life in pursuit of God and spiritual comfort springs from a life of loneliness and even abandonment. Abraham must leave his home, and according to rabbinic legend, must rebel against his father, to know God. Isaac, famously, is nearly ritually murdered to demonstrate the strength of the bond between his father and God. Jacob, having been driven from his home in murderous rage by his brother, Esau, wrestles with a mysterious stranger and so receives the new name "Yisrael," which means that he will struggle with beings human and divine and prevail. These mythic combinations of aloneness and spiritual connection are found in the lives of the matriarchs as well. Sarah leaves her ancestral home no less than Abraham; Rebecca must leave as well, and though she seems possessed of a kind of power and charisma that jumps off the page, it is clear she comes from a family of schemers and connivers; the marriage of Jacob and Leah is no great love story, and Rachel, in her infertility, commands Jacob to lie with her handmaiden, "lest I die" without a child. As an adult, I came to understand the depth and profound pain of my father's abandonment, but I also came to recognize how the condition of being alone has been a foundation in Jewish tradition, from which one seeks out the comforts of love, purpose, and the pursuit of an elusive God.

There are many ways in which the motif of Jacob "wrestling" with God has become manifest in Jewish tradition. In our time, much of that wrestling has been viewed as argument, whether over the suffering of the Jewish people, the failures of those who were supposed to care for us, or the unfortunate and tragic circumstances that befall everyone. But there is another aspect to this wrestling that is bound up in moments of wonder even as we call out from the depths of being alone. It may be that both our loneliness as well as our burgeoning hope are prompted by the nature of a God who is paradoxically present and hidden at the same time.

God Revealed and Hidden

In my reading of Jewish tradition, we are challenged to wrestle with a God who promises abiding presence, yet is most known through the quality of being hidden. In the Torah, there are two great moments of God's self-revelation, when God is closest to humanity. Ironically, both of these moments of God saying, "Here I am" yield the inescapable feature of God's hiddenness. There is the moment of *Beresheet*, the very beginning of the book of Genesis, in which God sets our created world in motion on the condition that the first humans, Adam and Eve, are supposed to be kept in the dark as to who God is. Their closeness to God lasts only as long as they obey God's command not to eat from the Tree of Knowledge of Good and Evil. Once they both eat the fruit and know everything the heavenly beings know, they are banished from the garden and lose their intimacy with God.

The second great moment of God's revelation is the encounter at Sinai and the giving of the Ten Commandments, when God appears to all the Israelites leaving Egypt and proclaims *"Anokhi,"* "I am *Adonai,* your God."[5] It is a moment of explicit and yet inchoate power in which God conveys, "I (*Anokhi*) am *Adonai,* your God, who liberated you from Egypt to be your God. I, *Adonai,* am your God." But for all of its power of revelation, God's proclamation of *"Anokhi"* ("I") emphasizes how inscrutable God remains. One apparent reason is sheer terror, as the people assembled at Sinai were so overwhelmed by the accompanying thunder and fire that they heard barely anything. But another reason, one that develops amid the evolution in Jewish thought, is that the essence of God's own self-disclosure is mystery. The more we know of God, the more we realize how much God is hidden from us.

According to the rabbis of the Talmud, the people were so overwhelmed that they heard only the first two commandments, *"Anokhi,"* "I am Adonai your God," and "You shall not have any gods before me." Another Talmudic opinion was that these, and possibly all of the other commandments as well, were bound up in one single utterance. About 1,000 years after the rabbis, the great philosopher Moses Maimonides claimed that the people did not hear any specific words, but rather had an encounter with a generalized, disembodied "voice." And finally, a Hasidic interpretation I have heard but never seen written down suggests that the people did not even hear that first word, only the silence before the utterance of the Hebrew letter *Alef* (א) of *"Anokhi"* (אנכי). Ultimately, God's revelation of everything is wrapped up in silence.

However, the earliest strata of Jewish tradition show how human beings wrestle with this paradox of a God both distant and close at the same time. It is a conflict that reaches a pinnacle with the story of the golden calf, and Moses' attempt to persuade God to reveal more of God's being to the people. Moses successfully persuades God to refrain from destroying the people, explaining how they are unsure and afraid. More gingerly, Moses suggests that the fault partially lies with God himself for being so remote. This negotiation between Moses and God is found in Exodus 33:12–23:

> Moses said to God, "See, You say to me, 'Lead this people forward,' but You have not made known to me whom You will send

5. Exodus 20.

with me. . . . Now, if I have truly gained Your favor, let me know
Your ways, that I may know You and continue in Your favor."

Moses wins a partial concession as God promises, "I will go in the lead
and will lighten your burden."

But Moses wants a more full disclosure from God, and so Moses
demands,

> Unless You go in the lead, do not make us leave this place. For
> how shall it be known that Your people have gained Your favor
> unless You go with us, so that we may be distinguished, Your
> people and I, from every people on the face of the earth?

In effect, Moses is asking an emotional question, not just a theological
one: "How can I trust You? How do I know You love me and us? Only by
being with us and feeling Your presence will we know that You are reliable."

God responds positively to this moral and spiritual logic by agreeing
unequivocally, "I will do this thing that you have asked; for you have truly
gained My favor and I have singled you out by name."

But there is more. God's protection of the people being secured, Moses
demands of God, "Oh, let me behold Your Presence!"

It could be to a lost lover or an absent parent to whom Moses pleads,
"show me your true self, the being, essence of the *'Anokhi'* that you showed
us at Sinai." God will deny this request, but by demurring, revealing enough
of the divine personality to satisfy Moses, but concealing enough so that
Moses will always harbor a fundamental yearning.

> I will make all my goodness pass before you, and I will proclaim
> before you the name Adonai, and the grace that I grant and the
> compassion that I show. But, you cannot see My face, for a hu-
> man being may not see my face and live.

To reinforce the dynamic of God's simultaneous revelation and
distance, the text continues:

> See there is a place near Me. Station yourself on the rock and, as
> My Presence passes by, I will put you in a cleft of the rock and
> shield you with My hand until I have passed by. Then I will take
> My hand away and you will see My back; but My face must not
> be seen.

Between lovers, the act of withholding, outside of a momentary and
playful seduction, destroys all love. But the nature of God is such that the
sense of mystery, of elusiveness, is its own kind of joy and exultation. God's
revelation to Moses—"No human being may see My face and live"—is not

a defeat for humanity, but rather, a statement about the pleasures of sacred encounter. Were we to know, with all certainly, the nature of God, there wouldn't be any joy in the chase. We "live" by yearning, seeking, investigating, acting on our curiosity about what God is or may be. In contrast to our experience with human beings, God's ultimate elusiveness sustains us with its own awe and grandeur.

Tzimtzum — God Also Withdraws

Kabbalah, the Jewish mystical tradition, asserts that our experience of God's remoteness, as well as our experience of being fundamentally alone, may be necessary for our own spiritual awakening. This idea is a central component of the mystical philosophy of Rabbi Isaac Luria, who lived in the sixteenth century in Tzfat, in the Land of Israel. Originally from Egypt, Luria was a spice trader, and came to live in the land of Israel. He settled in Tzfat, in the green, rolling, and occasionally severe hills of the northern Galilee, where there was a circle of passionate and almost hermetic devotees of Kabbalah. The tradition of mystical Kabbalah was only a few centuries into its maturity since the emergence of the Zohar, the pillar of Jewish mysticism, in the thirteenth century. Aside from Luria, perhaps the most famous among the rabbis of Tzfat was Joseph Karo, who, in addition to writing about his mystical visions, composed a practical code of law, the *Shulkhan Arukh* (set table), which has been the foundation of normative Jewish practice since its publication. Although Luria was new to the circle in Tzfat, he learned quickly through a combination of intellectual, spiritual, and also emotional genius. It is said of him that he could speak the language of birds, that he learned everything there is to know, and that he was the most selfless and loyal friend. By the time he died after just a few years of living in Tzfat at the age of thirty-eight, he changed the face of Judaism forever. Although he did not write anything by his own hand, we have an encyclopedic compilation of his thought through his student, Rabbi Chayim Vital. His book, the *Etz Chayim* (Tree of Life, or Tree of Chayim), is supposed to be a faithful transposition of everything that Luria taught concerning the inner life of God.

According to Luria, the first act of God was not creation as we know it in a literal sense. In the opening chapters of Genesis, we read of creation as a conjoining of forces that flow from God's closeness to humanity. When the Torah speaks of human beings as created in the image of God, it does so in a predictable manner: just as God created the first human being, so we transmit the divine image through creating another generation.

But for Isaac Luria, the first creative moment of God was an act of retreat and not intimacy, what Luria and Kabbalah have come to call *tzimtzum*, or withdrawal.

> Know, that before all things emanated and all of creation came into being, only the supernal light filled all of existence, and that there was no place full of this light so as to be void or emptiness. Rather, all was filled with the infinite light (*En Sof*) itself, and it did not have any beginning or end. Rather, all was one pure light, simple, perfectly balanced and consistent that was called the Light of the *En Sof* (infinite). And as it arose in the absolute will to create the worlds and to bring about the emanation of all reality, so as to bring to light the completeness of God's acts and names and forms of address, for this is the reason for the creation of the worlds as it is known in our circle . . . see that God withdrew into Godself (*tzimtzem et atzmo*) the infinite light (*En Sof*) to a single, central point, at whose very center was the light itself. And the light was withdrawn to a distance, toward the sides surrounding the one middle point. And so there was left a place that was free, spacious nothingness around that central point itself. And see, that this withdrawal was completely a symmetrical nothingness around that one central point, in the manner of that nothingness forming a circle in all of its surrounding area in complete symmetry.[6]

While this text expresses itself in its own idiosyncratic style, the essential idea is simple. God, being infinite energy (in Hebrew, *En Sof*, "without end"), was all that existed before the creation of the universe. But God, in wanting to be revealed as Godself, so as to express the "wholeness" or "perfection" of God's ways, needs to be something other than undifferentiated light. There has to exist some kind of "other" in order for God to be known. And so, for the universe to come into being, there had to be created a negative space, a vacuum, something that is "other" than God, within the infinite continuum of energy we conceptualize as God. In order to create that space, God drew that bit of the divine presence inward, like a cosmic breath, and through this initial act of divine contraction, the space was created within which all creation could exist.

In a gloss on the passage above, a commentator compares the relationship between God and the universe to that of the soul and the body:[7]

6. Vital, *Etz Chayim*, 1:2.
7. Helperin, *Hagahot u'Be'urim* on *Etz Chayim* 1:2.

> God's light, going out from its essence, is similar to the way in
> which the soul takes up no space. Rather, its "light" permeates
> the entire body to give it life. So it is with all of these matters, in
> which the light goes out from its source.

As a story of origins, *tzimtzum* creates a beginning different from any
beginning we might understand intuitively. As the origin of all creation,
tzimtzum emphasizes distance, not closeness, between God and humanity,
even as God yearns to be known by humanity—actually by all of creation.
In the eyes of Isaac Luria, the story of Adam and Eve, of coupling, procre-
ation, and companionship is ultimately a veil, a concealment of the truth
regarding the divine retreat. Ironically, Luria, as a mystic, sought a direct,
unmediated experience of God that is otherwise shrouded by stories and
text. Why, then, would he believe that God would initiate this relationship
in an act of withdrawal?

According to Gershom Scholem, the great twentieth-century scholar
of Jewish mysticism, the Jews' expulsion from Spain in the late fifteenth
century was the historical trauma that gave rise to Luria's idea of *tzimtzum*.
For Scholem, this event, something on a scale unknown since the Roman
destruction of the temple in Jerusalem, created a sense of pervasive brokenness and the unfathomable remoteness of God. Luria's idea of *tzimtzum*,
then, arose as a way to make sense of arbitrary suffering, experienced both
individually and collectively.

For people trying to stitch together a sense of God amid the fabric
of our lives, Scholem's view leaves us with a provocative insight: the first
task of a spiritual life is to recognize that God is, in a basic sense, *absent*.
Understandably, when we suffer, we may strive to find God's presence close
as a means of comfort. But if we follow Scholem's logic, the real comfort
may be found in the belief that God has nothing to do with the events that
produce human suffering. In fact, God, by definition, cannot have anything
to do with those events, because God is fundamentally removed from human experience. While God's fundamental distance may disturb some of
us, the insight is potentially liberating, for once we come to grips with that
fundamental divine absence, we may begin to seek out the myriad ways
of filling in that void, and discovering shards of divine presence revealed
through our own experience. In a strange, counterintuitive way, the absence
of God yields its own comfort. It's not necessarily an idea that makes intellectual sense, but perhaps it does in experience. Through God's absence, we
seek attachment. The seeking contains its own promise of connecting, often
evoking overlapping senses of hope, longing, even joy.

Alone, Finding Comfort in the Seeking

When I confronted my father, his "*anokhi*," his "I am," merely revealed emptiness and impotence. But at the same time, confronting my father's absolute retreat prompted my search for a different kind of abiding presence. It is not so much that I sought God to compensate for my father's abandonment, or as a surrogate for what my father could not provide. But confronting my father made me aware of how critical it was to face ultimate and unanswered questions about what was present and absent in my life.

I initially resolved to confront my father because I was curious. I needed to know if I had missed something in simply accepting my life as it was. And once I faced the truth of his own admission, I found that the curiosity didn't end. His expressed reason for his absence concealed more, and I was driven to explore the unknown. I wondered how any father, especially my father, could just turn his back and leave, and leave me in particular, a great kid.

But that explicit question was really a way to face a deeper and unspoken question: how, in the absence of my father, do I seek out and find a real foundation of connection and love that will never leave me? Would it be found through loving other people? Through service to others? Through an awareness of the connections we all share as human beings and as part of creation? Through learning about the Jewish God?

As I will come back to again and again, Jewish spirituality is shot through with the notion that all authentic connection requires yearning and questioning, and my life is just one example. But there are countless others. In the biblical story that I will weave through this book, the prophet Elisha inaugurates his independence and his maturation with the cry for Elijah his mentor as he is taken up to heaven. In the story of Elisha, and in my story and perhaps in all of our stories, that cry is often for a closeness that will never be had. These few examples bear witness to a primary mode of spiritual engagement, that *we encounter the holy when we long for it in its absence*.

But while yearning may be prompted by loss, the Jewish sense of God's simultaneous presence and eclipse endures as a hopeful paradox. God may never be truly found, but in the seeking, God may be revealed as closer than we thought. This dialectic of absence and presence turns the losses we experience in social relationships on their head. The loss of a friend, or a parent, or a lover leaves a stinging pain that we absorb or transcend through our own resilience. But as both an idea and an experience, we may find that the elusiveness of God beckons us to draw closer.

Elisha—A Prophet Abandoned and Connected

Turning to the story of Elisha, we see that the prophets of the Hebrew Bible similarly suggest that a fundamental sense of being alone, adrift, and disassociated from a home that provides us succor and support may be necessary in order to draw close to God. The primary requirement for being a prophet is the ability to live alone and have no interest other than God's truth. Having relinquished their origins, prophets dedicate themselves to healing the world of its injustice, callousness, and spiritual blindness. Each of the prophets, including both Elijah and Elisha, only has a scant biography, perhaps some mention about where they are from or who their father was, but that is all. When we meet them, we may witness their inauguration as prophets, but mostly, we know them as fully formed, engaged in their role as mature adults proclaiming God's truth. It is as though their relationships of origin, so important for us contemporary people to understand ourselves, are completely irrelevant to the lives of the prophets. Once prophets are fully engaged, they never express any nostalgia for "home," for their parents, or for a place they came from. It is as if they have accepted their isolation and abandonment as normal. Even Moses, about whom we know more than all the rest, never expresses any desire to be reunited with his mother or father, who left him to be raised in Pharaoh's palace.

In this vein, Elisha's cry of *"Avi, Avi,"* over Elijah's departure from this earth is an illuminating glimpse into a prophet drawing on his own loneliness to galvanize his life of devotion to God and humanity. From 2 Kings 2:9–14, we witness the core of Elisha's moment of simultaneous abandonment and discovery:

> (9) As they were crossing, Elijah said to Elisha, "Ask what I shall do for you before I am taken from you." Elisha said, "May a double portion of your spirit be upon me." (10) He said, "You have asked something difficult. If you see me as I am taken from you, it will be so. And if not, it will not be so." (11) As they were walking and speaking with each other, there was a chariot of fire, and horses of fire. They separated the two of them and raised Elijah to heaven in a whirlwind. (12) Elisha saw it, and he cried out, *"Avi, Avi!* My father, my father! Chariot of Israel and its horsemen!" And then he saw no more. He grabbed his garments and rent them in two strips."
>
> (13) He raised the mantle of Elijah which had fallen from him, and returned and stood on the bank of the Jordan. (14) He took the mantle of Elijah which had fallen from him and struck the water and said, "Where is Adonai, the God of Elijah?!" And

even he, as he struck the water, divided it evenly in two and Elisha crossed over.

As Elijah is taken up to heaven, so now Elisha must literally take up his mentor's mantle and begin his mature, prophetic mission by himself. In this sense, Elisha's cry of *"Avi, Avi"* is both a cry of mourning and a declaration of spiritual closeness in the same breath. In one sense, *"Avi, Avi"* expresses the longing for the departed spiritual father, Elijah, who has truly shepherded his charge.

But even as he cries in mourning, Elisha is not longing for an unfulfilled past, as if Elijah were a surrogate for a missing or abusive father. Instead, Elisha expresses a simultaneous longing for what Elijah has shown him but which me must now do himself: connect with the stream of thought from the ever-living God. From this moment forth, Elisha's mind will not be in the past, on the warm, pastoral life and family he left behind, or on the mentor who showed him love through his constant companionship. Rather, Elisha will be focused solely on the present and future in all its obscurity, fueled by nothing more than his absolute devotion to the wellbeing of the downtrodden and outcast and his willingness to be a conduit for divine power. And so, *"Avi, Avi"* is both mourning and recognition, a cry and a declaration, a statement of loss but also a statement of faith. Elisha's cry reflects the paradox of being alone and yet at the same time close to something unseen, yet real.

Judaism is an often-confounding path without a clear starting point. At its center is a God, distant and unseen, yet forever close and loving. It doesn't make sense, rationally or emotionally. Can we really be expected to jump into Jewish spiritual life without some concrete touchstone—a reassuring idea, adage, old saw—that God is palpable and present? And yet, that is what Judaism (the Torah, the Talmud, Jewish philosophy, ethics, and all the rest) asks us to do.

For me, Judaism requires no "leap of faith." Rather, it entails a confrontation with an existential conundrum: that we must live with some degree of isolation so as to induce longing, which prompts us to seek an existential and spiritual foundation that we feel we need. In a world in which we work and suffer through the trauma of abandonment, we learn, like Moses, to "live" without fully seeing the face of another. Like Elisha, we somehow learn that moving on despite the loss of someone or something foundational is its own path toward maturity and a new kind of closeness.

Looking back, I wonder how it was that I didn't try to numb the pain of my father's abandonment through the predictable paths of teenage self-destruction. The paths were there but I did not even seek them out. Instead,

I sought something new and almost completely undefined. Perhaps I had intuitively sensed that presence of mystery, and like Elisha who reaches out after losing his surrogate father Elijah, I have spent my life seeking contact with that mystery that comforts with its unique sense of belonging. As with Elisha, my first, mature contact with the truth of loss catalyzed my own spiritual beginning, a *Beresheet* of concealment and distance, confronting the *"Anokhi"* of absence, and in doing so, paving the way to embrace a new sense of presence.

Chapter 2

Turning Toward

In the Torah, Shabbat, the seventh day, appears to mark the cessation of the creative process set in motion with the word "*Beresheet*." As it evolved in Jewish tradition, Shabbat became its own spiritual beginning and source of renewal, week after week. Complementing its role as a day to experience rest and an expansive consciousness, Shabbat especially invites us to feel our longings. This dynamic tension springs from the emotional logic of Shabbat: when we imagine wholeness in having everything we need, we call to mind what is missing.

The prayer book ushers us into this spirit of yearning at the very beginning of Shabbat. Sephardic communities begin Shabbat in community by chanting the Song of Songs, those exquisitely charged erotic poems in which two lovers seek, but never quite find each other. That spirit of unrequited love continues to be evoked in many communities with the singing of a mystical love poem from the sixteenth century, *Yedid Nefesh*, Beloved of My Soul. The poem, written by the great Hebrew poet Eleazar Azikri, who lived among the same mystical circle in Tsfat as Isaac Luria, begins with the words, "Beloved of my soul, Merciful Father." With the mixed metaphors of lover and parent, this first line of the poem encapsulates the yearning for a source of ultimate, unquestioned, and unconditional love.

> "Beloved of my soul, Merciful Father, draw your servant to Your will.
> Like a deer I will run to You, bowing before Your splendor.
> Let Your sweet love delight me more than the honey of the honeycomb,
> or
> Other sensual thrill.

Splendid, calming, light of the world, my soul pines for Your love,
Please God, heal her; show her Your soothing light;
Then will she be strengthened and healed, and will be bound to You forever.

Elder, Wise One, show Your gentle compassion, cast your shelter on Your beloved child,
For so have I longed for You, to behold the grandeur of Your strength,
Please, my God, the desire of my heart, care for me, do not turn away.

Reveal Yourself, and spread over me, Beloved, the shelter of Your peace,
Illumine the Earth with Your presence, and we will celebrate and delight in You.
Quickly, Beloved, for the time is approaching, show me Your favor, as in days of old.

With this poem, each Shabbat becomes the renewal of a spiritual connection from our longing for a total, protective, and sustaining love. During the week, our experience may have been dominated by the experience of withdrawal, *tzimtzum*, into the demands that tax our emotional and spiritual capacities. But the arrival of Shabbat promises the return to a state of a renewed soul, heart, and mind that has been muted by the labors of the week. By reciting *Yedid Nefesh* and taking its yearning on as our own, we begin Shabbat with the recognition that the capacity for reconnection lies within us, even as we have felt burdened and lonely.

It is this ability to turn toward something outside ourselves, whatever that something may be, that infuses so much of life with the Jewish God. So much depends upon our innate inner ability to turn toward. I believe it is more essential than some of the qualities we usually associate with religious life, such as faith or loyalty. These latter qualities are acts of will, and while important, they are intermittent and fragile. But the longing for love and connection is constant, and while driven by our own vulnerability, it is also a great source of strength. The ability to yearn reveals our conviction that we are able to form sustaining relationships despite whatever has happened in the past.

Elijah and Elisha—Overcoming Loneliness

Longing and the innate drive for relationship lie at the heart of the Elijah and Elisha stories. The central experience of all prophets is to be connected to the "other," whether that "other" is human or divine. But with Elijah and

Elisha, we see personalities who express a heightened yearning for these connections as they experience utter isolation and abandonment. Additionally, their yearning is so raw that they are satisfied merely by an intimation or allusion to God's presence. In these stories of Elijah and Elisha, we see how even the faintest echo of a voice, or just the awareness of mystery, is enough to sustain these prophets in their loneliness. Their extraordinary ability to find comfort in the most remote "Other" demonstrates the strength of their inner resilience, one that is fortified by the power of their longing.

I believe these stories of Elijah and Elisha are universal and archetypal, holding out the prospect that each of us is similarly endowed to seek another presence from our deepest alienation. As the prophets draw on their yearnings to propel them to lives of communion, relationship, and service, so I believe we may be similarly prompted by similar feelings to seek comfort and renewal in the "Other," even one who is nebulous or remote.

In the story of Elijah, we see a prophet propelled by circumstance and his own actions to the depths of alienation and despair. But from the nadir of his loneliness, Elijah surprisingly discovers renewed strength in the most ethereal manifestation of God's presence. Elijah's story, in the 18th chapter of the First Book of Kings, begins with the decisive confrontation of his life. Seeking to undo King Ahab and his rejection of the God of Israel, Elijah sets a wager with the king, challenging his priests of *Ba'al* before all Israel at Mount Carmel, the site of modern day Haifa. Elijah's proposal is that he and the 450 priests of Ba'al in Ahab's service construct competing altars. Once these altars were set up, the 450 priests of Ba'al would call out to their god, and Elijah would call out to the God of Israel, and whichever deity answered would be known to everyone as the "God" of all. Clearly, Elijah assumed that Ba'al would do nothing, because he did not exist, while Elijah's altar would be visited by the God of Israel. At a public presentation of the wager, the people in attendance responded, "this is a good thing."

For almost an entire day, with Elijah's encouragement, the priests of Ba'al called to their god to take up their offering, only to evoke complete silence. The Bible tells us that in response to their pleas, there was, "no voice, no answer, no sound." Toward the end of the day, Elijah set up his altar, pointedly drenched in water and surrounded by a moat filled by the overflow. Elijah pleaded, "*Adonai*, God of Abraham, Isaac, and Israel, today let it be known that You are God of Israel, and I am Your servant; by Your instruction have I done all these things. Answer me God, answer me, so that this people will know that You are *Adonai* God, so You shall bring their hearts back." After reciting his prayer, Elijah's offering, and all the water around it, is vaporized by a fire from heaven. The people bow down to acknowledge and praise Elijah's God, and then Elijah proceeds to slaughter all of the 450 priests of *Ba'al*. This brutal conclusion to Elijah's proof of God forces Elijah to flee for his life from King Ahab, who employed the priests and will no doubt seek retribution.

Elijah—Attaching to a "Voice"

Surprisingly, Elijah's bravery and devotion throw him into an existential crisis. In the aftermath of his victory against Ahab, Elijah realizes that his triumph renders him utterly alone. The biblical text provides us with a stark portrayal of Elijah's existential crisis, this from 1 Kings 19:2ff.:

> Ahab told Jezebel all that Elijah had done, and all that he had done in killing all of priests of Ba'al. (2) And Jezebel sent a messenger to Elijah saying, "So shall God do and more, for at this time tomorrow I will make of you as of one of them." (3) And he saw, and arose, and left for his life, and he arrived at Be'er Sheva in Judah, and he left his servant there. (4) And he proceeded into the desert the length of a day, when he arrived and sat beneath a "rotem," a solitary date tree, and he asked that his life be taken in death; and he said, "It is too much! Now, *Adonai*, take my soul, for I am no better than my ancestors."

After routing the priests of Ba'al and facing retribution from Queen Jezebel, Elijah runs to the desert, fleeing for his life and taking no joy or satisfaction from his victory. Instead, he despairs of the burdens of being a prophet and, isolated from all human society, begs God to end his life. As with Moses, who also asks God to end his life multiple times on the journey through the desert, Elijah's feeling of abandonment is not merely social, but also spiritual. He has previously lived on the margins of society, and so living alone is not new to him. But now, Elijah's sense of abandonment is extreme, and he can no longer bear the costs of being a prophet, or even of living at all.

In answer to Elijah's plea, a form of gentle yet emphatic rebuke arrives from a messenger of God, who provides him food in the desert and instructs him to continue on his journey.

> (5) He lay down and slept beneath the solitary broom shrub, when all of a sudden there was a messenger of God touching him saying, "Get up. Eat." (6) He looked, and saw by the place he lay his head some cakes arranged in a row and a water skin, and he ate and drank, and sat back down and lay down. (7) The Messenger of *Adonai* returned a second time and touched him and said, "Get up. Eat. For the journey is too long for you." (8) He

rose and ate and drank, and walked on the strength of that meal
forty days and forty nights, to the Mountain of God at *Horeb*. (9)
He arrived there at a cave and slept there, and behold, the word
of *Adonai* came to him and said to him, "What are you doing
here, Elijah?" (10) He said, "I was truly zealous for *Adonai*, the
God of Hosts, for the Children of Israel, they abandoned Your
covenant. They ruined Your altars and murdered Your prophets
by the sword. I was left all alone, and they sought to take my life."

There is something so poignant, moving, and intimate about this
exchange. It feels as if Elijah is being gently taught how to live again, and
the first gesture in his revival is to listen to a nurturing and compassionate
divine messenger, and do what is most basic. It is as if the instruction to
"Get up" and "eat" is implicitly accompanied by an unspoken imperative,
"Listen to someone who cares about you." And the result it impressive. It
is clearly not only the food that sustains Elijah on his forty-day journey
to Horeb (an alternative place name for Sinai). Rather, it is the newfound
companionship and closeness to God that propels him and sustains him on
his journey. Everyone knows that no one can survive very long in the desert
on such meager provisions. And so Elijah's journey becomes a metaphorical
statement: to live, we have to turn toward something, and know that we
are not alone. And more importantly, we are to know that it is within our
capacity to do so.

The arrival at Horeb, or Sinai, is of course highly evocative, as it is
the place where Moses originally received the divine revelation. Among the
multitude of symbolic resonances here is the expectation that Elijah will,
like Moses, speak with God face to face. But before that happens, Elijah
discloses the source of his own despair, namely his feeling of utter abandonment. After being "truly zealous for God," he faced the fact that his only
human contact is among those who have "abandoned the covenant" of God
and seek Elijah's life, leaving him "left all alone."

That confession by Elijah of his own loneliness becomes the prelude
to God's momentous revelation to him, and by extension, to all humanity.
Fitting the existential circumstance, God's disclosure here will not be the
dramatic and unambiguous *"Anokhi,"* "I am," as it was to Moses and the
people coming out of Egypt. Instead, Elijah will be witness to something
much more enigmatic. Whereas God earlier issued the commandments in
a voice that shattered the boundaries of natural experience, God now comforts Elijah with a manifestation of the divine voice that will be soft, fragile,
and fleeting.

> And God said, "Go and stand on the mountain before *Adonai*, and behold, *Adonai* will pass. A great and fierce wind will break through the mountains and shatter rocks before *Adonai*. *Adonai* will not be in the wind. And after the wind, thunder, and *Adonai* is not in the thunder. (12) And after the thunder, fire; *Adonai* is not in the fire. And after the fire, the *kol d'mah mah dakkah*, the still, fragile voice."

In this moment of poetic stillness, the text imagines the divine voice as drifting off in the middle of a sentence, suggesting that Elijah will ultimately find relief from utter loneliness in a sense of God's mystery. Of the many lessons implied by this moment, one is that our inherent drive to connect is so strong that we are reassured by only the faintest hint of another presence. Instead of seeking refuge in a dramatic and concrete manifestation of God, Elijah will find his spiritual foundation in the sounds of silence, just as his ancestors at Sinai heard everything merely in the unvocalized first letter, *alef* (א), of "*Anokhi*" (אנכי), God's declaration of "I am." God implies in this promise to Elijah that God's mystery, unbound by anything earthly, has always been with Elijah and always will be, and that Elijah's capacity to turn toward that mystery survives the brutality of his prophetic life and the alienation he suffers. Interestingly, the biblical passage imagines the *kol d'mah mah dakkah*, the still, fragile voice, resonating in the external world. In later Jewish tradition, teachers and poets will imagine it arising from within the human soul.

The revelation of God's presence as a still, fragile voice does not completely relieve Elijah of his loneliness. We see that, after the revelation, he appears to feel the same way as before. But unlike previously, he seems possessed of a newfound strength—not superhuman, but just enough to carry on. Perhaps that's all any of us are really seeking.

> (13) As Elijah listened, he wrapped his face in his mantle, and went and stood at the opening to the cave. And behold, a voice came to him and said, "What are you doing here, Elijah?" (14) He answered, "I was truly zealous for *Adonai*, the God of hosts, for the Children of Israel abandoned Your covenant; they ruined Your altars and Your prophets they murdered by the sword. I am left alone, and they seek my life to take it." (15) *Adonai* said to him, "Go, return to your journey toward the wilderness in the direction of Damascus. You will reach and anoint Hazael as King of Aram. (16) And Yehu son of Nimshi you shall anoint as king of Israel; and Elisha son of Shafar from *Evel M'cholah* you shall anoint as a prophet after you."

Elijah's story of hearing the *kol d'mah mah dakkah*, the still fragile voice, powerfully reminds us how we are never alone. I image that each of us can summon some kind of experience of connecting with such a voice. Some of us feel a persistent hum when we are alone in nature; some of us find a great source of healing in meditating on each breath. We may connect spiritually through writing, art, exercise, or yoga. If we are willing to give ourselves the time and space, there seem to be innumerable opportunities to be alone and listen to the real and metaphorical sounds that escape our attention moment to moment. But there is something almost superhuman about Elijah. Is it too much of a stretch to draw a comparison, much less a parallel, between our lives and the story of Elijah? What if, like Elijah, we truly lost everyone and everything? What if we truly felt utterly bereft of God and human companionship? Would we be strong enough to turn toward the nearly imperceptible sources of connection that could ease our loneliness?

Elisha—Only Connect

On a more familiar scale, Elisha's early story advances the argument for our inner capacity to connect despite the losses we endure. Like Elijah, Elisha will experience a signature moment of great loss, abandonment, and consolation, albeit under a different circumstance, when his mentor is taken to heaven in a whirlwind. But in Elisha's story, the Bible supplies an important background detail by showing us how Elisha was rooted in a series of loving relationships with family and community before beginning his apprenticeship with Elijah. Perhaps this network of warm relationships taught Elisha how to connect as a boy and a young man. As he goes off with Elijah, whatever he has been given will be tested, because in order to become a prophet, Elisha will have to leave all of these relationships behind. Nevertheless, Elisha will demonstrate how the desire to connect and serve is so strong that it can survive the trauma of losing everyone he has loved.

Following immediately on the heels of what we have already seen of the biblical text, here is the account of Elisha's introduction to Elijah:

> (19) He (Elijah) went from there and found Elisha son of Shafat, and he was plowing, twelve pairs of animals before him, and he was with the twelfth; Elijah passed him and cast his mantle toward him. (20) He abandoned the cattle and ran after Elijah saying, "Let me kiss my father and mother, and I will surely follow you." And he said, "Go, return, for what have I done for you?" (21) He returned and took a pair of cattle and sacrificed

them, and in the pot of the cattle he cooked the meat, and gave
to the people and they ate it; then he rose and followed Elijah
and served him.

When we are introduced to Elisha, all seems right with him. He is a
country shepherd in a prosperous, shepherding family. He is not, like Elijah,
an urban prophet, exposed to all the vanity and corruption of the city and
the royal court. Instead, Elisha seems content to be ensconced in pastoral
wholeness. Elijah summons Elisha abruptly and decisively, and the biblical
text allows no opening for Elisha to refuse. But before leaving with Elijah,
Elisha says, "Let me kiss my father and mother, and then I will go with you."
As if to further emphasize his rootedness in the close network of community,
Elisha then slaughters oxen and feeds them to the people of his village. On a
final note to emphasize Elisha's relinquishing his old attachments in pursuit
of a new life, the text reads, "He arose and followed Elijah, and served him."
While Elisha's prophetic life comes at the cost of connections to family and
community, he is sustained by his new relationship to Elijah as they wander
accompanied only by each other and the still, quiet voice of God.

When tested by the crisis of losing his mentor Elijah, Elisha's inner
capacities for love and constancy sustain him and help him find renewed
purpose. As Elijah ascends to heaven, and Elisha cries out, "*Avi, Avi*! Father,
Father!" a reader should be startled by this novel and singular burst of emotion. Never before has another prophet or character in the Hebrew Bible
expressed their loss in such an explicit and personal way.

Certainly, other biblical characters, particularly in the Book of Genesis, are deeply connected to their parents. But with Elisha, it seems as if the
Bible is trying to show how the capacity for spiritual connection exists independently of one's actual relationships with beloved companions, whether
they are alive or in the next world, present or absent. As Elisha cries, "*Avi,
Avi,*" there is the sense that he carries with him the best that he has been
given. Early experiences of nurturing relationships primed Elisha to attach
himself to Elijah, even at the cost of leaving his family and community. But
with Elijah's passing, Elisha has truly lost everything. Without his parents,
his community, and now bereft of his greatest teacher and surrogate father,
Elisha is left only with his inner attributes of love and loyalty. Nevertheless,
as he is sustained by these attributes cultivated in his family and community, Elisha is able to emerge seamlessly into his new identity as a prophet.
As Elisha takes up Elijah's mantle to live in service to God and humanity,
Elisha demonstrates his understanding that he is never alone, despite losing
everyone who has loved him.

Jewishness from Nothing

For me, the ways in which Elijah and Elisha are sustained by mere intimations of connection capture an essential part of my being Jewish. Although I was born of two Jewish parents and raised in a Jewish household, there was almost nothing in my early life that would have fostered a sense that Jewish tradition, much less the Jewish God, could be a source of depth and wonder.

Instead, my first real exposure to being Jewish came from my father's mother, a woman with the faraway name of Bina, whom I called *Savta*. In ways old and new, Savta was a charismatic conduit of everything Jewish. Despite my estrangement from my father, Savta remains my most palpable connection to the Jewish past. Her love of me, but also her love of the *Yiddishkeit*, the Jewishness she embodied and transmitted, transcends my father's leaving me behind.

As a child, I felt that Savta came from another world. When I knew her, Savta was in her sixties and early seventies, and while vigorous, nevertheless seemed old. She had a Polish accent and old-world ways, and was completely oblivious to the music, sports, and pop culture that were the primary language for my cousins and me. Savta was a Zionist who tried to teach me rudimentary Hebrew and Yiddish before I began religious school. In a humorous and most probably unintentional rebuke to the forces of assimilation, she took my decidedly un-Jewish name of Justin, the appellation of one of the greatest Roman anti-Semites, and Yiddishized it into "Justele."

As a child, I understood that Savta escaped from Poland, but then I also came to understand from Romania, and then later, Ukraine also. From early stories, it was clear that, in fleeing Europe's gathering cloud of murderous anti-Semitism in the 1930s, Savta, her siblings, and her extended family suffered, losing relatives along the way. I will always remember Savta talking about a cousin who "died of a broken heart." By sharing her story with me, Savta imbued me with a sense of belonging to the grand canvas of the collective Jewish memory. Her presence and her stories galvanized my curiosity about what it meant for me to be the inheritor of these stories and this history.

Later, I came to understand that Savta loved literature, and that my parents met because Savta and my mother's parents knew each other from a "great books seminar" at a New England college. I share this because it shows that Savta was not merely an old-world elder worthy of veneration, but something more powerful: a bridge between worlds. I was a child of this country after the '60s, with its pop culture, sports, and fast food. My mother's parents, who raised me, showed me art, books, and classical music, but their Judaism was almost totally cultural and assimilated. Arguably, without Savta, my father's mother, I wouldn't have known that a real Jewish world of flavor, bite, and pain ever existed.

Once my father stopped contacting me, my relationship with Savta also ended. In the years after, she called me from time to time, and I could hear the earnestness bordering on desperation in her voice as she tried to keep me connected to her, my cousins, and my father. But as a teenager, I was simply too filled with anger and fear to really talk to her, so I listened politely and hoped she wouldn't call again. Losing Savta was emotionally devastating, even if I didn't acknowledge the cost at the time. But even after almost four decades without her, Savta's love of Judaism and the Jewish people continues to be a part of me, transcending the pain of abandonment, preserved in a child-like capsule at the center of my soul.

Strength and Consolation in Longing—*Devekut*

As with Elijah and Elisha, my longing, then, is not only a reminder of loss or woundedness, but a great and redeeming strength, more powerful than the forces of alienation that created it in the first place. Longing has prompted me to seek renewed connection in the wake of isolation. It has propelled me not only toward personal fulfillment, but to a broader sense of connectedness that reaches its pinnacle in ongoing love and social responsibility.

In Jewish mysticism, this kind of longing that is its own form of attachment is referred to as *Devekut*. *Devekut* is a rich subject of its own, certainly worth its own book of stories interwoven with teachings from the masters of Kabbalah and Hasidism. In one sense, *Devekut*, attachment of the soul to its source in God, is the only thing that matters. It should be the only thing with which one's mind, heart, and energies should be occupied. This is the view of the great Hasidic master Barukh of Medzhibuzh, who lived in the eighteenth century and was a student of the great exemplar of Hasidism, Rabbi Israel Ba'al Shem Tov. He says, "Everything is secondary to the attachment (*devekut*) of the soul to the Exalted One."

And yet, there is a recognition that some of the most powerful experiences of *devekut*, or spiritual attachment, occur through the reality of longing. In one central teaching, the optimal moment for *devekut*, deep cleaving to God, is precisely when that kind of soul attachment seems impossible. In a simple yet profound statement, this selection from a work from the early eighteenth century, *The Statement of the Ba'al Shem Tov*, teaches that real equanimity, the state of being able to completely detach from day-to-day life, was brought on by *devekut*, attachment to God. However, such *devekut* was to take place not only in moments designed for prayer and contemplation, but at the most pedestrian moments of a person's life, such as when we are eating, engaging in business, or otherwise going about our day.

> "I hold God before me always . . ." (Psalms 16:8) "Hold" (*sh'viti*) implies "equanimity" (*hishtavut*). For every matter that befalls one, everything should be equal (*shaveh*) before him or her; whether this is a matter for which people express praise or ridicule. Similarly, this is how it should be with all other matters, as with food; whether one eats a fine meal or other things, all should be equal in his or her eyes[1]

Elsewhere, the *Ba'al Shem Tov* explicitly reminds us that the kind of spiritual attachment we seek should occur precisely when we feel it is unattainable:

> The intention should be the following: there are times when a person goes about his or her business in the world, and is unable to study, but nevertheless needs to be in a state of cleaving to God (*devekut*). Similarly, when a person goes on his or her way and is unable to pray or study as usual, and needs to serve God through other opportunities.
>
> A person should not cause oneself pain over this! For God wants people to serve Him in every way possible—sometimes in one mode and sometimes in another. Therefore, we find the opportunity to go on our way, or to do our dealings with other people, in order to serve God in another manner.[2]

Finding spiritual connection in the decidedly un-spiritual moments of our lives seems like a contradiction, and in fact, the *Ba'al Shem Tov* reminds us that only the great spiritual masters are able to do this with any consistency. And yet, he also suggests that such is the creative tension that fuels our inner lives. When we feel ourselves to be most isolated—put off, distracted, under duress, disgusted, even ridiculed—those are the ideal situations in which we find within us the capacity to attach most strongly.

Longing—The Gift of Space

From a mystical perspective, such longing is part of the spiritual structure of the universe that sustains the divine/human partnership over a seemingly infinite gulf. For Isaac Luria in the sixteenth century, the first act of God's creating the universe was an act of withdrawal, or *tzimtzum*, that would

1. *Tzva'at ha-Rivash*, 2.
2. Ibid., 3.

allow for the space that would become inhabited by all of creation. This includes not only the Earth and its creatures, but also the stars, celestial beings, and almost infinite space. As a parent provides a child with independence, so God withdrew to a distance from creation in order that it should flourish on its own. In turn, God's distance instilled within humanity a desire to bridge the relational gap, just as a growing child seeks to be reunited with a parent. And just as a wise parent anticipates how a child will run back with open arms, so Luria's God knows that human beings' drive to reach back to the source of creation will keep us from being forever alone.

Drawing on our own painful experiences of people being remote, we may balk at Luria's idea that God's *tzimtzum*, or withdrawal, can help us. But we should keep in mind that the mystical analogy is not exact, and that God is ultimately different from people. For mystics, God's *tzimtzum*, or retreat, is not abandonment, but generosity. God constricts the divine being so as to create the negative space in which everything else can exist. I am struck by the description of mystical *tzimtzum* in its earliest written form, from the book *Etz Chaim* (Tree of Life) by Rabbi Chaim Vital from the sixteenth century, faithfully related as the ideas of his teacher, Rabbi Isaac Luria. Here, *tzimtzum*, withdrawal, or God's distance is a kind of cosmic gift. Here are the opening lines of this encyclopedic book about the divine inner life:

> When it arose in the mind of God to create the universe, so as to bring good things to his created things, that they would know His greatness and . . . cleave to the exalted divine being, He brought forth just one point, that contained everything, even though everything was not revealed. It is like a human being composed of the four elements, without knowing that one is composed of each part by itself. In this matter as well, within this point was included ten at the beginning of (God's) emanation . . . and so all of the stream and life force of infinite being (*En Sof*) is drawn from this one point. And even as this light descended from the One who emanates, it was attached to a vessel, along with its soul, as if wearing a humble garment.[3]

Ultimately, the goal of creation, in the mind of God, is to give us the ability to "cleave to the exalted divine being," and so to "know" the unfathomable grandeur of the creator. But the pure light cannot exist in its pure form if we are to become attached to it in some way. There is a part of the divine that always must be hidden, just as we, as human beings, retain a part of ourselves that is always unknown and concealed. A vessel is devised

3. Vital, *Etz Chayim*, 1:1.

for the transmission of divine light to creation, but it is a vessel, a "humble garment," and not the light itself.

At first glance, then, the gulf between ourselves and God would seem to be an unfortunate obstacle. Except we, with our inherent desire to connect and bridge that gulf even a little, make it possible for God and humanity to exist in a constant and close relationship, even at a distance. In fact, the gulf between God and humanity is a necessary feature of creation, the cost of being created things. Interestingly, it is not through any fault of our own, or any kind of trauma brought on by an act of rebellion against God that accounts for this distance. It is simply the way things are, so that God can be known, and so that we may exist. The *Etz Chayim* continues:

> Know that . . . just as the great, supernal light is as the sun, and one does not have the strength to gaze upon it, except by diminishing its strength through a window or by means of a veil, or by the distance of space or a small hole. In the initial time of creation, the light came, not through a veil at all, and so when it shone as endless light, there was nothing strong enough to contain it, except by means of distance.[4]

Most simply, we need distance from God in order to live, even as God wishes to be known and our greatest delight is to "cleave" to God. But, God being infinite energy, the only way for God and humanity to begin to exist simultaneously is for there to be a protective and absolute separation. Otherwise, the pure and unadulterated divine energy would swallow us up. There is a gamble here. The creative dynamic between God and humanity depends not only upon God's power to reach us, but also upon our inherent yearning to connect. In the enforced separation from God and the ensuing loneliness that the *Etz Chayim* envisions, all depends upon our inherent desire to draw closer to the God we cannot see or fathom.

Vital's vision of creation shows that, with our drive to bridge that gulf, we may look into the presumed nothingness that separates us from God and instead discover something, however momentary and elusive that "something" may be. With respect to God, Vital suggests that reaching for such a connection, presumably through prayer, meditation, and acts of kindness or study, may yield just enough of a faint glimpse of the supernal "light" through the veil. By analogy, perhaps this vision promises that the mere act of reaching out from our isolation and loneliness may be all we need to remind ourselves that we are never alone. After all, we are "created" of God's impulse to be known. And while it may often seem as if we are alone, our simple desire to be known is itself proof of the "Knower" who created us in

4. Ibid.

the first place. From this mystical perspective, the Creator wants us to see our way out of the isolation between God and humanity, and relies on our inner capacity for connection do so, much like a parent and child depend upon each other.

A Child's Fear and Comfort

A great Hasidic master from the last century, Rabbi Kalonymus Kalman Shapira of Piaceszno, otherwise known as the Piaceszner Rebbe, sheds some light on the mechanism by which we discover our capacity for connection at our moments of greatest abandonment. To do so, he personalizes the Kabbalistic view of the gulf between each of us and the "other," whomever that other may be. Most importantly, he shows us how the mere awareness of our longings points to the existence of some other being in close proximity, easing our sense of isolation. The style of the Piaceszner is one of authority complemented by gentleness, a style that was probably linked to his being a Rosh Yeshiva, the director of a religious school for boys, in the 1920s and 1930s in Piaceszno, a suburb of Warsaw. In fact, there is something deeply significant and poignant that this great spiritual teacher was someone so concerned with and attuned to the souls of children.

A brief survey of Kalonymus' concerns about children in the modern world reveals much about his thoughts on the spiritual life. At root, Kalonymus believed modern culture alienates the child from his or her own inner self, the *neshama*, or soul given by God. Kalonymus observed that the modern world imbued children with a kind of authority that did not match their actual emotional, intellectual, or spiritual maturation. His particular objection was not that children were becoming too urbane or sexualized before an appropriate age, though these things concerned him. Rather, he felt that children were expected to embody a kind of autonomy and maturity before their minds and souls really had developed the ability to feel and understand as adults. In contrast to the rush to conformity demanded by the modern world, Kalonymus believed the goal of education was to imbue in each child a sense of their own unique "path" on which they could grow in understanding, closeness to God, and kindness to other people. And at the root of this endeavor was the imperative to make sure that children appreciate their own inner grandeur from being descendants of the prophets of Israel. Kalonymus does not specify which specific aspects of the prophetic legacy he had in mind. But perhaps it is enough to see in his constant calls to *devekut*, cleaving to God, the imperative to devote ourselves to finding the divine within all relationships.

In a short work that has come to be known as *B'nai Machshavah Tovah*, literally the "Community of Proper Consciousness," Kalonymus explores a typical moment between a child and parent that illustrates how our basic yearnings to bond form the core of our spiritual lives. All too often, says Kalonymus, we are impeded in our inner lives by relying on the conventions that shape our persona and outward actions. These are behaviors, habits of mind and heart that we learn over a lifetime. As adults, we have allowed this repertoire of ingrained habit to dominate us, separating ourselves from our inner lives. And so, says Kalonymus, we should look to children to unlearn the adult habits that dampen the life of the soul. This passage, in the middle of a longer discourse on the role of attending to our inner yearnings through the vehicle of music, draws its wisdom from the childlike core in each of us.

> There are times when words will not arise from within you, nor will you feel any explicit plea. Nevertheless, you will feel a kind of stirring for which it will be impossible for you to express what it is you feel, a kind of embrace. It is like a child who pesters one's father. He or she does not want anything from the father, except to call and intone, *"Avi, Avi*, Father, Father." The father asks, "What do you want, my child?" "Nothing," answers the child, and resumes beckoning and intoning, *"Avi, Avi*, Father, Father."[5]

In this recollection of childhood, Kalonymus suggests that we are like the child. Ironically, we too may feel an ongoing existential embrace as well as a constant need to reassure ourselves that there is a source behind that embrace. We may need nothing, but like the child, feel an inner need to call out, like Elisha, *"Avi, Avi."* However, unlike Elisha, a child has not yet internalized the sense of presence to understand that the parent is always there. If anything, the presence of the parent does little to reassure the child! In an unfiltered display of a human being's fear of loneliness, the child is always calling out, *"Avi, Avi."*

For Kalonymus, the child expresses the constant yearning of our soul.

> Know, that in the matter of the soul's revelation, there are many instances in which we can learn from children. All of their actions are without intention. Their souls readily reveal them- selves in different aspects, and they act and move according to the ways in which their souls move them. Even this pestering is the pouring out of the child's soul to the soul of the father. And so you may occasionally feel in your singing a kind of murmur- ing or pleading: voiceless, wordless and unattached to any need.

5. Shapira, *B'nai Machshavah Tovah*, 43.

It is simply your soul pouring itself out and expressing, "Master
of the Universe, Master of the Universe."[6]

Just as we see with a child, so it is with us. When we are aware of our
simple and basic longing, we know that we are the company of the One who
is always there, yet revealed only in faint whispers.

Like a child, we may feel ourselves cut off and alone. And in that state,
whether we know it our not, we are reaching out constantly. We call out
without any specific need, desire or prayer in mind. That constant plea is
the autonomic gesture of our soul to attach itself to something greater than
ourselves. And to be satisfied, we do not require any kind of response, proof
or visitation. It is as if the calling out is itself our soul's act of self-soothing to
remind us that we exist, at all times, in the presence of another.

It would seem that we would learn this spiritual understanding by being cared for as children by our parents. Perhaps the early, nurturing web
of relationships that the prophet Elisha experienced facilitated his ability to
carry on once his mentor Elijah left this earth.

But I believe that, for Kalonymus, as with the story of Elisha, the analogy runs deeper. The soul's constant calling out is simply a part of our being
human, regardless of what we received or didn't receive from our parents.
In fact, for Kalonymus, we require some disruption in that parent-child
bonding, a feeling of abandonment, if only for a moment, to learn that we
are in the midst of a presence more transcendent and abiding than even
our parents. The feeling of being abandoned evokes our yearnings, which,
if we attend to them, may confirm that we are always in the presence of
something unknowable, but real and loving. Just like Elisha, who leaves his
loving parents to become an apprentice and then loses his surrogate father
to become a prophet, we, too, may need to experience a bit of the void to
discover that our capacity for attachment is stronger and more constant than
the external forces of alienation. Our constant yearning to connect restores
our sense of belonging when we feel abandoned by God, lose people in our
lives, or simply despair over a world whose rhythms and customs enforce
our collective separation and fragmentation.

There is a way in which the life of this teaching, and particularly the life
of Kalonymus Kalman Shapira, bears witness to the strength of our yearnings over the forces of destruction and loss. *B'nai Machshavah Tovah* was
not published during the lifetime of Kalonymus Kalman Shapira, but was
discovered by chance following his death. After the Nazis invaded Poland
in 1939, the home of the Shapira family fell within the confines of the Warsaw Ghetto. As the deprivations increased and the liquidation proceeded

6. Ibid.

through the Spring of 1942, Kalonymus continued to write and teach, even as he lost his wife, son, and mother, as well as daughter-in-law and sister-in-law. He collected a series of manuscripts and placed them in a milk can, which he then stored underground with instructions that, should he not survive the war, the manuscripts were to be sent to his brother in B'nai Brak, outside Tel Aviv, who would publish them. Kalonymus survived the liquidation of the ghetto, but ultimately died in Warsaw in 1943, presumably executed with a group of Jews held in a prison camp, all bound by a pact not to escape unless they could all leave together. Amazingly, his writings were discovered and the finder followed his instructions, and we are blessed to learn from this great soul who sought and found holiness amidst barbarism and dehumanization. One can imagine Kalonymus modeling his life on his reverence for the prophets of Israel, fully living out his mission as a spiritual teacher, like both Elijah and Elisha, just as everything that constituted his life and world went up in flames.

I find this teaching, and all teachings of Kalonymus, incomparably deep and full of empathy. I especially find his example of a yearning child discovering the quiet reassurance of presence to be familiar, especially now in my adult life, as I have had time to experience how childhood yearnings nurture and strengthen the soul. Kalonymus seems to see what I have seen in the lives of Elijah and Elisha, in the mystical idea of *tzimtzum,* and in my own life of struggling with the reality of an absent father: that an innate capacity to seek closeness may be more enduring than a sense of abandonment, and that even the smallest hint of abiding presence is enough to show that our constant reaching out is meaningful, based on something real apart from our own desires. We may have our isolation imposed upon us, or we may bring it about through our own actions and decisions. But perhaps, like Elisha, and like the childlike part of us, we may also discover that our loneliness awakens us to our inner longings, which may ultimately reveal the source to which they are directed in the first place.

Chapter 3

Finding a Voice

A round the time I prepared to confront my father at the age of sixteen, I was taking a class in creative writing at my high school. My school was the LaGuardia High School of Music and the Arts in New York City, the combination of the renowned Music and Art High School and the High School of Performing Arts, of "Fame" fame. Among the school's charms was its ability to attract teachers who were eccentric and passionate and who in turn inspired their students. One of those teachers was my creative writing teacher, Karyn Kay.

Ms. Kay was in her mid-thirties and dressed like David Byrne, lead singer of the group Talking Heads, in the concert movie *Stop Making Sense* (1984)—oversized clothes with weird folds everywhere, the effect of which was to make her look like someone who spent a lot of time in avant-garde art galleries and art movie houses, which she did. Ms. Kay would bring her experience in these places into class as we read James Joyce, Joseph Conrad, Hemingway, and other modernist masters whom we were supposed to learn from. She also helped me get my first internship, writing press releases and doing assorted grunt work for an art cinema collective in Greenwich Village.

Not surprisingly, I always remembered something Ms. Kay stressed to us in our writing, which was to cultivate our own sense of "voice." I understood that she didn't mean style, or an ability to sound cleverly ironic or have a facility with a turn of phrase. Instead, I knew she was trying to convey the ability to imprint upon our work a signature that only we could, through the prism of our life experience.

In a moving passage, Kalonymus Kalman Shapira finds this sense of one's authentic voice in music, in particular in the experience of singing a *niggun*, or wordless melody.

> Take for yourself some part of a *niggun* (melody). Turn your face to the wall, or simply close your eyes and continue meditating, as if you are standing before the Throne of Glory. And with your broken heart you have come to pour out your soul before God in song and melody that emanates from the depths of your heart. Then, from within, you will feel your soul break out in song. Even if from the beginning you felt as if you were singing to your soul to rouse it from its slumber, little by little you will feel your soul has already begun to sing on its own.[1]

In art, as in this teaching, there is the assumption that one's authentic spiritual voice is found in solitude. A writer will speak with great hope but also great fear about a blank page, and a painter the same way about a blank canvas, and here Kalonymus speaks of a moment of one's soul singing in private meditation. But really, all of these experiences partake of community. All forms of art take place within a tradition and in relationship to some audience, even if it is merely the invention of the creator's imagination.

This inherent irony in finding one's artistic or spiritual inner voice highlights the inherently confounding nature of community. In our series of overlapping relationships, none provide an absolute sense of communion, and yet together they form a holistic sense of belonging. Within these relationships, or perhaps transcending all of them, God is remote, ethereal, and elusive. Human beings on the other hand are very much present, but often preoccupied with themselves and occasionally unpredictable in how available they will be for us. To temper these personal idiosyncrasies, human beings organize into communities and these communities may create a sense of order and constancy. But they also may become a forum for the most offensive and disturbing behavior, and while they may at times provide us an existential anchor in life, they are in fact are constantly changing.

And so, among all of these relationships, there is always a breach, a point at which there is an absence of connection. In the striving to connect, we inadvertently create an absence of connection. And yet, we depend on this highly imperfect structure of community to cultivate our own Jewish spiritual "voices," whether through the teachings we absorb, the acts of kindness we engage in, and the ways in which we participate in rituals and interact around official and informal customs.

1. Ibid., 43.

To live as a Jew is to take on this effort of finding one's spiritual voice while engaging among these complex relationships with God, individual human beings, and shifting groups of people. At our best, we are enriched and ennobled by the best each has to give. We also may be challenged to sacrifice, endure pain, and give up part of ourselves in the process.

The Breach as an Impossible Struggle

The isolation of living in the breach, and the promise of finding some kind of internal spiritual voice within it, is a conundrum that stretches back to the Hebrew prophets. Caught between God and humanity, the prophets are profound examples of how unbearable and how untenable living in this breach can be. And yet, the prophets embrace their unique isolation and transcend it in order to fully become themselves. No other figures in the Bible except the prophets so vociferously argue with God as they alternatively excoriate and comfort human beings. In doing so, the prophets evoke the full range of experience we encounter everyday: loss, failure, and despair, but also hope, justice, and universal love. Although it may appear impossible to live in this breach while also discovering and marshaling this internal, spiritual voice, the prophets show us how it not only can be done, but that it must be done.

God's lament to the prophet Ezekiel expresses both the extreme challenge and the promise of the breach. Ezekiel lived in exile in Babylonia, just before the conquest of Jerusalem by Nebuchadnezzar, in the early sixth century BCE. He offers promises of renewal and visions of a restored temple and a restored Jerusalem, complete with its rituals and sacrifices. But in order to place the renewal and return in context, he must remind the people why they were exiled to Babylonia in the first place. In this passage, we see what is actually a familiar lament by God over the complete corruption of Israelite society before the destruction of the temple in Jerusalem in 586 BCE. In this description, a familiar description emerges: the public officials are totally corrupt and rapacious; the false prophets lie; the people abuse one another in every imaginable way.

However, what is new here is the role of the prophet. God, as usual, does not intervene in the day-to-day affairs of human beings, instead leaving them to their own devices to succeed or fail. But, even for God, there is a breaking point at which the anger and capacity for punishment will be triggered. When it is, it will be like a switch going off, and nothing can stop it once it has started. In this revealing passage, God expresses the desire for a prophet who will, literally, occupy the breach between God and the people, so as to defend the people and arouse God's compassion, thereby averting the inevitable destruction that comes as a predictable consequence of the people's moral degradation. This passage is from Ezekiel 22:30–31.

> Her officials are like wolves rending prey in her midst; they shed blood and destroy lives to win ill-gotten gain. Her prophets, too, daub the wall for them with plaster. They prophesy falsely and deceitfully for them; they say, "Thus said Adonai God," when God had not spoken. And the people of the land have practiced fraud and committed robbery; they have wronged the poor and needy, have defrauded the stranger without redress. And so I searched for a man, a fence-mender, somebody who would stand in the breach before Me on behalf of the land, that I not destroy the land. But I did not find one . . . .

Unfortunately, as God laments, not one human being, no matter how spiritually gifted, is capable of standing in the breach between God and humanity. It is a remarkable statement. All the prophets who came before were failures. A reader familiar with biblical history will have in mind the great prophet Jeremiah, who lived in Jerusalem at the time of the destruction and who over thirty-three biblical chapters browbeats the people while imploring them to pursue simple, daily justice to redeem the world. One may also have in mind Moses' breathtaking arguments, in which he protests that God cannot destroy the Israelites leaving Egypt when they rebel because it would be against God's nature to do so. And yet, neither prophet succeeds in his task. Despite Jeremiah's devotion to the people and to God, Jerusalem is destroyed and its elite exiled. Moses, after leading the people for forty years in the desert, is denied entry into the promised land, failing when all eyes are upon him.

These apparent failures prove God's lament that none of us are truly fit to tolerate the in-between state between living with the constancy of God's presence and the lonely, daily grind of living when God seems hidden. And yet, Jewish tradition has sought fit to preserve this prophetic legacy, in large part so that we absorb some bit of the prophetic archetype as part of our lives as people who yearn for moral wholeness in our world as well as spiritual closeness with people and with God. And so, living in the breach endures as a hopeful contradiction in our lives: true wholeness and communion may be impossible, but the effort to achieve it may be necessary to our own evolving humanity.

When Elisha cries *"Avi, Avi,* Father, Father" as his mentor Elijah leaves this world, he resolves to live this impossible and contradictory fence-mender's life. Upon losing Elijah, Elisha immediately takes up his mentor's mantle, and so embedded in that cry of longing must be some sign of the qualities that enable him to endure it and carry on. Elisha's cry of *"Avi, Avi"* may have meant, "my spiritual father is gone," but also "I will take on the work of my spiritual father," "I will seek comfort and purpose in my devotion to others," "I will seek strength in the reality that is hidden." Notably, Elisha's cry it is quite different from his mentor Elijah's response to loss and abandonment, which was to first give up all hope for living. Only after being instructed by the messenger of God does Elijah listen for the still, fragile voice of all creation. By contrast, Elisha reaches into himself to express the loss but also connect to the constant spiritual reality that will be his focus as he moves on. These two prophets were so close to each other, and yet both discover very different internal spiritual voices as they confront the breach in their own lives. We invite the spirit of Elijah every Saturday evening at *Havdalah* and at each Passover *seder*. But it is really Elisha who provides the model for how we straddle the worlds of security and loss, the holy and the everyday.

Confronting and Accepting the Breach

Like most children of divorce, I was all too familiar with living in the breach. Often, I was caught in the impossible middle between my father on one side and my mother and grandmother on the other, especially when conflicts arose. I coped with this breach by retreating into silence when it was clear that expressing my real desires would disappoint someone.

From the time just before my ninth birthday until a few months after I turned ten, I developed a sense of dread as I became aware of a widening gulf between me and my father over where I should live. Ironically, the tension began to build exactly at the point when we had grown closest. Between 3rd and 4th grade, I had spent the month of a summer with my father, my stepmother Lauren, and two-year-old half-brother Max in Brooklyn. I loved my summer in the city, with its newfound independence, outings only the city could offer, and warm family time. It had gone so well that my father proposed that I come live with him, Lauren, and Max. On paper it seemed ideal. But I wanted to stay where I was, on Long Island with my grandparents, the school and friends I had known. My preference was unequivocal, and yet my response was a deafening silence.

After that summer, most weekend visits with my father came to include an excruciating conversation in which he would ask if I wanted to come live with him. I never did, but I could also never bring myself to say "no." I let my silence do the talking for me—no argument, no tears, and no demonstrative sadness. Eventually, I learned that my father formally filed for custody, which implanted in me the greatest fear, that I would have to go on record as both judge and jury and risk losing my father's love forever. And, in fact, that is exactly what happened. After about a year and a half, the family court dismissed my father's petition, and following a ten-day visit over school vacation, my father stopped calling and there were no more visits. As I held the breach in silence during the year-and-a-half custody battle, so I kept my silence in the years after my father retreated from my life. In all that time, I didn't cry or express anxiety over my father's absence. If anything, it was a relief not to have to respond to his requests and be a part of those painful conversations.

But after a couple of years, I had to break my silence as I confronted the breach again, this time in the form of an invitation to my cousin Adam's bar mitzvah. Adam was my father's nephew, my first cousin, and we were especially close. By the time my father broke off from me, Adam was more than my first cousin. We had become best friends, sharing the deepest childhood secrets anyone would cringe to recall later. But there was also a cultural and perhaps even spiritual layer to our bond. It was through Adam and his family that I came to know about Judaism as it was lived and practiced. Seders happened every year at Adam's house, and if I found myself at Adam's on a Friday night, we would have a full *Shabbes* dinner, with *Kiddush* and blessings. My first experience away from home was with Adam at a Zionist summer camp. But I had not seen nor heard from Adam for almost three years after my father broke off contact.

When I received an invitation to Adam's bar mitzvah, I knew with complete certainty that I simply could not attend. My grandparents and my mother encouraged me to go, but in my mind, there was no deliberation—it was just accepted fact, totally impossible. Not even my love for Adam, the closest person I had to a brother that I always longed for, could pull me over the abyss into a confrontation with my father.

Once I let it be known that I wasn't going, my grandmother Diana, ever respectful of social convention, insisted that I write a note declining. I dreaded this simple gesture, as declining the invitation forced me to explicitly say "no" to my father. As I sat in my room, ready to put pen to paper, I just sobbed and sobbed like I never had before. In my mind, I cried not over my father, but over losing my connection to Adam. But in reality, crying over Adam was a way to channel all of the pent-up rage toward my father for his deception, his weakness, and the unfairness with which he set me up. In the adult world, we can often cherry-pick our relationships, even those that are in a larger web. But for a child, who depends on parents for relationships within a family, making these in-between selections is impossible. I knew this intuitively.

I also knew that I did not want to be with my father. During our conversations when he would ask me to come live with him, he said that he wanted me to be happy. But in his absence, I knew he revealed his true intentions by distancing himself when he couldn't get what he wanted. And so I declined Adam's bar mitzvah invitation, crying with sadness and fury for a long time, alone, until I was done. Although it would be another three years before I would reach out to my father, I never again cried over anything that had to do with him.

The Rabbinic Abraham—Model of Living in the Breach

As I look back on this moment, I see it as an episode critical to developing my own internal voice in the face of loss and an uncertain future. Like Elisha, my cry allowed me to let go of an either/or life and begin to accept the reality of living in between. I felt and recognized my loss, accepted my life as less than ideal, but nevertheless trusted that there would be something else to anchor me, even if I didn't know what that something else would be. I have absolutely no idea where this kind of emotional confidence came from.

The rabbis imply that finding one's voice between love and loss is an inherently Jewish gesture. In a series of complex and provocative *midrashim* about Abraham, stories composed by the rabbis roughly 1,800 years ago and elaborated upon in the Middle Ages, there is an argument that negotiating the twin prospects of abandonment and love is a necessary and archetypal struggle. Following Kalonymus, parts of this story have been taught to young children for generations, and its first half was the first *midrash* I ever learned on my first day of Sunday school.

The story concerns the growing animosity between Abraham and his father, Terach, and like all *midrashim* composed by the rabbis it supplies information that is not in the Torah. While the original text of the Torah depicts a quiet, uncomplicated relationship between Abraham and his father, the *midrash* envisions irreconcilable conflict. According to the story the rabbis tell in the Middle Ages, the conflict begins before Abraham's birth, when the evil and mighty King Nimrod predicts the greatness and eventual dominance of Abraham. Feeling threatened, Nimrod offers Terach an abundance of silver and gold if he will kill his child, who is soon to be born. Terach refuses the offer and chooses instead to hide Abraham in a cave, where he lives alone for three years. When he emerges from the cave, baby Abraham demonstrates his great spiritual sensitivity as he tries to discern who created the sun, the moon, and him. As the sun, the moon, and the stars all fade from view, Abraham realizes there must be something else. He asks his father, who shows Abraham his idols, which he claims are the things that created the sun, the moon, and the stars.

Of course, Abraham has a sense that his father's ideas are completely worthless, and the original *midrash*, composed by the rabbis nearly 1,800 years ago, depict Abraham's great spiritual sensitivity and intelligence, which lead him to defy his father.

> Terach was a worshipper of statues and sold them. One time he went out and had Abraham sell in his place. A man came in asking to purchase. Abraham asked, "How old are you?" That man said, "I am fifty or sixty." Abraham said, "Woe to the man who is sixty and wishes to worship something made yesterday!" The man was embarrassed and went away. Another time a woman came in carrying in her hand a large cask of flour. She said to him, "Take some of this and lay it in front of the statues as a sacrifice." Abraham took a hammer and shattered the statues, placing a hammer in the hand of the biggest among them. When his father returned, he asked, "Who did all of this?" Abraham said, "What can I say? A woman came in with a cask of flour and asked me to present it before them as a sacrifice. One said, 'I will eat it first.' Then another said, 'I will eat it first.' Then the biggest of them took a hammer and shattered them."[2]

Generations of Jewish teachers have told this story to young children because it seems like a playful and comic introduction to Judaism's central tenet: one God, anything else is a fake. But its staying power, I believe, stems from the way it captures the universal crisis all children face in separating from and even rejecting their parents as they discover their own view of the world, essentially, their own voice. For most people, this willing step into the breach is a necessary part of becoming most fully ourselves. In Abraham's case, it seems he has no choice but to reject everything his father believes and stands for. Instead of his father, Abraham places his trust in a God he knows only by inference, a God who seems absent, hidden, and without form. Abraham therefore lives in an impossible state of in-between, rejecting the father who has protected and cared for him, but attaching himself to a God who is invisible and unreal to everyone but him. Remarkably, Abraham exhibits no concern about living in this breach, as he is confident that the unseen God he chooses is more reliable and constant than his father of flesh and blood. Sotto voce, the *midrash* makes a revolutionary and

2. *Midrash Rabbah*, Genesis 38:19.

enduring statement: in a world of violence and falsehoods, each of us may follow our own internal search for authenticity to a universal God who is unseen and rarely heard.

Abraham Betrayed

The second part of the story, which we keep from young children because it is simply too frightening, suggests that a person's internal spiritual connection is more enduring than anything, whether that be the dangers of the world or even the love of one's parent. As the story continues, Terach reveals his cynicism and does the unthinkable, bringing Abraham back to Nimrod to be put to death for his disobedience.

> Terach said to Abraham, "You are lying to me. Do they know anything?" Abraham answered, "You say they cannot. Your ears do not hear what your mouth is saying!" Terach took Abraham and submitted him to punishment before Nimrod. Nimrod said, "Let us bow to the fire." Abraham said, "Let us bow to the water that quenches the fire." Nimrod said, "Let us bow to the water." Abraham said, "If so, let us bow to the clouds that hold the water." Nimrod said, "Let us bow to the clouds." Abraham said, "Let us bow to the winds that scatter the clouds." Nimrod said, "Let us bow to the wind." Abraham said, "Let us bow to a human being that withstands the wind." Nimrod said, "You are speaking empty words. As for me, I only bow down to the fire, and now I will cast you into it. Perhaps your god to whom you bow will save you from it."[3]

Of course, God saves Abraham from the fiery furnace. The tragic figure in this story is ultimately Terach. Obviously, he loses his relationship with Abraham. But Abraham had a brother, Haran, who actually dies because of the ordeal that Abraham had to endure. As Abraham's punishment by the hands of Nimrod is unfolding, the *midrash* imagines Haran thinking to himself about where his allegiance lies.

> Haran thought to himself, "If Abraham prevails then I will say that I am for Abraham. If Nimrod prevails then I will say that I am for Nimrod." Whereupon Abraham descended into the fiery pit and was saved. They asked Haran, "Who are you for?" He said, "I am with Abraham," whereupon they took him and cast him into the fire where his insides were devoured, and then he

3. Ibid.

emerged and died in front of Terach, his father. Therefore, it is written, "Haran died in front of Terach, his father."[4]

Terach says nothing. As Abraham is about to be cast to his grisly death, God saves Abraham, and Nimrod and Terach are not so much chastened as rendered completely silent and impotent. Terach, though, loses everything, and so this story becomes as much about the consequences of not living in the breach as the risks of doing so.

Ultimately, embedded in this story is both a horrifying reality as well as a radical strategy. People are imperfect and unpredictable, and even those charged with protecting us may contribute to our own pain and suffering. The antidote to the danger of this world is to seek the source of truth that we know through our internal capacities to absorb the wonder and mystery of all things. Following our inherent, childlike curiosity of this mystery will eventually force us to confront the half-truths, rationalizations, and other falsities we are given, sometimes for our own protection. But once we have experienced even a glimpse of this mystery, like Abraham in his years after emerging from the cave, that seed of curiosity stays with us, and develops into both an evolving understanding of the world as well as an internalized yearning to understand more. Over time, that yearning matures into something unique to each of us yet shared in common, and abides in a life that may very well continue to have its share of trial and disillusionment.

Living *in the Breach*—Moving towards Judaism

From my earliest encounters with Judaism, I always felt that it promised something more, even though I couldn't articulate what that "more" was. As I reflect now, it's remarkable to me that as a child, I not only sought out that sense of "more" in Judaism, but I believed it was there. Even though my family never spoke about a Jewish education, as my friends started going to Hebrew school, I knew it was time.

When I was twelve and approaching bar mitzvah, Judaism was beginning to become a vehicle for my own spiritual voice, just as I was becoming aware of the breaches in my own life. Six months after declining my cousin Adam's invitation, I would celebrate my own bar mitzvah, with my mother, my new stepfather, and my grandparents. Looking at a portrait of all of us in the synagogue, I feel warmly toward that moment, because I now see how a new spiritual foundation was forming beneath my childhood experience of loss. Among the adults in the photo, each in their own way looks a fish out

---

4. Ibid.

of water against the backdrop of the upscale Temple Sinai sanctuary. But I, with my prayer book open and my *tallit*, look comfortable. I recall feeling at home with my rabbi and cantor, excited with a sense of accomplishment to be reading the Torah and chanting the *Haftara*, eager to take my place in Jewish tradition and among the Jewish people. I had no idea what God was. But I also knew that despite living with my religiously alienated grandparents, despite being silently bereft of a father, brother, and cousin, I had reached into something profound—beyond my father, beyond my family, beyond myself.

Like Elisha when he leaves with Elijah, I set out to do something that was part of the broader structure of my family's world, but essentially alien to them. I looked to my synagogue as a place where I could begin to seek out a different kind of voice, both from within and without. As a child, stepping into synagogue gave me a sense of presence and belonging, both intimate and foreign, qualities I found equally compelling. I did not feel a personal sense of God in the synagogue, but I did sense a kind of indifferent presence when I was there. Ironically, this non-personalized, indifferent sense of presence imparted its own kind of reassurance. It fostered an expectation that the adults, and particularly the rabbis, would somehow be wise, kind, and learned because they were accountable to something more grand than the rest of us. There was a feeling, particularly in an almost empty sanctuary, that we were not alone. The indifferent presence set an expectation that even Hebrew school, for all of its inconvenience and boredom, was important, because it was part of something larger. I had a feeling that if that disembodied presence with no form or name was there before I stepped into the Temple, I could count on it always being there. Whether I pleased the adults around me or disappointed them, there would be something bigger and constant in my experience. An indifferent presence, as opposed to my father, would not, could not, be angry with me, and it would never leave me. The choice, whether to stay or go, was entirely my own.

A Paradox: God as Present When Absent

Looking back to how I invested my childhood synagogue with something more grand, I realize that I experienced something of how different voices in Jewish tradition understand *tzimtzum* as both the withdrawal as well as concentration of God's presence. Even in the casual expectations many of us have that a synagogue, an exceedingly human institution, be a "house of God," we actually hold an ancient expectation. In the way Jewish mystics think about God, the retreat of God's presence brought about a heightened intensity of God as concentrated, focused in a smaller space.

It's this side of *tzimtzum*, the aspect of God being present and concentrated, that has its roots among the rabbis of the Talmud, about 1,200–1,300 years before Isaac Luria. The rabbis of the Talmud and the Midrash express the paradox of God's in-between state in the following way: "God is the place of the universe, but the universe is not God's place." How can it be, wonder the rabbis, that the *Shekhinah*, God's presence, exists everywhere, and yet, "dwells among the people," as the Torah promises.

The rabbis' answer is that the *Shekhinah*, the divine presence, "contracts" itself, engages in an act of *tzimtzum*, so as to become encountered at that one particular point, even as God is infinite. According to the rabbis, God was found, concentrated, or embodied uniquely in the *mishkan*, the portable sanctuary in the desert, and in the temple in Jerusalem. After all, the Bible shows us in a number of places how the divine presence retains a special power inside the *mishkan* in the desert as well as the temple in Jerusalem: the divine voice issues from between the two images of *keruvim*, heavenly angels, above the ark; those who trespass the sacred boundaries of the sanctuary will be vaporized by the power that resides there; a cloud of God's "glory" filled the sanctuary upon Solomon's dedication of the temple in Jerusalem. These examples prompt the question, how far can God go in such embodiment and contraction? Since God is limitless, so God's capacity for *tzimtzum* is limitless. According to the rabbis, God can contract Godself to an infinitesimal point between the two images of the heavenly beings in the *mishkan*, and even be found between the two hairs on a person's head.[5]

But for Isaac Luria via his student Rabbi Chayim Vital, the contracted state of God at this point is actually a reminder of God's fundamental withdrawal into Godself, and so a reminder of both presence and absence at the same time. At the beginning of the book *Etz Chayim*, Vital reflects on how God had, by necessity, to contract the unending light of *En Sof*, of infinity, in order to make space for creation. Of course, a breach had to be created, a distance between God and the created world, lest the created world be absorbed by God's energy. And so there was *tzimtzum*, withdrawal, God's self-retraction to make room for the creation whose ultimate purpose is to know God. The ultimate emblem of this simultaneous absence and presence is found at that point between the two heavenly creatures.

> "And I shall speak with you . . . from between the two *keruvim* . . ." (Exodus 25:18), for the *Shekhinah* (divine presence) was contracted there, and from this one point emanated ten points

5. Heschel, *Torah min HaShamayim*, 59-61.

from *Keter* (the highest divine potency) to *Malkhut* (the divine potency closest to humanity).[6]

At that one point, God is, in a very real sense, clothed in a form that serves as a kind of protective barrier between God and humanity. There is a real distance as God takes on the form of the ten "*sefirot*," or potencies whose power and energy is always shifting. But at the same time, it is the ability of the infinite God to be clothed in these forms that renders God accessible. The disguise is also the revelation. The absence of God, the space that induces longing, is also the vehicle through which God is known to human beings.

And so, as much as the *mishkan* addresses the human need for closeness, it is more an emblem of the in-between states of closeness and distance. This becomes clear in a single image at the end of the Book of Exodus, when the building of the *mishkan* is finally complete. After all of the detailed instructions incumbent upon Moses and the people, and after the Torah records that they executed all of these instructions perfectly, we may expect a new kind of intimacy between God and humanity as a reward for all of this labor. But strangely, at this moment of unprecedented harmony between God and humanity, the Torah instead introduces an image of separation. In the concluding lines of the Book of Exodus, the Torah tells us that while the "Glory of God" filled the *mishkan*, a cloud surrounded it, and so Moses was unable to enter. Why, at the moment when God could be so close to the people does God impose a barrier to communication and intimacy?

A compelling answer is provided by a sixteenth-seventeenth-century commentator of a mystical bent, Rabbi Efraim ben Aaron Luntschitz, in his book the *Kli Yakar*. Luntschitz was the rabbi of Prague for the final fifteen years of his life, from 1604–19. His commentary emerges as part of a great period of Jewish creative flowering, both in general and among Jews in Eastern Europe. His life overlaps somewhat with the mystical renaissance in Israel that produced and was also generated by the presence of Isaac Luria and his teachings on the ever-unfolding creative cycle enumerated in this book. His lifespan also overlaps with that of the Polish Rabbi Moses Isserles from Krakow, whose compendium of *halakhah* (Jewish law) was published around the same time as the great *Shulkhan Arukh* (set table) of Joseph Karo, who like Luria lived in Tzfat among the mystics. Today, a traditional edition of the *Shulkhan Arukh* is almost always printed with the glosses of Rabbi Moses Isserles. It is in this context that Luntschitz wrote the *Kli Yakar*, which takes a somewhat transcendent view of the biblical text,

6. Vital, *Etz Chayim*, 1:1.

often reaching for the deepest levels of "meta" philosophical and mystical interpretation.

On this last image from the Book of Exodus, we see the author of the *Kli Yakar* meditating on the paradox of God being close and remote at the same time. Specifically, God is made manifest to the people in a way whose only parallel is the moment of God's self-disclosure at Mount Sinai. But inevitably, God must preserve some distance between Godself and the people for the relationship to even be possible, in this case, for the people to gaze upon the "Glory of God."

> "The cloud covered the Mishkan and the Glory of God filled the Mishkan . . ." (Exodus 40:35). It appears that the "Glory of God" is not the cloud, but rather the fire and the light, which is to say that the "Glory of God" is that which appeared from *amid* the cloud. For without the cloud, one could not look at it (meaning the Glory of God). For just as one is unable to peer directly at the light of sun, all the more so is one unable to gaze at the resplendent light of the *Shekhinah* (divine presence). Therefore, the holy light was always viewed from the midst of the cloud. But when the Mishkan was established, they separated one from the other. For when the divine light would enter the Mishkan, for that is the place of its holiness, the cloud would remain outside.[7]

Under usual circumstances, the divine fire and protecting cloud would combine so as to provide the people with a "vision" of the "Glory of God" they could sustain. The cloud was a filter to the overwhelming, sun-like power of the divine fire, which no human being could reasonably behold. Ironically, at the moment of the building of the *mishkan*, when God and humanity should draw into a new closeness, the divine fire and protecting cloud separated—not totally, but just enough, so that the fire filled the *mishkan* while a cloud surrounded the *mishkan* itself. In this way, at this moment of greatest intimacy, there is a true barrier to divine-human closeness. Perhaps the shielding cloud still protects the people from the absolute power of the divine fire. But the price is that the domain of the *mishkan*, that meeting point between people and God, is too filled with God's presence to be useful. And so, for the moment, entry is blocked. Once the divine fire recedes from the *mishkan*, then Moses can enter and draw closer, on behalf of himself and on behalf of the people.

To substantiate his interpretation, the author of the *Kli Yakar* hearkens back to the end of God's self-disclosure on Sinai, recorded in Exodus chapter 24, during which God invites Moses to draw closer to sanctify the

7. Lunschitz, *Kli Yakar* on Exodus 40:35, in *Miqra'ot Gedolot*.

covenant between God and the people. Why, we may wonder, does Moses enter a cloud there, but is unable to do so after he has finished building the *mishkan*? Again, it comes back to the way in which we may only draw close when the Glory of God is shielded from us. Such was the case, says the *Kli Yakar*, at Sinai. But here, once the *mishkan* is built, the divine fire of God's "Glory" is no longer protected in the same way, and so Moses and the people must remain at a distance.

> For there, since the Glory of God was covered by a cloud, it was possible for Moses to enter. But now, since they have separated one from the other, with the cloud being outside and the Glory of God without the cloud inside the Tent of Meeting, Moses was therefore unable to enter the Tent. . . . By these words are solved many doubts in this matter that troubled the traditional biblical commentators.[8]

What were these "many doubts" that he alludes to? On one level, it's a textual question as to why Moses is unable to enter, the relative position of the "Glory of God" and protecting cloud, and how they work. But on a deeper level, I believe he is responding to the paradoxical intimacy as well as the sense of confounding distance that people find with the God of the Torah. In order to draw close to God, there must be a veil, and the closer we come to any kind of intimacy with the transcendent presence of the divine, the less we are able to "see," which is to say, comprehend or translate into everyday language.

The *Kli Yakar* suggests that the final image of Exodus embodies both sides of the experience of *tzimtzum* in a single moment: the necessary remoteness of God, but also concentrated grandeur and awe. This interpretation touches on a common experience: we are always living between communion and isolation, even or especially as we live with their mediating forms, be they the *mishkan*, the covenant, Torah, community, a synagogue, a text, or some other element of what we call "religious" life. These mediating forms can become our vehicles to draw closer, but at times they may also obscure the connection we are seeking. Each of us being different, we approach both the distance and prospect of closeness in our own way. The mediating forms then, imbued with the *tzimtzum*, the contraction of the divine presence but also the absence or withdrawal of God, form the basis of our shared spiritual vocabulary to give shape to our individual, inchoate voices.

For me, I encounter this *tzimtzum*, this concentration of inexplicable energy and healing, in the vehicles of relationship. More than study, or

8. Ibid.

prayer, or holiday rituals, the myriad ways in which Judaism and all of life provide us the means to connect are the conduits for my spiritual voice. In a life in which I have often been afraid of being alone, moments of generosity from others have given me a vision of something beyond what I had known, as well as invested mundane, everyday reality with a compelling sense of mystery. In my early life, my father established himself as impossibly remote, and as I came to discover later, retreated into his sacred myth. But that deeply sad and traumatic event did not stop me from finding love, friends, teachers, mentors, and communities. In each of these contexts, every kindness from another was itself like a revelation, an unexpected surprise. It is part of my "*anokhi*" ("I"), my understanding of who I am at my core, that I seek out and open myself to these experiences, even as no one human being can provide everything I seek.

The Garden: Seeking Presence from Absence

Amid these sources about the beginnings of a spiritual life, I feel compelled to share a final story from the Talmud. It is, to my mind, the ultimate story about pursuing a remote God, seeking certainty and failing in the pursuit, and so struggling to find a voice while living between the real world and the spiritual one we may believe has some kind of existence.

The story is known as the "The Four Who Entered the Garden (*Pardes*)." It is widely viewed as a foundation of Jewish mysticism, of seeking God without mediating barriers, and it is found in Tractate *Hagigah* 14b.

> Our Rabbis taught: Four entered the Garden and these are they: Ben Azzai, Ben Zoma, Acher (the Other One), and Rabbi Akiva. Rabbi Akiva said to them, "When you reach the place where there are stones of pure marble, do not call out 'Water, Water.' For it is written, 'One who speaks falsely shall no longer stand before me' (Psalms 101:7) . . . ."[9]

As the Talmud relates in other places, the four Sages, Ben Azzai, Ben Zoma, Rabbi Akiva, and Elisha ben Abuya were of unique stature. To be among them meant to have memorized all of the written scripture of the Hebrew Bible and a sizable portion of the oral tradition of interpretation that had grown up around it for several hundred years. Arguably, without Ben Zoma, we may not have the Passover *Haggadah*. Their act of "entering the Garden" is code for a mode of a highly specialized mystical soul ascent, one clearly fraught with its own danger. And so, Rabbi Akiva reminds his

9. Babylonian Talmud, Tractate *Hagigah*, 14b.

friends and colleagues, "When you reach the place of pure marble, do not call out "water, water," for it says in Psalms, "those who tell falsehoods shall not stand before me." Which is to say, the vision they experience may produce an image of the floor of heaven that appears to them as water. But, if they call it "water," they will be speaking words of illusion, succumbing to their own preconceptions instead of being open to the truth of their visions.

Unfortunately, Rabbi Akiva's warning turns out to be well founded, as each of the sages meets a different fate in pursuing their face-to-face contact with God, with only Rabbi Akiva emerging whole. The story continues:

> Ben Azzai looked and died. Of him it is written, "How precious in the eyes of *Adonai* are the deaths of the righteous" (Psalms 116:15). . . . Ben Zoma looked and became insane. About him it is written, "You have found honey. Eat only your fill, lest you become satisfied from it and vomit it up" (Proverbs 25:16) . . . . *Acher* (the Other) looked and cut the shoots. Rabbi Akiva emerged in peace.[10]

The economy of language gives us a haunting glimpse of the perils of venturing too far outside the breach, of pushing one's consciousness to its limits in pursuit of knowing God. Ben Azzai died, Ben Zoma became insane, and Elisha ben Abuya became "*Acher*," or "The Other," by becoming an apostate and abandoning the life of *mitzvot*.

What does this story mean? At first glance, it seems to be an object lesson against trying to transcend our daily lives: if only Rabbi Akiva can do it, the rest of us should be extremely wary. We may find the prospect of a deeper knowledge of God to be spiritually or intellectually compelling, but few, if any of us, are prepared to handle it. As with looking directly at the sun, it is dangerous for most of us. And so, the story seems to be teaching us, be satisfied with living in the breach, color between the lines, be satisfied with the imperfect knowledge and abiding loneliness of everyday life.

But this is not where the story ends. The text continues a little farther on:

> It happened that Rabbi Yehoshua ben Hananiah was standing on the steps of the Temple Mount and saw Ben Zoma, who did not rise to greet him. He asked of him, "What is on your mind Ben Zoma?" He said to him, "I was gazing at the distance between the upper waters and the lower waters, and found that there are only three fingerbreadths between them, as it is written, 'a wind of God hovered over the waters' (Genesis 1:2), just as a dove hovers over her young but does not make contact."

10. Ibid.

Rabbi Yehoshua said to his students, "Ben Zoma is still on the outside."[11]

This passage rings of broken connections and the yearning for wholeness, basically, life in the breach. The setting is the site of the ruins of the Second Temple, destroyed about two generations earlier in 70 CE. If we can imagine Ben Zoma, now supposedly insane after his attempt at a soul ascent, sitting among these ruins and staring off into the stratosphere. His friend, Rabbi Yehoshua, noting how Ben Zoma fails to engage in the most conventional social greeting between sages, tries to prompt a conversation. The answer he receives from Ben Zoma, that the difference between heaven and earth is but three fingerbreadths, leads Rabbi Yehoshua to believe that his friend has not recovered from losing his mind.

But then the logic of the Talmud turns this seeming object lesson into an affirmation of the virtues of wonder. Yes, we may be consigned to our everyday lives, but that does not mean we cannot or should not be occupied with questions about transcendence, and our closeness to a reality that eludes us as it envelopes us.

Immediately following Rabbi Yehoshua's assessment of Ben Zoma and his perseveration on the wind of God hovering over the water, the Talmud offers an alternative perspective.

> Is this really so? "a wind of God hovered over the waters." When was this? On the first day! The separation happened only on the second day of creation, as it is written, "there was a separation between the waters" (Genesis 1:6). And how much was this separation? Rav Acha bar Ya'akov said, "as the width of a hair." The Rabbis said, "as the space between boards on a bridge." Mar Zutra, or one may say Rav Assi said, "like two cloaks lying on top of each other." And they said to him, "Like two glasses inverted over each other."[12]

Far from being "outside," Ben Zoma seems to be the catalyst for an ongoing debate among later generations of sages, who are very much on the "inside" of their communities and even outdo Ben Zoma in their speculation. Instead of being the product of a mystical experience, their discussion appears to be part of the accepted give and take of Talmudic debate. Going beyond Ben Zoma's three fingerbreadths as the distance between heaven and earth, these later rabbis imagine the distance as that between two hairs, overlapping boards, cups and coats.

11. Ibid., 15a.
12. Ibid.

One implication of these juxtaposing stories is that while Ben Zoma may have had to go to the edge of his own sanity to understand his relationship to creation and to God, we do not. It appears we may live within our very earthly lives, and yet imagine how we are both rooted in this world and yet simultaneously occupy a part in the cosmos. Living in the middle, we have the unique advantage of being able to survey the entire landscape of heaven and earth from the vantage point of our lives as they are. Even if we feel that by imagining something beyond or undergirding our lives we are venturing to the limits of rational thought, the Talmud reminds us that it is part of how we find our place—within ourselves and within a community of seekers.

But perhaps the first step in seeking is not some dissatisfaction with the state of the ordered, rational world, but with the emotional and existential dimensions of our lives. For me, the first true step in uncovering any kind of confronting the breach and finding an internal spiritual voice was to confront my father, six years after he dropped out of my life. While facing him forced me to confront the true depth of my loss, doing so revealed my own internal sources of happiness and resilience. The day I met him, I had several hours between the end of the school and our dinner, and so I spent it doing things I loved. I hung out with friends in Central Park; I walked a mile or so along the bustling streets of midtown New York at rush hour; with some extra time I browsed a bookstore and picked something up. I was both eager and anxious to see my father again, but more than that, I just felt so fully vital—connected, engaged, curious, open.

This very impulse to engage, from the reality of loneliness, I would later discover as essential to finding a spiritual voice in Jewish tradition. Because contrary to most of our assumptions, the Jewish God doesn't really promise anything. There is no clear path to knowing God or guarantee for what that pursuit will bring to our lives. In fact, the deepest, most true and authentic "self" of God will always remain hidden, and nowhere is a path prescribed by which we may draw closer. And so, as we wander, our inner capacities for discovery propel us to seek and ask questions. With time and practice, certain ideas and motifs, like familiar markers, become part of our lives, giving a collective shape to our individual and idiosyncratic longings. There are many things that have happened to allow me to live a happy and purposeful life instead of a life of suffering, and among these have been countless moments spent stepping into the rhythm of Jewish ritual and the spaces of Jewish community. Often, these experiences have been simple moments in a daily or weekly routine, nothing extraordinary. But, they have also been responses to the great revelation, the "I am" at Sinai, as well as to the creative chaos of beginning, or *Beresheet*. Somewhere in between the grandeur and the mundane is my own internalized sense of what binds me to the wonders of this world, to other people, and to that which transcends all created things in time and space. And when this world falls short, as it often does, it's that same inner voice that compels me to begin seeking again.

Part 2

Shattering the Vessels

The Creative Destruction of Elisha the Prophet

2 Kings 2

(19) The men of the city said to Elisha, "Behold, this is a good city of settlement as my master sees. But the water is bad and the land barren." (20) He said, "Get me a new flask." And they placed in it salt and brought it to him. (21) He went out to a water source and cast salt there. He said, "Thus said Adonai, I have healed these waters. Death and famine will no longer be from there." (22) And the water was made pure until this day, according to the word of Elisha as he spoke it. (23) He went up from there to Beit El. As he was walking on the path young children came out from the city. They taunted him and called him, "Get out of here baldy, get out of here baldy!" (24) He turned around and saw them, and cursed them in the name of Adonai. Then two she-bears came out from the woods and slaughtered forty-two children. And from there he traveled to Mount Carmel, and from there to Samaria.

Chapter 4

Only I-You

A Teacher and Student Connect

I remember the moment when I considered my first serious thought about God. I was alone in my room, lying in bed, toward the end of my sophomore year in high school. I was fifteen, and had just completed what was called Confirmation in our synagogue. It was a good, meaningful experience in which I connected with a number of the kids in my cohort and our new, young rabbi, Rabbi Ron. That summer, he would take us to Israel for what would become one of the formative experiences of my life. As part of our Confirmation class, I remember we looked critically at the prayer book and at the beginning of Genesis. We also had to read books on our own, and I read Elie Wiesel's *Night*, in which the author emerges from Auschwitz, without a father and angry at God, at fifteen.

From the vantage point of almost twenty-five years in Jewish education, I realize now how haphazard this Confirmation program was. But at the time, I knew that I was having my first mature encounter with Judaism, considering what God, ritual, and Jewish community meant to me through the lens of personal experience. The Confirmation class culminated in May during Shavuot, the holiday that celebrates and reenacts God's giving of the Torah on Mount Sinai. In the days leading up to the celebration, I felt that it was time to make my own internal commitment to something big that lay at the heart of these new interactions with my rabbi, my friends, and impending journey to Israel. I thought about the question of God, and realized that

I probably didn't believe in God in any meaningful, personal way. Nevertheless, I had a sense that Judaism gave the question of God a unique degree of depth and grandeur, and that it would be worthy, perhaps imperative, for me to know more about what Judaism had to say. The choice to agree or disagree would be entirely my own, but learning what Judaism taught about God seemed like a compelling obligation I could take on as my own. And so, I resolved that I would devote myself to learning about the Jewish God, even though I did not feel the personal sense of God's immediacy or nearness that for many people constitutes their belief.

About six months later, I had a moment that would galvanize all of my future thoughts and explorations about God in Jewish tradition. I was hanging out with a few friends in Rabbi Ron's office. Among the books that lined his walls, I noticed at least a dozen by Martin Buber. I had never heard of Martin Buber, but with the more than dozen books on Rabbi Ron's shelf, I figured he must be important. In a quiet moment, I asked Rabbi Ron, "Who is Martin Buber?" Rabbi Ron told me that Martin Buber was a Jewish scholar from Germany. He described Buber's philosophy by explaining that there are two basic relationships. There are I-It relationships, in which we connect so as to get something in return. I remember him saying, "Like with this ashtray." And then, Rabbi Ron explained, there are I-You relationships, and these are the kind of relationships we have with people we love, and with God.

It was such a simple explanation, and yet so powerful and enduring. With my burgeoning sense of awareness of the brokenness of my family and my yearning for something different, it felt like a liberating revelation to know that God could be understood through the sincerity of everyday interactions. Driven to overcome the pain within my own family, I found within Rabbi Ron's explanation of Buber the first glimpses of myself in relation to God, Jewish tradition, and the Jewish people. Friendships and relationships, which were surrogates for what I lacked in my own family, were now cast in ultimate terms. Buber, as explained by Rabbi Ron, showed me that my yearnings for depth, openness, and honesty were part of something greater than myself.

Of course, I was not only looking for a sense of affirmation, or relationship, but so much more. In that moment of discovering Buber, I was really opening up myself, and seeking a way out of the patterns of avoidance, denial, and abandonment I had experienced in my own family. On a very basic level, I wanted a father, not my father exactly, but at least a "partial father" who could provide some kind of guidance without expectation or judgment. Throughout my late teens and early twenties, I found myself seeking mentorship from loving, thoughtful men who could nourish continuing explorations of myself and my aspirations. Rabbi Ron was the first of these men. And so, learning about Buber from Rabbi Ron, and how the alienation and loneliness of life could be overcome by reaching out toward the eternal "You," I was taking on Rabbi Ron as a teacher to make whole again the broken shards left by my father.

Rabbi Ron knew it too. He knew my story and my family, and he looked out for me. In retrospect, I realize that Rabbi Ron's role in my life also partook of his own search for wholeness. As I have come to understand, many rabbis have a deep-seated need to teach and connect, and often that need is driven by some kind of pain and vulnerability. Some rabbis may be aware of these sources of pain but for various reasons will keep them private. However, Rabbi Ron openly shared his struggles in sermons and casual conversation.

Rabbi Ron's father was a famous rabbinic scholar, raised in Germany the world of "cultured Orthodoxy," as historians describe it. As a boy, Rabbi Ron's father was rescued and ferried to Scotland on a *kindertransport*, after which he studied in London and then became an eminent professor in America. Even during those teenage years when I knew Rabbi Ron, I was aware of how his towering father was both a blessing and a burden. A larger-than-life personality, Rabbi Ron's father was able to open a vista onto the depth of Jewish life that few others could. I remember feeling profoundly envious when Rabbi Ron related how his father made a practice of studying Talmud with him as a teenager. I pictured Rabbi Ron and his father with books open at a long table, debating the meaning of these texts for hours and hours, the father pushing his son to grow so as to emerge as his intellectual equal. I would have given anything to have had that kind of intimate give and take with a father or a mentor, made all the more rewarding for the intellectual and spiritual pleasures of studying Talmud. And yet, I also knew that Rabbi Ron struggled under the unfathomable weight of his father's legacy. No one could ever match the erudition of Rabbi Ron's father, and no son could possibly measure up against Rabbi Ron's father's portrait of survival, brilliance, and popular acclaim. Once, in a High Holiday sermon, Rabbi Ron encapsulated his struggles with his father in the words of a famous Cat Stevens song in which a son has no choice but to run away from a father who never listens.

Looking back, I imagine that Rabbi Ron was drawn to Buber for the same reasons I was: to break away from the pain of a remote father by immersing oneself in spiritual connection. Buber may have been a connection to Rabbi Ron's legacy of towering cultured Jewish scholarship, but Buber offered something more—what Rabbi Ron's father could never give him: the companionship known by all who reach out from the lonely "I" to the eternal "You." That "You" could be all the relationships we long for as human beings: a future lover, a circle of emotional companions, mentors, students, and somewhere in the mix, God. I know that when Rabbi Ron first uttered the words "I-You," all of these possibilities instantly sprang to mind, and they still do. But more than what I thought, I recall what I felt from Rabbi Ron in that moment. He spoke to me directly and quietly, and when he spoke those words, I felt a responsibility to listen and consider them closely. Without even saying anything, I knew that he sensed how closely I was paying attention.

And so, in sharing a simple idea, Rabbi Ron and I had a moment of what Buber would call "encounter," each of us reaching through our own worlds of "I," with all of their incompleteness and suffering. In that moment, we were both able to experience a respite from our yearnings, meeting in that archetypal and heartfelt exchange between teacher and student. And, more importantly, after the moment was over and we went about whatever it is we did next, I knew I had something to return to. Whatever my longings were, I knew that I could find something by reaching across the gulf that separated the lonely "I" from all the manifestations of "You."

Buber—An Iconoclast Seeking Healing

Although I could not have known this at the time, Buber was not a typical Jewish thinker that a rabbi in the early 1980s would share with a curious teen. Something like the works of Chaim Potok, the stories of the Hasidic masters, or the rabbinic work *Ethics of the Rabbis* would be a more conventional way to guide a young person at the time. In a uniquely modern vein, Buber speaks to a person's doubt, skepticism, and even cynicism, whether born of the times or one's personal experience, and he does so in a way that seems to transcend the conventions of Jewish discourse. Rarely in *I and Thou* does Buber quote the Bible, the Talmud, or some other part of the Jewish canon. He does not even try to wrestle with the promises, the rewards and punishments, or attributes that Jewish tradition assigned to God. Precedent seems to mean nothing. Instead, it seems more that Buber breaks with the past in order to formulate something new, perhaps because the recent past for Buber was so violent and dreadful that he believed humanity and Jewish tradition needed a fresh start.

It is hard to know where to begin with Buber because the writing in *I and Thou* is so elliptical, continually referring to its own ideas with a barely discernible beginning and end. But as Buber wrote *I and Thou* between 1919–21, we know that he was seeking a spiritual antidote to the horrors of

World War I. Characterizing an age that witnessed more destruction than at any point in history, Buber declared, "The sickness of our age is unlike that of any other . . . ." Buber saw in his time a prevailing "dogma" of despair which, left unchecked, would bring about an "ineluctable running down" toward "doom." But Buber also understood that the trauma of World War I was a function of the "It-world," and so while exceptional in degree, it nevertheless "belongs with the sicknesses of all."[1] Having diagnosed the illness, we could seek the cure. Therefore, even from amidst this oppressive trauma, human beings could rescue themselves by reaching out toward the "You," whether that "You" was viewed as other people, or God, or both:

> Whoever is overpowered by the It-world must consider the dogma of an ineluctable running down as a truth that creates a clearing in the jungle. In truth, this dogma only leads him deeper into the slavery of the It-world. But the world of the You is not locked up. Whoever proceeds toward it, concentrating his whole being, with his power to relate resurrected, beholds his freedom. And to gain freedom from the belief in unfreedom is to gain freedom.[2]

Whereas the cultural forces overwhelming us with dread "enslave" us, "proceeding" toward the "You," drawing on our inherent "power to relate" can set us free. And even though the encounter with "You" lasts but a moment, we may "return" to the world of the everyday with the spiritual strength to transform our surroundings by continuing to seek out true relationships of reciprocity. In Buber's words, we can "return," or as Jewish tradition might say, engage in *teshuvah*, turning inward, toward other people and God simultaneously, so as to bring healing. Buber's ideal is the person each of us can become, "the human being who overcomes the universal struggle by returning; . . . who rises above the spell of his class by returning; who by returning stirs up, rejuvenates, and changes the secure historical forms."[3]

The dehumanizing and alienating historical conditions can act against a person's capacity to connect, but then again, someone who is attuned to their own loneliness may see the opportunity to find healing in an "encounter" with the "You," an Other who is both human and divine. The way toward healing the day-to-day world of isolation, degradation, and loneliness is through recognizing that all relationships partake of the same, fundamental and universal "I-You" relationship:

1. Buber, *I and Thou*, 104.
2. Ibid., 107.
3. Ibid., 106.

I know nothing of a "world" and of "worldly life" that separate us from God. What is designated that way is life with an alienated It-world, the life of experience and use. Whoever goes forth in truth to the world, goes forth to God. Concentration and going forth, both in truth, the one-and-the-other which is the One, are what is needful.

God embraces but is not the universe; just so, God embraces but is not my self.[4]

Consolation in Relationships and in You

Because our entire lives are about relationships, and for Buber, all relationships ultimately lead to God, every aspect of our lives is bound up in the life of God. We may choose not to see the threads between our lives and the eternal life of the universe, but that eternal life still exists. Apart from any thoughts about God, the interconnectedness of all things means that our feelings of abject loneliness, of being cut off from everything, are themselves an illusion. Even when it seems like we are all alone, when all evidence seems to show that we are alone, we are in fact never alone. Also, our reaching out need not be internal or toward anything supernatural. All Buber says we have to do to overcome our feeling of separation is to "go forth in truth to the world," engage with everyday life with integrity simply as ourselves. Since God "embraces but is not the universe," we do not have to get caught up in all the pain of life to encounter the eternal You. Simply by greeting reality as it is, and accepting ourselves as we are, we come into contact with that which suffuses everything. Perhaps this explains that the time in my life when I confronted my father and the extent of his abandonment was also the time when I embraced my new community of friends through synagogue and took in the gentle mentorship of Rabbi Ron.

Of course, "going forth to the world" toward the eternal You is no easy solution to overcome loneliness. Because as much as Buber believes in the inherent power of each of us to create healing relationships, the nature of the universal "You" is paradoxically close and elusive, both a part of our lives in the world as well as transcending this world.

> One does not find God if one remains in the world; one does not find God if one leaves the world. Whoever goes forth to his You with his whole being and carries to it all the being of the world, finds him whom one cannot seek.

4. Ibid., 143.

> Of course, God is "the wholly other"; but he is also "the wholly same," the wholly present. Of course, he is (that which) . . . appears and overwhelms; but he is also the mystery of the obvious that is closer to me than my own I.[5]

If we seek consolation in a spiritual life, it is an incomplete consolation, because our experience and understanding of God will ultimately remain a paradox. We may inquire about God through our own experience, only to discover that if God does exist, God lives in a realm beyond all comprehension. And yet, we may also find that while God may be wholly remote and other from us, God may be closer to us than ourselves.

Different from total existential loneliness, these paradoxes in a life with God are also part of our deepest relationships with people. I think of discovering what it was like to be in love for the first time, also an experience that happened soon after Rabbi Ron introduced me to Buber. My love was "other," and I was passionate about drawing close to her. And yet, she had a greater intimacy with me than I had with myself. She experienced all of the unintentional quirks of my personality that I could never see, she experienced my body in a way I never could, she adored me and also bristled at things about me that I did not see in myself. The experience was one of surprise and delight, with occasional moments of facing difficult truths. And yet, as close as she was to me, she was also different from me, her own self, and sometimes remote. I discovered how love imparted a closeness that was intoxicating, and at the same time, could sometimes remind me of how much I was separate and independent.

Buber, then, leads one to a new understanding not only of being connected, but of being alone. All aloneness is challenging, because no matter how much we reach out to the eternal "You," we will never find perfect communion. But Buber's aloneness is a healing kind of aloneness, from which we are reassured by the very impulse to reach out. The impulse to connect is its own consolation. I believe that this is what Rabbi Ron was trying to show me—that the promise of aspiring to live in Buber's I-You mode is really a way to affirm the "I" who is always searching and yearning.

Elisha—Alone Again, But Not

This kind of aloneness, of being decisively independent yet deeply connected, lies at the heart of Elisha's maturity as a prophet. Being alone appears to be a central requirement of a prophet's life as he bridges the worlds of

5. Ibid., 127.

humanity and God as nobody else can. For Elisha, it is an especially radical way of being, connected as he is to family and community in his earlier, non-prophetic life. When Elijah comes for Elisha, we see how ensconced Elisha is in his family and shepherding community. And while he gives up everything to apprentice himself to Elijah, he must lose his mentor in order to emerge fully as a prophet in his own manner. Elisha, apart from all other prophets, expresses his sudden and radical aloneness by crying out *"Avi, Avi"* as Elijah is taken from this world. But is he really alone?

The first story of Elisha as an independent prophet establishes both his exceptional qualities to serve humanity but also his utter and complete alienation from normal human community. In the first episode immediately after taking up Elijah's mantle, Elisha restores fertility to a drought-ridden city, this from the second chapter of the Second Book of Kings:

> (19) The men of the city said to Elisha, "Behold, this is a good city of settlement as my master sees. But the water is bad and the land barren." (20) He said, "Get me a new flask." And they placed in it salt and brought it to him. (21) He went out to a water source and cast salt there. He said, "Thus said Adonai, I have healed these waters. Death and famine will no longer be from there." (22) And the water was made pure until this day, according to the word of Elisha as he spoke it.

Like Elijah, Elisha has the power to channel divine energy for healing purposes, a facility that will eventually become his unique hallmark as a prophet. But accompanying this ability is also a capacity for fierce destruction that inevitably sets him apart from all human society. Immediately after this work of wondrous natural renewal, we are witness to one of the oddest and most troubling episodes of the Hebrew Bible. Elisha's act of healing and compassion is followed immediately by one of wrathful and total destruction against a group of children:

> (23) He went up from there to Beit El. As he was walking on the path young children came out from the city. They taunted him and called him, "Get out of here baldy, get out of here baldy!" (24) He turned around and saw them, and cursed them in the name of Adonai. Then two she-bears came out from the woods and slaughtered forty-two children. And from there he traveled to Mount Carmel, and from there to Samaria.

This act of decisive and immediate retribution is meant to be shocking and haunting. Without any warning, and with no subsequent commentary or reflection by the biblical author, two bears emerge from the forest and slaughter forty-two children. The Jewish medieval biblical commentators, sources for the range of normative views of the text, do not raise any objection to the events of this story. They are generally silent on this incident of the mauling bears, as they see the children's deaths as an appropriate consequence for mocking God's authority and truth as represented by Elisha. The rejection of Elisha is a rejection of God, and the children's destruction is a microcosm of what would happen to the entire people if they were to similarly abandon God.

To flesh out the normative view just a bit, Elisha's complete lack of concern for the children is precisely the point. If Elisha is to be a prophet devoted to God's ways, his rebuke must be total, even if the offense comes from the mouths of babes. This incident, then, supports Elisha's prophetic role in a broader sense, which is to dispel all illusion and turn the people's hearts toward God. The role demands complete and total integrity to the point where a prophet cannot tolerate any denial of God's complete and total sovereignty in the universe. As an embodiment of the divine pathos, the prophet becomes a conduit of the uncompromising divine anger, just as he is also the conduit of God's limitless love. Where there is injustice, or an effort to ridicule the Creator, a prophet has no choice but to destroy things in this world that militate against God being known. And so, just as Abraham comes into his own by smashing his father's idols, so Elisha begins his mission by summoning the forces that destroy those who mock him and, by extension, God.

So goes the normative view, which definitely has its merits. But we are not completely beholden to the normative view, nor should we be. For one, this normative view implies a deeper problem. God may be able to embody the seemingly contradictory attributes of uncompromising love and unrelenting anger. But this is an impossible situation for any human being. Perhaps that is because, as Buber might say, we live in the It-world, where our primary task is to preserve and improve our relationships day to day, and that requires that we accommodate ourselves to our circumstances. As we say all too often, "It is what it is." The prophets, however, do not have either this need or this luxury, but live in what we call Buber's world of I-You, even as they contend with people day to day. And so, Elisha begins his mature life with God and humanity with a radical act of destruction. But, within this act of destruction, may there be seeds of a future healing?

The *Mitzvah* of Accompanying Strangers
—No One Should Be Left Alone

Interestingly, while the classic medieval commentators have no problems with this story, the rabbis of the Talmud who preceded them by roughly 1,000 years chafe against it. Their context for considering the Elisha story stems from their understanding that it was an obligation, a *mitzvah*, to accompany people on the open road. In the ancient world, the open road was full of dangers. To the rabbis of the Talmud, being alone between cities meant being vulnerable to demons, to the sexual temptation of prostitutes, and particularly to robbers. And so, by obligating themselves to accompany guests on the open road, the rabbis could ensure that any traveler could be safe.

In Tractate *Sotah* of the Talmud, the last chapter deals with the ritual, outlined in the Torah, of the "broken-necked heifer," an expiatory sacrifice offered when a corpse is found between two cities and no one city can claim responsibility for the victim. In such a situation, there is an elaborate ritual in which the elders of the city must proclaim, "Our hands did not shed this blood, nor did our eyes see." But in the Mishnah, the earliest compilation of rabbinic thought that emerged toward the end of the second century CE, the rabbis see more at stake than simply absolving themselves of the murder itself.

> The elders of the city wash their hands in water where the heifer was slaughtered and recite, "Our hands have not spilled this blood nor did our eyes see." Would it truly occur to you that the elders of the court were spillers of blood? Rather, they were declaring, "This person did not come to us, and we did not send him away without food, nor did we see him and leave him on his own unaccompanied."[6]

Later on, in the ongoing reflection provided by the Talmud, the rabbis elaborate on the obligation to accompany visiting strangers, which leads to the problem that Elisha was left by himself by the citizens of Jericho. These brief excerpts from the Talmudic discussion from Tractate *Sotah* 46b gives a sense of an obligation that, although not mandated explicitly by the Torah, appears to have the force of a true *mitzvah*:

> Rabbi Meir says, "We compel people to accompany, for the reward of accompanying has no measure." . . . Rav said, "One who accompanies one's fried four cubits in a city is protected

---

6. Babylonian Talmud, Tractate *Sotah*, 45a.

from injury." When Ravina accompanied Rava bar Yitzchak four cubits in a city he encountered a dangerous situation but was saved. The Rabbis taught, "A teacher should accompany a student up to the border of the city. A friend should accompany another friend as far as the limits of Shabbat (about a mile). For a student accompanying a teacher, there is no limit."[7]

Regarding the case of Elisha, the rabbis discuss the commandment to accompany people in the most absolute terms:

> Rabbi Yochanan says in the name of Rabbi Meir, "One who does not accompany another or is not accompanied is as one who sheds blood! For if the men of Jericho had accompanied Elisha, he would not have released the bears against the children."[8]

With the statement of Rabbi Yochanan, we move from the behavioral consideration of accompanying companions to its deeper underlying spiritual dynamics. To accompany someone is not only a gesture of protection—it is a gesture of friendship on the deepest level, of caring for the essential wellbeing of another.

But with Elisha, the act of accompanying him is not to protect him from any danger. This is unnecessary, since as a prophet, Elisha receives protection from God. Rather, Rabbi Yochanan suggests that Elisha requires protection from himself! In his extreme spiritual isolation, Elisha is liable to harbor distrust and even hatefulness toward the many who live up to God's demands imperfectly or not at all. Alone in his prophetic mission, Elisha risks becoming a fanatic, and allowing his zealotry to wreak destruction on those who are ignorant or disdainful of God's ways. And that is exactly what happens when Elisha is left to his own devices. True, Elisha is special and unique. But that doesn't mean he should go about the world "unaccompanied," meaning standing radically apart from humanity.

This is most meaningful not because of the insight it gives into Elisha, but into ourselves as we risk our own isolation in pursuit of a spiritual life. A life in pursuit of spiritual connection may very well impart its own kind of comfort and pleasure, but we should watch out for the destructive self-righteousness and extremism that may sometimes accompany religious devotion.

In this vein, another *midrash* imagines the prophet Jeremiah protesting to God against the destruction unleashed by his assuming his role of

7. Ibid., 46b.
8. Ibid.

the prophet. Against the supposedly normative, self-evident view of Elisha's encounter with the children, here Jeremiah is haunted by Elisha's example:

> Master of the Universe, I cannot prophesy to them. What prophet ever came before them whom they did not seek to slay? When You set up Moses and Aaron before them to act on their behalf, did they not wish to stone them? When you set up the curly-haired Elijah over them to act in their behalf, they mocked and ridiculed him. . . . And when You set up Elisha over them to act in their behalf, they said derisively to him, "Go away baldhead! Go away baldhead!"[9]

In this exchange, no less a prophet than Jeremiah shrinks from his task, knowing it will endanger his life. But I believe the deeper emotional resonance in this brief *midrash* stems from Jeremiah's fear that his unique relationship with God will destroy his relationships with other human beings. Notice how the *midrash* repeats the phrase "You set up . . . over them" to describe the career of each prophet. Through Jeremiah's concern, we are led to believe that God inaugurates each prophet with the expectation that they are the hierarchical leader of their era. Jeremiah seems to believe that because they are invested with God's moral authority, they are somehow "higher" than everybody else. But this is not the case in the Bible. While kings exert power over people, prophets do not. When God selects Moses, he is a shepherd, not a ruler. Elisha, especially, is identified with the most desperate of people rather than with any privileged group. Jeremiah, then, is less expressing the reality of being a prophet than his concern that being so close to God will inevitably provoke anger and hatred from human society.

And here is where the *midrash* ceases to become merely a gloss on the biblical text and speaks directly to us. Perhaps all of us share Jeremiah's fear to some extent. Yes, there is much that a spiritual life promises: solace, connection, renewal of the heart and mind. But as beautiful as it is to cultivate a life built upon prayer, study, meditation, and acts of kindness, the intensity and focus of a spiritual life can take us away from other people. Not only do these pursuits take time, and often require us to be alone, but they yield insights we may find impossible to put into words. Even if we can, it may often seem hard to find the people who will really hear and empathize with what we are trying to convey.

9. Pesikta Rabbati, 26:12, in Bialik and Ravnitzsky, *Book of Legends*, 478.

Setting Ourselves Apart—A Necessary Cost?

Paradoxically, even a sincere, thoughtful, and balanced religious life can bring about its own kind of isolation as we unintentionally set ourselves apart. On this score, I must admit that I have never resolved the inherent tension between my life of Jewish practice and spirituality and my connections to friends and family who do not share that life. When staying at the home of family or friends, I may easily feel self-conscious about taking time to pray in the morning with *tallit* and *tefillin*, afraid someone will spot me and think it's strange or weird. I feel both grateful but awkwardly indebted to friends and family who graciously accommodate my practice of not driving on Shabbat. During the normal get-togethers when we talk about our work and latest interests, I am hesitant to share my excitement over a page of Talmud I studied, or a beautiful song we sang for the first time as a community, or the peace I found in a quiet moment on Shabbat, as I am concerned that others just won't get it. I do find many ways to connect. But I am frequently aware of a gulf between the life I am drawn to and the priorities of many whom I know and love.

Buber himself was aware of the ways in which a spiritual life, the "I-You" encounter, suffers from being exclusive. Any connection to the "You" necessarily comes at the expense of being connected to everything in the "It-world." Even though the realm of "I-You" relationships represents the ideal, the world of "I-It" is the arena in which the diverse array of everyday relationships teach us and nurture us in their own way. Therefore, because of the way in which a spiritual encounter takes one away from the day-to-day reality of the world, Buber believed it could only last a moment. But after the moment was over, a person is newly invigorated with the desire to re-enter the world and change it. On its face this seems like a benevolent resolution to the inherent challenge of isolation in a spiritual life: leave other people behind, but only for a moment, and then go back and create some good. But actually, this push and pull in one's life between the worlds of spiritual encounter and the everyday is part of a more radical challenge. For Buber, each person is charged with changing the fundamental nature of this world from one based on utilization of the "other" to one of genuine relationship with the other. But in order to effect this change, each of us must live in two worlds at once: the world of aspiration toward ideal relationship, the world of You, and the world of the everyday, which we never transcend but always try to improve. In a sense, we are constantly engaged in a process of creative destruction.

This radical quality of separating from what came before to emerge into something new springs from the deepest strata of Jewish tradition. The unique Jewish story begins when God commands Abraham to leave his father's house so that he will "be a blessing" by walking in God's ways. In the next generation, Isaac must separate from Abraham, after almost being sacrificed to God, in order to have his own encounters with God independent of his father. Jacob must flee his home after robbing his brother of the blessing of being firstborn, and only then does he realize that he is in the presence of God. As if to emphasize the need for leaving everything behind, each of these figures affirms their covenantal relationship with God in a place that is not their original home. In each of these stories, embarking on a life with God entails a new kind of isolation and therefore its own unanticipated resolution, leaving behind what was known in order to form a relationship with a God who is real but ultimately unknowable.

As if reflecting upon the lives of the biblical patriarchs, the rabbis of the Talmud similarly express the idea that all real understanding entails breaking from our past. In the account of the Torah, there is already an arresting image of Moses shattering the Ten Commandments, written by God on two tablets of stone, when he descends from Mount Sinai to find the Israelites worshipping the golden calf. The question remains, after God provided Moses with a new set of tablets, what happened to the broken shards of the old ones? The rabbis' answer is succinct, elegant, and powerful: both the whole tablets and the shattered tablets were in the ark carried by the Israelites throughout the desert that found its home in the temple and Jerusalem. The image evokes the constant interplay between old forms of understanding, which must be broken to yield the new. Even more radically, the rabbis held that when there is a moment to do something "for the sake of God," we must "'break' the Torah" by going against a previous interpretation or even what the Torah actually says. According to this strain of rabbinic tradition, a growing repertoire of spiritual insight upsets our previous notions and compels us to jettison everything we have learned before.

We Live in Brokenness

The notion of creative destruction in the spiritual life reaches its most forceful and explicit formulation in the mysticism of Isaac Luria and his view of the "shattering of the vessels," *shevirat ha-kelim*. For Luria, this "shattering" is critical to the process of ongoing creation. As I reflected in the first part of this book, God initiates the creation of the universe by withdrawing into Godself so as to create space for the universe to exist. But Luria believed that the divine energy, though absorbed within God, had to go somewhere. And so, says Luria, God devised *kelim*, or vessels, to contain the excess of light from God's initial withdrawal, or *tzimtzum*. However, as Jewish tradition asserts in a variety of ways, there is no vessel, not even one created by God, that can withstand the force of divine energy. Luria himself spoke of the necessity of *tzimtzum* as akin to Earth's distance from the sun—we need the distance in order to survive. And so, unable to withstand the intensity of God's unmitigated energy, the successive vessels designed to contain the infinite light shattered, and those shards became the material of the created world. Even for the vessels that were further from God and therefore in theory not as closely exposed to the divine light, these too shattered:

> Perhaps the lower vessels would not be obliterated and could withstand the divine light because of their distance from God. For all that which is farther from God is more likely to withstand the divine energy. However, as each lower vessel was smaller than its higher vessel, therefore even the lower vessel, even though it was farther from God, was not able to withstand the divine light.[10]

As much as Luria's myth of the shattering of the vessels, or *shevirat ha-kelim*, accounts for the fragmentation and brokenness of creation, it also sets the stage for healing. For even though our universe is comprised of broken shards, they are broken shards containing divine light.

> When the vessels shattered . . . even so, there still remained a bit of the sparks of holiness in the vessels, and so they descended as "rent garments," and they continued to descend downward and became the root of the "husks" of creation . . . and this is what is left for us to restore by means of our prayer and acts of kindness.[11]

According to Luria, our acts of devotion to God and humanity release the divine light from the shards, returning the light back to its source in God, bringing about a cosmic healing. Later, I will reflect more on the process of *tikkun*, of the multitude of ways by which Jewish tradition has us bring those shards together in a new, maybe even more perfect, wholeness. But we should pause to think how profound it is that Jewish tradition has understood, possibly since the Bible and explicitly for the last six hundred years, that the shattering itself is necessary.

Rabbi Dov Baer of Mezritch, an early Hasidic master who was a disciple of the charismatic leader of early hasidism Rabbi Israel Ba'al Shem Tov, illustrates the phenomenon and the promise of the "shattering the vessels"

10. Vital, *Etz Chayim*, 1:2.
11. Ibid.

through two different parables. To place these teachings in context, we should consider that Rabbi Dov Baer was an early and formative leader of Hasidism in early eighteenth-century Poland. While the aims of Hasidism are subject to voluminous scholarly debate, we may broadly consider that Hasidism was a spiritual movement of revival. Among the striking features of this revival was the effort to internalize and democratize mystical concepts that had previously been reserved for an intellectual and spiritual elite. So, for example, while Isaac Luria devotes chapters upon chapters to painstaking analysis of the intricacies of God's being, Hasidic teachers such as Dov Baer reflect more on the ways in which the qualities and energies of God correspond to our own psychological dimensions.

While there are many legendary stories about Dov Baer and who he was, perhaps his most palpable legacy are the books he authored and the role he played in the growth of early Hasidism. He is considered to be the first true follower of the Rabbi Israel Ba'al Shem Tov, who is often referred to as the "founder" of Hasidism. However, the new historical thinking is that the Ba'al Shem Tov was not a founder at all, but a highly respected teacher and community leader. The myth that grew up around him occurred after his death. And so, to the extent that many of the supposed teachings of the Ba'al Shem Tov are championed in books actually authored by Rabbi Dov Baer and his disciples, it is believed that perhaps Dov Baer was himself responsible for the flavor and mystique of Hasidism as a popular movement with unprecedented reach.

Rav Dov Baer's talent for showing us how the mystical lens of shattering yields a profound vision of ourselves as simultaneously alone and connected becomes evident in these two parables. They are both taken from his book, *Maggid Devarav l'Ya'akov*, and although no translation exists of this book, these famous parables are found in anthologies of Hasidic writings.

In this first parable from *Maggid Devarav l'Ya'akov* # 31, Rabbi Dov Baer imagines God as a tailor. Most of us see only the torn tatters the tailor works with, but a trained eye will see the wholeness that can emerge.

> "Come my beloved, let us go out to the field (Song of Songs, 7:12), let us sleep in the villages" One may understand this by means of the verse, "The One who covers the heavens with clouds, who prepares rains for the earth . . ." (Ps. 147:8). For there are two kinds of giving: in one, a wealthy person gives a gift to one who is also wealthy, and in another, a wealthy person gives a gift to one who is poor. The difference between the two is that the wealthy person experiences no embarrassment over receiving a gift, whereas the poor person does. However, in order to insure that the poor person does not experience

embarrassment, the wealthy person must render him/herself as if s/he has nothing, so that giving a gift does not engender a feeling of being embarrassed.

And this is what is meant by "The One who covers the heavens." For this there is a parable in *Raya Mehemna* (Zoharic/mystical literature) of a tailor who took a whole piece of cloth and tore it into small, thin pieces. One who is not a skilled craftsperson will say that it is ruined, but one who understands that such a piece may become a glove or something else, this person recognizes and knows that everything needs to be rendered into small pieces. So it was before creation that only God existed, and afterwards created all the worlds . . . that before the current paucity of existence grandeur was unknown, and so it was necessary for there to be a great shattering, so that the light would be known.[12]

Even before he arrives at the charming and genius parable of the tailor, Rabbi Dov Baer reminds us of spiritual and social conundrums that reflect our aloneness in the world. The first is that, while we yearn like one of the lovers of the Song of Songs, the object of our yearning remains forever out of reach, as the "One" is covered in the clouds of the heavens. And then he turns our attention to this world, when we exist in a perpetual state of relationship and need, and even if we wish to satisfy the needs around us, we face the ethical obstacle of embarrassing another. The solution, surprisingly, is to render ourselves as if we are "nothing," to efface ourselves such that we can give *tzedakah* in a way that honors another human being.

The elusiveness of the You, whether that You is God, a lover, a friend in need, or even one's deepest self, points to the deepest existential/spiritual conundrum, namely, that our experience of the universe is fragmented. We are unable to see the whole, and so the One we seek is always obscured. And so it is to respond to this confounding reality that Rabbi Dov Baer provides us with the genius analogy of a tailor. In the tatters, the tailor sees the wholeness, whereas most of us see only the shreds.

So it is with our fundamental perception of the world. God shattered the vessels holding primordial light by necessity, and in our lack of awareness, we may behold only the brokenness of the world around us—our loneliness, our spiritual isolation, our embarrassment, and awkwardness. However, as we grow in our understanding of God's artistry, we learn to see how the shards of creation, or the strips of cloth, may be woven into something new. Of course, what is new does not bear any resemblance to the original cloth, even though its essence, the material, is the same. However,

12. Rabbi Dov Baer of Mezritsch, *Magid Devarav l'Ya'akov*, 31.

Rabbi Dov Baer explicitly emphasizes that there is no way around the tearing of the cloth or the shattering of God's light. Only through being blown up and embedded in the stuff of creation may the "light" of God be known. Or, to paraphrase Leonard Cohen, only through the cracks are we able to let the light in.

In the second parable, Rabbi Dov Baer invites us to think of the everyday occurrence of a chick hatching as a dual metaphor for the primordial cosmic shattering and also for our ongoing growth and change.

> Nothing is able to change from one manifestation to another manifestation, such as an egg becoming a chick, without first dissolving into nothing at all from its first manifestation, as with the egg. And only afterward may it become another manifestation. Everything must happen this way, to become Nothingness, and only then to become something else.[13]

In another place, Rabbi Dov Baer elaborates on this image:

> No change in this world is possible without Wisdom, which is to say, Nothingness. For our eyes see that an egg cannot become a chick until it loses its form as an egg entirely, when it enters for just one moment into the gate of Nothingness. And only afterwards may it change from an egg into a chick. . . . This is the energy of all creation, it is the stripping of all form and structure, and within it, change.[14]

There is a deep teaching here about the nature of Nothingness as the medium for change, which I will delve into more deeply in the next chapters. But for now, we can see how Rabbi Dov Baer draws a simple analogy between the creative destruction of Luria's vessels that underlies the cosmos and the changes that take place before us, and also within us, every day. Just as the vessels of divine light burst, so we who are also vessels of that same divine light undergo transformations. In this vein, Rabbi Dov Baer implies that we, like the egg, also become nothing before we can become something else, as is the way of all creation. To become new beings, we must first become unrecognizable both to other people and even ourselves. Everything, and even we by implication, must become "nothing, so that afterwards it may become something else."

Rabbi Dov Baer's radical understanding of how the simple progression of life changes us arouses my skepticism even as I revel in his poetic imagery. With Buber, we can feel the attraction of his thought as offering

13. Ibid., 54.
14. Ibid., 100.

the dual prospects of growing into independent, maybe even solitary people while never losing the fundamental connection to the You, whether that is the eternal You in God or another human being. But if we become "nothing," as Rabbi Dov Baer enjoins us, do we not risk losing these very connections we yearn for, as well as those who need "something" from us? I have seen relationships break up over one partner's deepening commitment to a spiritual life. But I believe there is another side to embracing the radical change inherent in this kind of life. While we may fear isolating ourselves by becoming someone different, there is also the prospect that with our new sense of self and practice we will invite others in. This would certainly be Buber's understanding. The more intense our spiritual exploration, the more we open ourselves up to an encounter with the "Other," the "You."

A Lonesomeness with Connection

For Buber, deepening spiritual engagement has to mean a greater openness to all people around us. In a striking passage in *I and Thou*, Buber shows how one may be alone, and yet decidedly connected in the pursuit of the "supreme" You.

> There are two kinds of lonesomeness, depending on what it turns away from. If lonesomeness means detaching oneself from experiencing and using things, then this is always required to achieve any act of relation, not only the supreme one. But if lonesomeness means the absence of relation: if other beings have forsaken us after we had spoken the true You to them, we will be accepted by God; but not if we ourselves have forsaken other beings.[15]

This passage sets us up to expect a "good" lonesomeness and a "bad" lonesomeness. But actually, they are both the result of seeking out the moment of communion in "I-You." And so, no "lonesomeness" is bad, so long as it is the kind that helps us remain open and generous. To form relationships, with people or with God, means "detaching oneself from experiencing and using things." Withdrawing from the everyday world of ephemera and demands, we may find ourselves "lonesome" from our habitual modes of engagement, but in doing so we are actually reviving ourselves as we seek out a new quality of connection. The other kind of "lonesomeness" similarly occurs through the act of drawing toward, making ourselves vulnerable by speaking the "true You" to another. Other people may not be ready to know

15. Buber, *I and Thou*, 152.

us as we really are, and so they may turn us away. But Buber consoles us by reminding us that, when we have truly and authentically shared ourselves, we are never alone, but accepted by the ultimate You, even if we can't feel that sense of communion. This kind of un-lonely "lonesomeness" is predicated on the condition that we are not totally shut off from other people even as we pursue connection to the "You." This is certainly a pitfall in a spiritual life. We have to be mindful not to become so wrapped up in our pursuit of the "You," that we are really just pursuing an idealized version of ourselves. "Other beings" must always be with us in our seeking the You—it can't be any other way.

Thirty years after Rabbi Ron introduced me to Buber's promising and radical idea of I-You, I am still trying to figure out how to reconcile the need for both a decisive break with the world and the imperative and promise of making new connections. As I look over the narrative of my life, I realize how my father consigned me to loneliness. But in taking on the kind of spiritual "lonesomeness" that Buber envisions in order to seek out the ever-elusive You, I can say that I have experienced something. I can't say what that "something" is. "Connection" is too pat and stable. "God" would be too grandiose and perhaps too much of my own projection rather than reality. But in pursuing both solitude and relationship, I can say that I have known experiences that no one could have prescribed or predicted for me.

For now, I very much believe in the "You," though I am often at a loss to translate these "You" moments into language. For me, the "You" is refracted into a seemingly infinite array of faces, voices, personalities, and sensations. They are moments rather than beliefs, ideas, or even thoughts. And so, though isolated from my father, I rarely feel truly alone in the world. From the scraps of our tattered relationship I have now for decades been weaving a new tapestry of people and the universe, along with whatever unites people and the universe, and perhaps with what lies beyond.

Chapter 5

God Is Not God

Not by Might, Not by Power

Elisha's life entails a radical transformation, and at the center of it is his relationship to power. When we first meet him, he is warmly ensconced in his family and community. But then as a mature prophet, he wastes no time summoning bears to maul the children who taunt him. He has attained the ability to summon God's limitless power, which means that all earthly power wielded by human beings is meaningless. And yet, Elisha must also be limitless in his compassion, concerned as he is with the poorest and most marginal people in his society, the people most exploited by the abuse of power at the hands of those who command armies and wealth. For us who are charged with walking the prophetic path, we must reconcile ourselves to a world in which we must both account for our relative privilege and the agency we do have, against the ever-present reality that the power from which we benefit will undoubtedly exploit or oppress someone else.

Through Elisha's example, we learn that the ideal is to divest ourselves of our conventional notions of power. Elisha's encounter with the taunting children, and the bears that consume them, makes the point as an object lesson against seeking power in expected places. From the scene in which the children appear and taunt him, "Get away, baldy! Get away, baldy!" we can imagine how the children viewed Elisha as a "nothing." Along with his baldness, Elisha probably embodied other unimposing physical qualities that went along with being a prophet: perhaps a slow, meditative gait, a

disheveled appearance, a singularly modest bearing that defied social convention. In the eyes of mischievous children, Elisha was a weakling they
could abuse with impunity. And so they taunted him mercilessly, drunk as
children can be on the exercise of their newfound power.

However, we learn immediately that Elisha's seeming "nothingness"
co-exists with frightening force. In response to the children's taunts, bears
come out of the woods and maul the children, forty-two to be exact. The
story, in its unapologetic gruesomeness, shocks us into realizing that real
power is found in places where it seems to be absent. Elisha, bald, alone, and
on the margins, appears to be one who can and should be forgotten, but he is
possessed of unlimited power in his ability to summon what is unseen. Going forward, Elisha will repeatedly demonstrate that the greatest abundance,
advantage, and access to God's power lies with precisely those who are most
vulnerable and forgotten. And the avenues for accessing God's power are
not those of privileged people. As opposed to those who garner their favor
of kings and princes through the advantage of wealth and connections, the
poor, bereft, and destitute will galvanize God's response through Elisha's
concern for them. According to these stories then, real power is built not
upon things, but upon the ability of human beings to see themselves in a
state of dependence upon each other and the force behind all creation.

These stories of Elisha similarly challenge us to assess how much we
divest ourselves of our attraction to power, and how much we open ourselves
to the kinds of relationships through which we support and heal. Looking
back, it is clear that confronting my father at sixteen was a moment in which
I turned toward something unknown and unseen as a way to oppose conventional power and authority. That moment also occurred at a time when I
was growing suspicious of mainstream values regarding power and prestige.
As a teen, I rejected the materialism I encountered in the forms of nouveau
riche Long Island and the go-go Wall Street days of the 1980s. Instead, I had
internalized an alternative set of values and aspirations. In place of money
and competition, I was drawn to music, art, and literature, and to community service as ways to find myself, connect with others, and feel like I was
making some kind of social contribution. That, simply, was what I wanted
out of my life, then as well as now.

Shattering Myths of Society and Self

As I began college, I supplanted the power and authority of my father by
constructing my own myth of total self-reliance. Banishing the prospect
of any relationship with him from my mind, I believed that I, of my own

accord, could become most fully myself by living independent of him. I expected that this period of my life and the experience of the school I would attend, Oberlin College, would play a critical role in my Elisha-like, deep and radical transformation. On an unspoken level, I also felt that the intellectual rigor of college would distinguish me over and against my absent father. Whatever my mother's and grandmother's feelings toward my father, they admired his academic brilliance and readily recounted his sailing through Brooklyn College and graduate school at the University of Chicago. When my father reached a crossroads in his career as a research scientist, he returned to law school, purportedly achieving a perfect score on the LSATs. Succeeding in college would therefore be my way to surpass my father and define myself, as I would find my voice, my profession, and my calling. I also looked toward college to provide me with the new companionship of friends who would be there for life, as surrogate family, with deep abiding love. All of this, I believed, would help me drive my father from my life, along with all the sadness, unfulfilled expectations, and pain he represented.

Oberlin helped me on my path toward independence by stripping away the beliefs I held about myself, about people, and about the world. Most often, I found myself thinking about different kinds of "power" other people ascribed to me as being white, male, and of relative privilege. "De-mythologization" was a word that described much of what was happening in classes and conversations, and I absorbed the zeitgeist such that I was always wondering if I was being inclusive enough, appropriately mindful of my privilege or adequately deconstructing my male power. There is perhaps little self-parody in this shorthand summary, a luxury of time and distance. But in truth, I engaged these questions with full earnestness and continue to consider them a cornerstone of how I engage with the world and make choices day to day.

Of all the de-mythologizing ways of thinking that were prominent at Oberlin, feminism was perhaps the overriding intellectual theme for much of my time in college. In feminist thought, I saw a thoroughgoing way of both deconstructing and reconstructing myself—intellectually, emotionally, and eventually spiritually. By coming to grips with the inherent power of being a man, and the ways in which this power infiltrated all interactions and all of society, I could make purposeful and meaningful choices about everything: the causes I supported, the career I would choose, the people I would befriend, the ways in which I would listen to and interact with people day to day and moment to moment. In a sense, feminism became a lens through which I could engage in Buber's dance of the worlds of I-It and I-You: by envisioning the egalitarian ideal, if but for a moment, I could immerse myself back in the world with an eye toward being an agent for change.

While I found feminist thought intellectually compelling, I felt as if I came to it as a matter of course through my mother, whose outlook was profoundly shaped by the women's movement of the late '60s and early '70s. While many people debate the nuances and subtleties of feminism, my mother lived it by necessity. As a divorced, single mother responsible for supporting her son with scant resources, my mother had to go to work at nineteen, confronting the rampant and demeaning sexism of the workplace at the time. She started as a secretary and, through the '70s, worked her way up to become an account executive for one of the most prestigious PR firms in New York, all with only one semester of college.

My mother marched in the women's liberation parades, and describes one of the most thrilling moments of her life as walking arm-in-arm with Betty Friedan down 5th Avenue. She read *Ms.* magazine and kept her checking account at the First Women's Bank of New York. Feminism reinforced my mother's sense that her life narrative could be different from what was expected of her by her parents. Like many feminists, particularly those who found their voice in the early '70s, my mother celebrated creativity and marginality, and participated in her own joyful assault on societal convention when she could. Feminism helped my mother see herself as a newly empowered woman, giving her hope when her life, in fact, was very challenging. With time, I have come to realize that I drew on my mother's feminism to envision my own future. If feminism could give my mother a sense of herself against the conventional and disempowering attitudes toward women, it could likewise help me define myself as I came into an awareness of how people, cultural myths, and structures of power undermined my own personhood, rather than supplying a meaningful foundation.

Feminism and the Jewish God

Feminism would also play the initial role in my deconstruction of God, a step that would be pivotal in discovering a new spirituality for myself. In truth, I was pretty indifferent toward living any kind of Jewish or spiritual life in my early college years. But the desire to learn about what people had to say about God was still there. That dormant but real interest was enough to push me to take a class called "God and Secularity," an upper-level class that was way over my head but exposed me to postmodern theology, all of it from a Christian perspective. I was taken by the feminist readings, in particular the sense of urgency that, if we are to devote ourselves to the earnest seeking of God, then we have to divest ourselves of the patriarchal imagery with which God is envisioned. In order to get to the "truth," assuming such a thing was even attainable, we would have to purge religious life of all traces of power that oppresses.

In particular, the intense focus on language impressed me. I was intrigued by examples, such as the titles of Mary Daly's books, in which the extremely intentional and spare use of language could not only correct the abuse of power in traditional religion, but suggest a new moral and spiritual vision for religious life. Daly's titles, such as *Beyond God the Father* and *Gyn/Ecology*, encapsulate much of what I and others have been drawn to in religious life over the last few decades: views of God that admit an almost limitless freedom of thought and relationship, and that insist on an inherent connection between preservation of the soul and preservation of our planet and all life.

I imagine that, for many people, such a deconstruction of God and God language can become tiresome. But for me, the evisceration of God language deepened my own sense of the urgency of a profound spiritual conundrum: how to give a name to a reality unseen, further divested of its artificial claims to authority and dominance, but perhaps nevertheless real. I was taken by how feminist scholars took the domineering God, with whom relationship was impossible, and threw Him on the junk heap, like Abraham smashing his father's statues. In the words of the pioneering Jewish feminist Judith Plaskow in her book *Standing Again at Sinai*, "When a metaphor is assumed and defended, it has ceased to be an image and become an idol." I also took to heart what many feminist writers considered the next step. In place of oppressive ways of thinking, we could "name" our supposedly marginal and personal experiences, granting them legitimacy by giving them a voice. I was not yet sure what those experiences would be for me, but I was taken by the prospect of getting rid of the old language of a domineering, distant, and patriarchal God, and in its place seeking language that expressed my aspirations to be part of a liberating social reality.

It wasn't until years later that I learned how Jewish tradition has its own version of deconstructing God from within. As I understand now, there is something very Jewish in the feminist method of paying close attention to language in order to introduce radical ideas. The rabbis of the Talmud, looking back on the God of the Bible, take stock of the plethora of images and recognize how the Bible speaks about God in *metaphor*. That realization gave the rabbis ample license to expand on the repertoire of motifs of God as a father, king, shepherd, and lover, just to name a few. Often, the rabbis revisited the biblical motifs to show how the motifs themselves are inadequate to "contain" God. For example, God may be depicted as a king, but the rabbis contended that whereas a king of "flesh and blood" is capricious, distant, and cruel, God as King is nurturing, compassionate, and generous, actually the opposite of what we may expect from a king. This is classic deconstruction: God as "King" is not really a "king" at all. Perhaps most poignantly for me, the rabbis imagine how God as a judgmental father forever regrets his domineering attitude and resulting estrangement from his children. Imagining God reflecting on the destruction of the temple in Jerusalem, the rabbis have God lament, "Woe to the father who sends his children from their father's table!" Through these and many more examples of parables and stories, the rabbis both expand upon and undercut the images of God in the Bible, preventing these metaphors from becoming clichés. In so doing, the rabbis invite us to name our experiences of God as deeply complex, contradictory, and transcending all description, essentially rendering God as mysterious and unknowable.

The Rabbis Defeat God

Even more radically, the rabbis' reflections have the cumulative effect of driving from our consciousness not only conventional notions of God's nature, but also our assumptions of God's power. With God's authority undermined, God is not merely the grand power of the universe, but also the One most vulnerable to our arguments, dissatisfactions, and desires to direct our lives and improve the world. At their most extreme, the rabbis almost completely restrict God's authority and ability to intercede in human affairs. In one of the most perplexing and haunting stories from the Talmud, the rabbis portray a God whose "voice" is banished from our experience. To use feminist language, the rabbis upend the hierarchy between God and human beings, and show that *we*, not God, have all authority over the course of our destiny.

This story from the Talmud begins innocently, as a group of rabbis argue about a rather arcane subject—whether an oven constructed of linked rings is susceptible to ritual impurity—when the discussions come to a standstill. Rabbi Eliezer marshals every rational argument he can think of to support his position, but none of the other rabbis agree with him. So he decides to reach beyond the limited scope of rational debate that is the norm with his colleagues. Here is an account of the story from the Talmud, *Bava Metzia* 59b:

> It is taught: on that day, Rabbi Eliezer responded with every argument that existed, and they (his rabbinic companions) did not accept his reasoning. He said to them, "If the halakhah (point of Jewish law) is as I say, let this carob tree prove it," at which point the carob tree became uprooted from its place and

moved 100 cubits. They said to him, "One does not bring proof from a carob tree." Rabbi Eliezer further said to them, "If the halakhah is as I say, let the stream prove it," at which point the stream began flowing backward. They said to him, "One does not bring proof from a stream." He responded to them, "If the halakhah is as I say, let the walls of the house of study prove it," at which point the walls of the house of study began to fall. But Rabbi Joshua objected and protested, "Where scholars contend with each other in halakhah, what is your purpose?!" The walls did not fall out of respect for Rabbi Joshua, but neither did they stand upright out of respect for Rabbi Eliezer, as they continue to both stand and lean."[1]

At this point, the story seems to be an ironic and almost comic way to insist upon the integrity of rabbinic debate. Where sages disagree, there is no recourse to anything beyond the natural world, no matter how emphatic the argument. And yet, how far can this go? What if the halakhah, this point of Jewish law, is as Rabbi Eliezer says? He would have the backing of the author of the halakhah, namely, God. If Rabbi Eliezer has God on his side, can anyone else truly object? Here is the surprising and haunting answer provided by the story:

Rabbi Eliezer responded to them, "If the halakhah is as I say, let it be proven from heaven!" A heavenly voice announced, "Why do you disagree with Rabbi Eliezer when the halakhah is as he says in every instance?" Rabbi Joshua stood up and said, "It is not in heaven" (Deuteronomy 30:12)! What does this mean, "It is not in heaven?!" Rabbi Jeremiah said, "Since Torah was already given at Mount Sinai, we do not seek counsel from a heavenly voice. For it has already been written in the Torah from Mount Sinai, ". . .after the majority must you incline" (Exodus 23:2). Rabbi Natan came upon Elijah. He asked him, "What did the Holy One do at that moment?" Elijah said, "God laughed and said, 'My children have defeated Me! My children have defeated Me!'"[2]

On one level, this story liberates humanity by limiting God's scope and authority, driving God away from the realm of day-to-day decision-making, going so far as to even silence God. In the story, Rabbi Joshua quotes God's own words from Deuteronomy to assert that, once given, the Torah is no longer God's but is given over to human beings who must now rely on our

---

1. Babylonian Talmud, Tractate *Baba Metzia* 59b.
2. Ibid.

own capacities of discernment to apply its teachings. By banishing God's voice from our everyday lives, we are free to live with maximal moral and spiritual authenticity, at least according to Rabbi Joshua. At Sinai, God revealed Godself and God's commandments, but we, with our capacities of reason and intuition, puzzle over how to apply these commandments day to day. Living in the space of our willing banishment of God, we hold the authority of Torah, but take upon ourselves total authority over its interpretation. Unburdened by God's control, we are free to determine the moral and spiritual course of our lives, and God's laughter seems to be a sign of approval that we have finally gotten it right.

For me, part of the enduring appeal of this story is that it takes away the requirement to view God with absolute and all-encompassing power. Doing so makes any kind of personal relationship to God both easier and harder. In one sense, God may be more comprehensible, more relatable, and human once taken off of the pedestal. And yet, the God whose power is diminished is also the God rendered even more remote once the divine voice is silenced.

According to this story, it is not only optional, but necessary to live at a remove from any sense of God's voice, and only with this distance does one become a devoted Jew. In fact, according to Rabbi Joshua, we should reject those who claim to speak in God's voice, and relinquish any prospect of hearing God's voice ourselves, even if it seems clear as day. Instead, we should only rely on the capacities we have been given as we strive, "after the majority," for a collective human understanding. As the rabbis say in the Talmud, "After the destruction of the temple, prophecy was given over to children and fools."[3] For those of us who sense God more as absent than present, this story invites us to recognize how our experience without God is actually an authentic and normative feature of Jewish tradition.

However, when I consider this story against the backdrop of being estranged from my own father, I must admit that this story is more haunting than triumphant. It invites me to consider us free of God, but that freedom comes with existential risk. Perhaps God's laughter is not joyful like that of a parent who relishes a child's independence, but sinister and cynical, like a father full of spite, countering the children's new maturity with rejection of his own. This is the risk taken on by all of us carving out our place in the world different from our parents, teachers, or mentors. When we do, we may not know if they will approve or disapprove. And so, along with the radical freedom from God, perhaps this story also reminds us of how we must live with the constant uncertainty of whether we are living in a

3. Tractate *Bara Bathra* 12b.

pleasing way, in a noble way, in the right way. Without the authority of those who have guided us up to a certain point in adulthood, we may not have any answer. This uncertainty may be transfigured into a yearning for pursuit of the unknown, with all its mystery and danger. But it also may instill an ongoing anxiety and fear that contributes to a lifetime of second-guessing and indecision.

The Death of God?

In college, before I knew of this story about Rabbi Joshua silencing God's voice, I was drawn to a view of religious life as far as the deconstruction of God could go. In the seminal book of essays *After Auschwitz*, Richard Rubenstein attempts to erase every traditional expectation of what we consider to be "God" from our consciousness. According to Rubenstein, the Holocaust revealed, once and for all, that the "God" of tradition was a fiction, a projection, and a childish fantasy of all that would protect us. God would not punish those who were evil or reward those who were pious, either immediately or along some kind of geologic time scale. In the wake of the trauma of the Holocaust, a life with God was incapable of providing any kind of transcendent meaning or real comfort. Instead, after Auschwitz, such a god (small "g" intentional) was, in Rubenstein's language, dead. There may be other gods, Rubenstein admitted, but that was beside the point. The primary task for a person, living in the wake of Auschwitz, who saw themselves as striving to be a religious person was to admit that the god we had been brought up to count on was "nothing." Only by first embracing the "nothingness" of God could we even begin a new journey toward a new understanding.

> The God who is the ground of being is not the transcendent, theistic God of Jewish patriarchal monotheism. Though many still believe in that God, they do so ignoring the questions of God and human freedom and God and human evil. For those who face these issues, the Father-God is a dead God.[4]

In my notes from that time, I wrote in the margins of my book, "God is resurrected. Shattered myths lead to rediscovered meaning." I must have believed at the time that admitting the "nothingness" of received God language, declaring God "dead," would yield a new, different and more mature spiritual life. I looked to Rubinstein the way that people who love culture look to anthropology, or the way people who study medicine analyze

---

4. Rubenstein, *After Auschwitz*, 238.

anatomy. Rubenstein helped me survey the landscape of God that I truly wanted to understand, but from which I was happy to live at a distance. Rubinstein, I believed, laid all the falsehoods about God and faith on the table, exposing everything. With that full accounting, I believed, would come understanding, and with understanding, truth. In this way, Rubinstein rang with power and possibility.

But from where would this new sense of understanding, insight, or truth emerge? According to Rubinstein, God as the "focus of ultimate concern" is not found through prayer, or through devotional contemplation, but rather, through "self-discovery." And so, Rubinstein's promise of wholeness would be found in what he calls "freedom." By this, he means the freedom to search, but also the freedom to not expect anything of God, save the dissolution of illusion and falsehood in oneself. Rubinstein illuminates this freedom through a concept of God who shatters all myths:

> Paradoxically God as ground of being does everything and nothing. He does nothing in that He is not the motive or active power which brings us to personal self-discovery or to the community of shared experience. Yet He does everything because He shatters and makes transparent the patent unreality of every false and inauthentic standard. God, as the ultimate measure of human truth and human potentiality, calls upon each man to face both the limitations and the opportunities of his finite predicament without disguise, illusion, or hope.[5]

I encountered Richard Rubenstein's book not through any kind of soul searching in college, or by pursuing a personal need to understand more about the Shoah. Rather, I came upon *After Auschwitz* by accident, as it was assigned in a course on modern Jewish thought that I selected in order to fill out my schedule one semester. But of course, I was searching without knowing I was doing so, seeking language for the experience of wanting to be free of my father and everything he represented, yet yearning to be connected to something at the same time.

Far from inducing me to feel sad or lonely by this deconstruction of God, Rubenstein's book energized me. I embraced his central idea that, once we accept our essential loneliness in the wake of God's nothingness, we are free. Even in traditional Jewish language, a Jew who throws off all Jewish obligations, who is secular and has no use for God, is called "frei," Yiddish for "free." Without my father, I really did feel free, even though friends who heard my story wondered how that could be possible. But honestly, I didn't really feel the pain of my father's absence during college, at least in any direct

5. Ibid., 240.

way. I was in love, immersed in ideas, and devoted to finding community. These ways of seeking to comprehend a deconstructed God propelled my own desire to free myself of the expected pain of what should and could have been, given the absence of my father. Following the feminists and Rubinstein, I realized that I did not need a personal God, and by extension my father, to wrestle with the limitations and embrace the opportunities of my life. All I needed was the courage and honesty to face myself. After all the myth busting, I would discover a new "ground of being," mostly human but also perhaps something else, through my thoroughly reconstructed sense of myself. Without a father, and without a personal God, I would have authenticity that I could abide with liberating insight and purpose. As a twenty-year-old, I was convinced that ultimate meaning was found in my power to re-invent myself, and that entailed embracing, rather than mourning, the absence of fathers human and divine.

With the perspective of years, I have to admit I may have read too much optimism into these radical deconstructions of God. Perhaps Rubenstein meant exactly what he said when he thought God was dead—end of story. Fellow travelers over the years—rabbinical students, rabbis, progressive Jews, and others—have always felt that Rubinstein really meant what he said: that God was dead and that was it. But I always thought he was saying that only the "father" God we have been taught to believe in was dead. I always resisted the fatalistic interpretation of Rubenstein and instead assumed that, beyond lifting the veil of patriarchal metaphors, beyond the dead nothingness, there was more, a new something that defied our ability to express what it was, but still something real.

Perhaps my belief that there is "something" amid the "nothing" comes from my deference to survivors of the Shoah who themselves have not given up the search for God, even as they exercise their right to draw on their experience as a righteous argument against God. There is a man in my congregation who escaped Poland twice and while in one moment will say that he does not believe in God, a few moments later will proudly declare himself a "Deist, like Thomas Jefferson," apparently willing to entertain some kind of transcendent order to the natural world. A woman in my community is a child survivor of one of the Lituanian ghettos in which close to 95 percent of the Jews perished. She's very fashionable and fun loving, and with a mischievous glint in her eye pronounces that she is "an agnostic," though she loves to study and celebrates her family's brisses, baby namings, and b'nai mitzvah with unbridled joy. The post-Holocaust theology by survivors themselves, particularly the great philosopher Emil Fackenheim, is remarkably deep. But I am particularly moved by what I once heard Elie Wiesel say in an interview, "I believe in God, but I don't like Him."

Whether my reading is the "correct" reading of Rubenstein or a creative misreading based on my own biases, I believe it sprang from my twin desires to debunk all power—of my father and of God—but at the same time remain connected to what my father could have given me, and to what Jewish tradition promised through the expressions of God's all-encompassing otherness and grandeur.

A Paradox: God's Nothingness Is Full

Regardless of what Rubenstein actually intended, there is a line of thinking, going all the way back to the Bible, that God is most fully manifest as nothingness. The formulation sounds strange, contradictory, and maybe even nihilistic. But it is backed up by scores of stories, parables, and reflections throughout all of Jewish tradition. The burning bush that draws Moses' attention to God may suggest that God is both a dying ember and everlasting life at the same time. Only Moses can fully attend to the overwhelming voice at Sinai, but that same voice, in the same place, reassures Elijah in a tone that is "quiet," "still," and "fragile," practically inaudible. In the rabbinic midrash, Abraham destroys his father's idols to demonstrate that the most real and powerful force is the God who is unseen. And in Kabbalah, the vessels holding the divine light shattered and became as nothing, so as to allow the world to be created, each particle concealing the hidden spark of God's presence.

Even more explicitly than these examples, the Jewish philosophical and mystical traditions proclaim God's "nothingness" to be something real. In fact, for some, God's "nothingness" may be God's most concrete attribute. Moses Maimonides, the great Jewish philosopher of the late twelfth, early thirteenth centuries, opens his magnum opus, *The Guide for the Perplexed,* by saying what Daly and the feminist theologians said, that God as we "know him" is not God at all, but a construction of our limited imaginations. The true God, according to Maimonides, lies beyond all language, intellectual conventions, and social conditions that give rise to our flawed understanding.

Maimonides does not exactly say that God is nothing, but he comes close. First, he demonstrates how popular conceptions of God, even those that the masses believe are enshrined in the sacred texts of the Torah and rabbinic commentaries, are simply wrong. Despite what is written in the first chapter of Genesis, God does not have an "image" or "likeness" from which human beings can be created. Similarly, God does not speak, talk, appear, make decisions, or do anything in which God changes from point

A to point B. Having laid out his belief in the absolute non-corporeality of God, Maimonides dispenses with all of the popular Jewish conceptions of God as if he were taking out the trash. But he doesn't stop there.

Once we have divested ourselves of any notion of God's corporeality, Maimonides notes that we may still believe that God has certain non-corporeal "attributes," be they compassion, justice, love, etc. Such a notion was advanced by the leading Christian and Islamic philosophers of his day. But, says Maimonides, to define God by attributes that we discern is to limit God. By saying of God that "God is good," or "God rewards and punishes," we violate the understanding of a God who is singular and unchanging, and so by giving God even abstract attributes, we nevertheless make God over in our image. The most we can do, says Maimonides, is assign God "negative attributes." We can never posit what God *is*, only what God *is not*. And it is this God, the God who cannot have attributes assigned, and who resists being seen, heard, or even conceived, that lies in wait to be known by those willing to devote their entire lives to searching out the ultimate truth.

Kabbalah, Jewish mystical tradition, shares and expands upon the idea of Maimonides' God who can only be known in the negative. For some mystics, the God to be known is *Ayin,* literally "nothingness." But God's "nothingness" and our "nothingness" are nowhere close to the same thing. Instead of God existing as a void, God's being as *Ayin* is actually the fullness of everything.

In the Middle Ages, the author David ben Judah he-Hasid describes a contemplative experience in which real communion with God is the ability to reach a state of "nothingness:"

> . . .concerning the Cause of Causes (a philosophical/mystical term for God, ed.) there is no aspect anywhere to search or probe; nothing can be known of It, for It is hidden and concealed in the mystery of absolute nothingness (*ha-ayin ve-ha-efes*). . . . So open your eyes and see this great, awesome secret. Happy is one whose eyes shine from the secret, in this world and the world that is coming![6]

Nothingness in the Fullness of Yearning

Notice how contemporary this is. God is nothingness. God is not even "God," or "He" or "She," but "It." God is not even an object who can be

---

6. Matt, "*Ayin*: The Mystical Concept of Nothingness," in Fine, *Essential Papers in Kabbalah*, 81.

known, searched, or probed. The great modern thinker Abraham Joshua Heschel wrote that we often think that we are the subject meditating upon God as the object. But it is, in fact, the opposite, says Heschel. We are the object, and God is the subject. But here, in this mystical text, there is not even a subject and object, only the Cause of Causes, which is really nothing, and yet "It" is hidden in everything! This may or may not be a text that stands up to Maimonides' rational scrutiny. I am sure that a towering logical mind such as his could find all of the internal contradictions. But for one seeking something real amid all of the incomplete and insufficient explanations of God that get in the way, this "nothingness" offers something refreshing and real. If we are able to dispel all illusion, we achieve the great experience of being rendered as "nothing." And yet, we may discover that "nothing" that is, in fact, everything.

As to the experience of nothingness and how we may gain a glimpse everyday, consider this text from the eighteenth century. It is another teaching by Rabbi Dov Baer of Mezritsch, whom I quote earlier in the book. Here, as in the previous chapter, his meditation alludes to the mystical notion of the "shattering of the vessels," which is the precondition of cosmic creation. Here he considers very directly and personally how each of us in a spiritual life may come into contact with that essential nothingness:

> A human being should think of him- or herself as Nothing, and put out of his or her mind the substance of his or her entire being, seeking everything in each prayer for the sake of the Shekhinah. Then will he or she be able to transcend time, that is, enter the world of thought where all is equal: life and death, sea and dry land.
>
> And this is what is alluded to in the *Zohar* (II, 52b), "For what reason are you crying out to Me?" "To Me," that is to say, that the matter alludes to the Ancient One. For they (the Israelites) need to render themselves selfless and detach from their troubles, so that they would enter the world of thought, in which everything is equal.
>
> This is impossible when one cleaves to material reality in this world. One is cleaved to the division between good and evil . . . and so how may one transcend time, where there is total unity. And similarly, when one concentrates on one's material needs and prays for ones material desires, the Holy One is unable to become garbed in him. For the Exalted One is Without End, without any vessel that can hold Him.
>
> Unless one considers oneself as Nothingness.[7]

7. Baer, *Maggid Devarav L'Ya'akov*, 1.

There is a bit of an ascetic strain here that may seem foreign to our experience of Jewish tradition. Put it aside for now, as that is not the main thrust of this passage. Instead, this passage calls to mind moments of real transcendence—making music, finding real comfort amid sorrow, deep study, meditation or prayer, connection to human community, lovemaking. All of these are experiences of the fullness of life, and yet they are all ways in which we "lose ourselves," and so perhaps may be glimpses of "*ayin*," our sense of nothingness, be it the nothingness of ourselves, of God, or that place where we simply meet the transcendent. From Rabbi Dov Baer and from Maimonides, I infer that in these experiences in which we "lose ourselves," we are actually most fully ourselves. Rabbi Dov Baer names the experience of leaving one's sense of self behind as becoming absorbed in the reality of God, that encompasses and transcends everything. As we "lose ourselves" and become "nothing," we encounter that paradoxical sense of "nothing," which is actually everything. In the language of Rabbi Dov Baer, we meet God in our shared state of "nothingness."

From Nothing to Something

In the encounter between "all" and "nothing." I believe that my sympathy for the "God is not" way has long seemed for me a way to reconcile the experience of an absent father with that of a remote God. My father's abandonment forced me to give up all illusion and hope for what he should have been and given me. But in these radical ways of thinking about God as "nothing," I feel myself turning toward something that emerges once I have dispensed with all pretense and illusion and accepted the reality of living with contradictions. In my life, one of the great existential paradoxes was how my father seemed to love being with me, and yet he was determined not to make space for me in his life. In Judaism, God always seemed impossibly remote, and yet, in this hiddenness, was intriguingly real. The view of God as essentially "nothing" speaks to my reflex to confront pain, entertain despair and cynicism, but ultimately reject it, believing that hiddenness and absence is instead a kind of mystery, promising to yield something real yet unknowable.

Even as I lived happily without my father, I lived with the longing engendered by his absence. I did not long for my actual father, necessarily, but for the ultimacy, the love, and the constancy he could have provided. That longing drove me to find satisfaction in experiences without him, and it made me a musician, fueled my studies and friendships, and most of all, drove me to love. It drove me to engage in my own *shevirat ha-kelim*, my own shattering of assumptions of what I wanted and how I lived my life, rejecting various conventions and pieties so that I may discover some kind of underlying truth. And yet, despite all the de-mythologizing and decon-struction of God that I embraced, I felt there had to be more. Destroying the idols was necessary, and continues to be, but not for the sake of uncovering only absolute nothingness, but in the hope that the absence of illusion will yield something new.

Chapter 6

Sifting through the Broken Images

New Wholeness—A Daunting Prospect

From the perspective of Kabbalah, the shattering of vessels may have been a necessary stage in creation, but its cost is that we live in a world that is inherently flawed and broken. As long as the universe is comprised of the shards of divine light trapped within the "husks" of the created world, nothing is as it is supposed to be. Everything, whether we are talking about the material world, our souls, or even God, requires a new wholeness, what in Hebrew we call *tikkun*. Amazingly, the task of this restoration becomes the obligation of human beings with our fragile hands, our confusion, and our inconsistency. Living in the world of brokenness is a lonely and uncertain prospect.

During my time in college, I think I accepted a measure of existential loneliness, even as I was engaged and connected to other people. My willingness to accept Rubenstein's God as "nothing" was a good emotional fit as I sought to drive my father from my own memory. But as I have said, believing that God was "nothing" was for me a prelude to believing that God was actually "something" else. My reflex was to embrace the deconstruction of God so as to entertain new ideas about God and religious experiences that I had yet to encounter. I willingly stepped into a kind of spiritual loneliness expecting that I would eventually step out of it. While optimistic about my growing understanding of God, or at least of ideas about God, I did not feel the same way about my father. I still yearned for teachers and mentors who could provide the experience I needed from my father, never seriously considering that my father would be one of them.

I look back on this time now and realize how disjointedly I was seeking a kind of healing. The various ways in which I explored new understandings of God in the classroom and eventually in community brought me both intellectual excitement and joy. But as I continued to completely ignore my father, I was avoiding the great source of my pain, which of course I had to face in order to move forward. Ideally, these two explorations—of my father and God—should have worked in tandem. But in the reality made from the shards of shattered vessels, my own healing began in a way that was haphazard and piecemeal as I remained committed to living separate from my father, but always reaching toward something else.

As I reflect on how I embraced both the alienation from my father and the beginnings of an adult spiritual search, I see how the biblical Elisha similarly relies on his loneliness as part of his mission of bringing healing to the world. In this way, the episode with the boys stands out as so completely contrary to who the prophet Elisha will become. He will live this life with great devotion and humility, not once deviating from his commitment to humanity or questioning the capacities of God. And so, while Elisha is devoted to healing, he must be uncompromising. Not even the presumed innocence of children will deter him from standing against the forces of cruelty and dehumanization.

Elisha's complete lack of sentimentality is a key to a deeper kind of radical aloneness in his role as a prophet. Other prophets must also live alone and endure scorn. But all of them participate in an ongoing, reciprocal communication with God that not only gives them authority, but strength in which they battle against callousness, tyranny, and spiritual blindness. However, Elisha is not known for being God's vessel for any grand, poetic pronouncements. Unlike all other prophets, and most notably his mentor Elijah, Elisha will never have any kind of verbal exchange, attain any kind of direct encounter or vision, or receive any sign from God. As the stories of Elisha continue, he lives more like us, addressing the pain of the world without any clear avenue to encountering God's presence. He knows he must find ways to bring healing, but he also knows that he must do so while living in almost complete isolation from any kind of connection, whether to other people or to God.

Wholeness Follows Isolation: Elisha ben Abuya

While the biblical Elisha may live and engage with the world from almost total aloneness, the rabbis of the Talmud seem to suggest that such complete isolation is impossible, even if we are driven to seek it out. Instead, even if we try to completely distance ourselves from the injustices of this world and even from God, the rabbis seem to believe there may be an inner impulse compelling us to find some kind of connection. Among the rabbis, there is another Elisha, Elisha ben Abuya, who comes to represent an extreme example of one who refuses to abide the unjust suffering of this world and shuns the refuge of God and community. There is a story that, when confronted by the death of a child, Elisha ben Abuya comes to the despairing conclusion, "There is no judgment and there is no judge." But even though the rabbinic Elisha appears absolute in his rejection of God and the rabbinic community, his broader narrative suggests that we can never extinguish our desire for greater understanding, for the gifts of human connection, or the possibility that our lives mean something outside ourselves.

This rabbinic Elisha is depicted as living in the late second century CE, about a thousand years after the period of the biblical Elisha. I have actually alluded to him earlier in this book, in the story of the four who entered the *Pardes*, the garden of mystical speculation. Of the four who entered, he is the one who is said to have "broken the shoots," which is to say, he became an apostate, completely rejecting God. For this reason, he is called "*Acher*," the Other one, a name that he is given after this story about the mystical soul ascents, and not before.

According to the Talmud the deeper reason for Elisha's denial of God is his belief that God has rejected him.

> *Acher* cut the shoots. Of him Scripture says, "Do not allow your mouth to sway your flesh" (Ecclesiastes 5:5). What happened? He beheld *Metatron* (a divine being), who was given the ability to advocate for the merit of Israel (before God). (*Acher*) said, "Have we not learned that in heaven there is no sitting, no strife, no end and no weariness? Perhaps, let it not be so, that there are two powers (in heaven?)" At that moment he was brought before *Metatron* and struck with sixty beams of lightning. (*Metatron*) said to him, "How is that when you saw us you did not rise?" He was then given the authority to erase the merit of *Acher*. A divine voice went forth and proclaimed, "Return O backsliding children (Jeremiah 3:14), except for *Acher*." *Acher* said, "Since this man (*Acher*) was expelled from that world (heaven), let him go forth and enjoy this world (earth)." *Acher* pursued a

disreputable path. He went forth and found a prostitute and had
sex with her. She said, "Aren't you Elisha ben Abuyah?" He then
plucked a radish from its vine on Shabbat and gave it to her. She
said, "He is another (*Acher*)."[1]

According to the Talmudic story, all this stems from Elisha's traumatic
encounter with *Metatron*, which occurred during his quest to draw closer
to the presence of God. Contrary to his expectation, in which heaven is
a place of formlessness and the absence of suffering, Elisha beholds what
appears to be a man, the divine archangel *Metatron*, passing judgment on
humanity. Elisha's attempt to think out loud so as to make sense of a contradictory divine reality arouses heavenly anger. What he hears is a divine
voice quote the prophet Jeremiah, "Return, O backsliding children," which
the rabbis viewed as epitomizing the call to *teshuvah*, or repentance. This
ongoing invitation from God is supposed to reflect the constancy of divine
compassion, like the unconditional love of a parent who believe that one's
child is fundamentally good and always capable of returning to the ways
of kindness, justice, and integrity. Except Elisha heard something different.
Instead of the universal, constant beckoning to return to God, Elisha heard
every child's worst nightmare, that his divine parent no longer believed in
him or loved him, and that he was the only one among all human beings to
whom God's love did not extend: "Return, O backsliding children—everyone except Elisha ben Abuya!" Upon hearing of his own banishment from
the company of God, effectively being thrown out of the home of the human
family, Elisha resolved to focus solely on his own pleasure in this world.

From the observation of the prostitute comes the greatest insight: by
rejecting God and the ways of the rabbis, Elisha has transformed himself
into "another," "*Acher*," the archetypal "other." The Talmud then takes on
the insight of the prostitute as its own. And in reading this Talmudic passage, we take on the extreme isolation of Elisha, the prostitute, and now this
text, as our own. We are no longer reading "about" the "other," but rather,
through getting inside this story, we too are becoming that "other."

But as the text continues, we see that even in the most extreme state of
being "other," alone and despised, there is always the prospect of return. Despite rejecting God and God's laws, the Talmud's Elisha remains a passionate
student of God's Torah, a venerated teacher, and a generous companion to
the rabbis whose worldview and society he has rejected.

The same page of Talmud (*Hagigah* 15a) that recounts the apostasy of
Elisha also portrays his close relationship with his student, Rabbi Meir.

---

1. Babylonian Talmud, Tractate *Hagigah*, 15a.

After going down the path of disrepute, *Acher* asked Rabbi Meir, "What is the meaning of the verse, 'This one no less than the other is God's doing' (Ecclesiastes 7:14)?" Rabbi Meir said to him, "Each thing that the Holy One created, He created its counterpart. He created the mountains, He created the hills. He created the seas, He created the rivers." *Acher* said to him, "This is not what your teacher Akiva taught you! Rather, God created the righteous and created the wicked, created the garden of Eden and created Hell. Each person has two portions: one in the Garden of Eden and one in Hell. If one rises to the merit of being righteous, one takes one's own portion and that of one's friend in the Garden of Eden. If one is judged as wicked, one takes one's portion and that of one's friend in Hell."[2]

Elisha, disillusioned, has clearly resigned himself to living out his life on the path of being the "wicked" one, at least in his own mind. But even in the depths of his complete abandonment, both imposed upon him and of his own free will, Elisha is still a great teacher. His charisma jumps off of the page. He not only has great depth of insight, but he knows how to make a dramatic and enduring point, alluding to his own inner struggles in a way so as to make them universal. Although Elisha projects an outward attitude of resignation to his life of moral degradation and spiritual isolation, he appears to long for a return to the rabbinic community.

While Elisha knows his connection to God is completely broken, his companions believe they can help him ease his spiritual loneliness. Their concern emerges in another exchange with Rabbi Meir.

After following the path of disrepute, *Acher* asked Rabbi Meir, "What is the meaning of the verse, "Gold or glass cannot match the value (of wisdom,) Nor vessels of fine gold be exchanged for it?" (Job 28:17). He (Rabbi Meir) said to him, "This refers to words of Torah, which are difficult to acquire as vessels of fine gold, and easy to lose as vessels of fine glass." (Acher) said to him, "This is not what your teacher Rabbi Akiva said! Rather, just as vessels of fine gold and fine glass may be broken but can be fixed, so while a student of Torah may stray, he still has a means of repair." (Rabbi Meir) said to him (*Acher*), "And so you should return." But Acher said to him, "I have already heard from behind the veil, 'Return, O backsliding children—except for *Acher* (the "other," Elisha)!'"[3]

2. Ibid.
3. Ibid.

Immediately following is a second story in which Rabbi Meir tries to nurture his teacher Elisha's inner desire to overcome his isolation:

> Our Rabbis taught: There was a story of *Acher* riding on his horse on Shabbat, with Rabbi Meir walking behind him so as to learn Torah from him. He said, "Meir, turn back, for I have measured by the footsteps of my horse that we are coming upon the permitted distance of travel on Shabbat." He (Rabbi Meir) said to him, "Really, you should return." He (*Acher*) said to him, "But I have already heard from behind the veil, 'Return, O back-sliding children—except for *Acher*!'"[4]

Ironically, from a rabbinic point of view, the tragedy of Elisha was not his rejection of God or even his personal inclination to live over the edge. If anything, the rabbis admired their Elisha for his extraordinary insight, moral clarity, and forcefulness that made him such a beloved and charismatic teacher. For the rabbis, the real tragedy of Elisha was his refusal to allow his friends to help him heal from the pain of his own, self-imposed isolation. Even if God completely abandoned Elisha ben Abuya, as he believed, his fellow rabbis did not think he required God's intervention to find a new wholeness. All Elisha needed was to "come back" to living with his beloved friends within the norms of the rabbinic community.

While Elisha was unable to weave this new wholeness during his lifetime, his rabbinic companions make it possible after his death. In the mythology of the rabbis, there was a concern as to where Elisha's soul would come to rest—in heaven, with all of the righteous, or in a kind of in-between, restless state for all eternity. Although Elisha judged himself as irredeemably wicked, the rabbis saw him as one who lived with such ongoing devotion to Torah that he could eventually merit being counted among the righteous, although it would take some doing.

> When *Acher* died they said, "There is no one among us who can affect his judgment, nor is there anyone in the World to Come. There is no one among us because he busied himself with Torah, and not in the World to Come because he was a great sinner." Rabbi Meir said, "When I die, I will cause smoke to go up from his grave." He (Rabbi Meir) died, smoke rose from the grave of *Acher*. Rabbi Yochanan said, "He was a student among us and followed a degraded path. We do not have the strength to bring him to the World to Come. And even if I could take him with me, who would take him from me (to remain in the World to Come)? When I die, the smoke will cease from the grave of

4. Ibid.

Acher (meaning he would be finally welcomed into the World to Come)." When Rabbi Yochanan died, the smoke ceased from the grave of *Acher*. A mourner wailed about him, "Not even the guardian of Hell's gate could stand before you, our teacher!"[5]

Finding a Teacher

As a college student, I believed that I was living completely independently of my father, but in reality, I was living like both Elishas. Like the biblical Elisha, I moved on and pursued my happiness without him, through love, friends, and my studies. And like the rabbinic Elisha, though I never entertained the possibility of a return to our relationship, I hungered for and sought out what my father should have given me.

Not surprisingly, my way back toward Jewish life began with a search for a mentor. For my first three years of college, I had a number of thoughtful professors and advisors. But then, almost by accident, I signed up for a course in modern Jewish thought, led by Professor Ginsburg, who really became my "teacher." In my Jewish world, there is a way in which many of us yearn to find a "teacher." The yearning is actually hardwired into the culture from antiquity. In the first chapter of the rabbinic collection *Pirke Avot*, the great sage Yehoshua ben Perachia says, "Make yourself a teacher, and acquire for yourself a friend." The injunction appears intentionally ambiguous. A teacher is not necessarily a friend, but a true teacher is someone whose influence touches that part of our soul where we yearn for spiritual companionship. In other places in rabbinic literature, a teacher is a father figure, one who sometimes supplants one's own biological father. To prove their point in a Talmudic passage, the rabbis actually invoke Elisha lamenting the loss of his mentor Elisha with the words, *"Avi, Avi*, my father, my father!" Famously, the rabbis of the Talmud teach that if there is a disagreement between one's father and one's teacher, the teacher has the final say. Although I was completely unaware of these Jewish teachings on teachers and students, there is no doubt that my missing a father fueled my longing for a teacher of insight and wisdom, and in meeting Professor Ginsburg I sensed that he wanted to give of himself as much as he wanted to share his ideas.

Professor Ginsburg was a loving teacher, laying out texts and ideas, and then truly listening to our responses and reactions. He would carefully attend to what students said, nodding, stroking his beard, thrusting his neck forward and hunching his shoulders. All of these bodily movements were

5. Ibid., 15b.

no doubt unconscious, but seemingly cultivated over time to communicate, "your responses to my ideas are more important than the ideas in the first place." Professor Ginsburg was the kind of teacher who would readily agree to accompany a couple of students to the campus pub for "bring your prof and get a free pitcher" on Thursday. On one of these Thursdays, I was impressed when he responded with real interest as a fellow student shared her plan to buck convention and spend part of her summer traveling to hear the Dalai Lama.

Professor Ginsburg was also one of the most demonstrably erudite people I had ever met. He seemed to have complete fluency in the history of Jewish thought, from the central ideas of the great rabbis and philosophers to the minutiae of specific texts and their interpretation. To each lecture he brought an accompanying stack of books bursting with post-its, and at any point seemed ready to weave in ideas we were encountering in other classes, whether they be principles of Maslow's psychology of self-realization, literary deconstruction, feminism, or Asian religious ideas. Most of all, Professor Ginsburg endeared himself to us as someone whose natural humility and humor was the perfect accompaniment to his brilliance. He clearly loved books, and it was easy to see how he could lose himself in his texts and ideas, but he was first and foremost a mensch. Once, when he passed me on campus, he took a moment to stop and say to me, "That was a brilliant paper. Really, a brilliant paper." No one had ever said that to me before—my papers weren't really so great. But also, no teacher had ever taken that kind of personal notice of me, and since then, no other piece of feedback has so changed the way I saw my potential to make a statement with my thoughts and my writing.

It turned out that Professor Ginsburg was a seeker as well. My first inkling came when once, in a class on Jewish mysticism, there was a moment when his passion for the material transcended his responsibilities as an academic instructor. I forget what Professor Ginsburg was talking about, but he was standing, emphasizing the words "the richness of the tradition," while repeatedly pounding his fist into his palm. The passion and earnestness in his voice and body language conveyed that there was something deeper in these books, texts, and ideas toward which our formal academic study was only a first step. As I stayed in touch with Professor Ginsburg over the years I saw how he was actually a seeker first and a professor second, teaching a wide variety of students at retreats and conferences, embracing meditation practices and perhaps devising some of his own.

The Romantic Counterstroke

Through Professor Ginsburg, I encountered a way of thinking that helped me see my mix of curiosity about God and skepticism about conventional notions about God as part of the universal quest for spiritual understanding. In his introductory class on Jewish mysticism, Professor Ginsburg assigned Gershom Scholem's *Major Trends in Jewish Mysticism*. Scholem was raised in Berlin in a Jewish secular family in the early part of the twentieth century. Scholem had a brother who became a Communist but nevertheless maintained good relations with his bourgeois father. But when Scholem became a Zionist, his father kicked him out of the house.

Scholem became passionately curious about Jewish history and thought, especially about Jewish mystical traditions. At the time, no one in the highly trained, academically superb world of European Jewish studies even touched Jewish mysticism. At most it was viewed as baroque superstition and nonsense. But Scholem had an intense curiosity about the ways in which people understood their world and processed their impressions through received literature and language. He was both a friend and, to some extent, disciple, of the great writer and thinker Walter Benjamin. Scholem received his PhD by writing on a long-forgotten and little-studied precursor to the Zohar, and after emigrating to Palestine, set about accumulating both an encyclopedic knowledge as well as unparalleled library of Jewish mysticism. He also had the rare gift of a synthetic mind and a writing style that is clear and lyrical even as he parades through any number of obscure texts, ideas, and references.

But for all of Scholem's great erudition about particular mystical texts, their authors, and the movements that spawned them, he articulated a foundational idea about religious life that may be one of his most enduring contributions. It was a radical departure from the accepted methodology of presenting Jewish history as an orderly, linear progression whose greatest achievement was the ability to critically and rationally examine classical sources from the outside. By contrast, Scholem viewed Judaism as messy, in a perpetual state of flux, of action and reaction, all toward the goal of human beings overcoming their inherent existential loneliness.

Scholem proposed a threefold theory of religious evolution—not just for Judaism, but for all cultures. In the first stage, people feel uniquely and especially close to their gods. This example is especially strong in pagan, earth-bound religions, in which people perceive God, or divinity, to be embedded in the material world. Judaism fell into this pattern, not because it was exemplary, but because it was particular but unexceptional, striving to rediscover God through the lenses provided by its own unique historical experience.

> The first stage represents the world as being full of gods whom man encounters at every step and whose presence can be experienced without recourse to ecstatic meditation. In other words, there is no room for mysticism as long as the abyss between Man and God has not become a fact of the inner consciousness. That, however, is the case only while the childhood of mankind, its mythical epoch, lasts. The immediate consciousness of the interrelations and interdependence of things, their essential unity which precedes duality and in fact knows nothing of it, the truly monistic universe of man's mythical age, all this is alien to the spirit of mysticism. . . . In this first stage, Nature is the scene of man's relation to God.[6]

Notice here how the closeness between God (or more accurately, "gods") is likened to a spiritual childhood. There is not distance, certainly no gulf or "abyss" in this first stage. But there is also no religious or spiritual "consciousness" that we would be familiar with. The kinds of things we strive for in an adult understanding of the world: how people and things are connected, how causes may or may not be related to each other, the myriad ways in which we seek to make meaning, all this is impossible when there is such an extreme closeness of divinity and humanity. As Luria and so many others emphasize, there needs to be distance in order for there to be an awareness of oneself in relationship to others, to the world, to all being.

That gulf occurs in what Scholem refers to as the second stage. In this stage, it may be that the consciousness of humanity changes such that people realize while divinity may be present everywhere, the contact with divinity is more elusive. During this stage, societies develop all the mediating mechanisms—rituals, temples, priests, spiritual bureaucracies, texts, ideas, etc.—that help people address their gods, but these conventions have the added effect of creating an even deeper gulf.

> The second period . . . is the creative epoch in which the emergence, the break-through of religion occurs. Religion's supreme function is to destroy the dream-harmony of Man, Universe, and God, to isolate Man from the other elements of the dream stage of his mythical and primitive consciousness. For in its classical form, religion signifies the creation of a vast abyss, conceived as absolute, between God, the infinite and transcendental Being, and Man, the finite creature. . . . Man becomes aware

6. Scholem, *Major Trends in Jewish Mysticism*, 7.

of a fundamental duality, of a vast gulf which can be crossed by nothing but the *voice;* the voice of God, directing and law-giving in His revelation, and the voice of man in prayer. The great monotheistic religions live and unfold in the ever-present consciousness of this bipolarity, of the existence of an abyss which can never be bridged. To them the scene of religion is no longer Nature, but the moral and religious action of Man and the community of Men, whose interplay brings about history as, in a sense, the stage on which the drama of Man's relation to God unfolds.[7]

This is where we live. The "dream-harmony" of the ever-present God as parent is disrupted. The myth of an ever-present God, in constant relationship with us as with a parent to a young child, is gone as well. Instead, we have to reconcile ourselves to the distance, satisfied only by the faintest intimations of any kind of divine "voice," and relying on our meager rituals to facilitate some kind of awareness, not of the relationship necessarily, but of the gulf that exists between ourselves and God. As I think back on the story of Rabbi Eliezer and the rabbis from the last chapter in which they banish God's voice, I am struck that classical Judaism embraces that gulf as much as it tries to bridge it. Many people popularly describe Judaism as a practical, this-world religion, and perhaps they are right to a degree. But that affirmation here is seen as a strategy for accommodation, perhaps to render the existential isolation that Scholem notices a little more bearable.

But then there is the third stage, what Scholem referred to as the period of the "romantic counterstroke," in which humanity attempts to bridge that gulf of alienation they feel between themselves and God. In this stage, people seek the unmediated contact they imagined their ancestors having in humanity's spiritual infancy, dispensing with or circumventing the religious conventions that have been established. And so, people seek the means to transcend those rituals, texts, ideas, priests, and customs so as to have an intensely personal and immediate experience of God.

And only now that religion has received, in history, its classical expression in a certain communal way of living and believing, only now do we witness the phenomenon called mysticism; its rise coincides with what may be called the romantic period of religion. Mysticism does not deny or overlook the abyss; on the contrary, it begins by realizing its existence, but from there it proceeds to a quest for the secret that will close it in, the hidden path that will span it. It strives to piece together the fragments

7. Ibid.

broken by the religious cataclysm, to bring back the old unity which religion has destroyed, but on a new plane. . . . Thus the soul becomes its scene and the soul's path through the abysmal multiplicity of things to the experience of the Divine Reality, now conceived as the primordial unity of all things . . . .[8]

If this last stage seems familiar, it is because, says Scholem, it is the epoch in which we find ourselves. It is inherent in the vocabulary of our age to "quest" and "strive" after an experience that avoids the alienating traps of conventional religion. We seek not to be isolated, but engulfed in the "unity of all things." Instead of pursuing the needs of society, or satisfying the requirements of religious hierarchies, we seek the fulfillment of the soul. In the grand scope of religious history, we, as a human civilization, are profoundly aware of this gulf and we are devoted to transcending it.

Although Scholem wrote in a style of formal and scholarly detachment, I have always felt as if he was speaking directly to me from the depths of a personal experience. I have seen myself in the stages of connection, alienation, and yearning that Scholem describes. While the object of these stages was a conflated muddle of my father, God, and a vague desire for deep relationships, it was all bound up in a longing for the "Other." I felt Scholem's invitation to explore mystical thought as a way to see a mirror of how we live in the gulf between connection and loneliness, with despair, disillusionment, and skepticism as common experiences standing in that breach. I was intrigued, as was Scholem, by the steps we take, be they through ritual, texts, or community, to bridge that separation between ourselves and the great "Other." At the time when I encountered these ideas for the first time, I began to take some steps of my own. Sometimes, I would pray or study the Torah or another sacred text by myself. I also began taking my first tentative steps toward re-engaging with Jewish community. And while much of the impetus for these steps was toward seeking the "Other" that I began to think might be real, I also had some practical questions on my mind.

Bringing It All Back Home—Learning and Community

Toward the end of college, I began to think about the direction my life would take. When I began college, I initially thought I would study music and literature so that I might become a music journalist. After I dropped music, I embraced being an English major so that I might become a professor or a teacher. But toward the end of college, I realized that these paths were not

8. Ibid., 8.

compelling me. As I reflected on what had been important and meaningful to me, I thought of my desire (largely unrealized) to be an activist, as well as my ongoing aspiration to work one-to-one with people in an emotional and intimate way. I knew that I wanted to do something creative, where I could indulge a life of the mind and heart. I also thought about the papers that had gone well, and that they had explored the themes of contemplation and spiritual growth in various literary characters. I recalled moments of study when it seemed as if everything came together, in particular the way in which the ideas in Professor Ginsburg's class left me with a sense of ongoing and unfinished work.

An old intuition returned—one that originated when I was fifteen, seeing Israel for the first time through the eyes of my friends and most of all through Rabbi Ron. At the time, I imagined how rewarding it would be to do for other people what Rabbi Ron did for me, opening up connections to Jewish history and tradition, to other people, and to thoughts about God. I imagined a life of study, of sharing my ideas, of the warmth and reward of sharing people's most meaningful moments, and the joy and pathos of being connected to the Jewish story. Now, after several years of walking my own path—through study, music, and love—I was seriously revisiting these thoughts and feelings again. I realized that I wanted to become a rabbi.

Except I knew almost nothing—certainly no Hebrew beyond what I had learned in Hebrew school, and I was minimally familiar with what took place at a synagogue service. I really did not know what it felt like or meant to present in front of a group—the intensity and brilliance of people around me in college canceled that out. There was so much I didn't know about Jewish history and ideas, despite having done some good reading in modern Jewish thought. And yet, while outwardly embarrassed to share my aspiration with anyone, I was inwardly convinced. This was spring of my junior year, and so with summer coming up, I dove in on my own. I read anything Jewish that looked interesting. At home over the summer, I went to the small, mostly older, Saturday morning service in my synagogue library. I reconnected with Rabbi Ron and I became a little more familiar with the prayer book and tried praying on my own. I made a point of reading the Torah portion on Shabbat from the book my mother and stepfather gave me when I was fifteen and back from Israel.

But I had also realized that, if I really wanted to learn about Judaism from the inside, I couldn't do it alone. I would need community. I remember a student at Oberlin, younger than I was and who had spent time in Israel, leading a study session in which he contrasted learning in college vs. learning in a traditional Jewish manner. As opposed to the inherent isolation of study carrels and the silence of college libraries, traditional Jewish study was done in *chevruta*, or conversational partnership, with another. That simple difference conveyed that Jewish learning is not about accumulating knowledge (though there certainly is much of that) but a more holistic sense of growing in multiple ways through contact with other people.

In addition to appreciating this concept of *chevruta*, I held onto the conviction I learned from feminism that community was essential to the transformation of society. Even as a teenager, I believed that the purpose of religious life was to bring about *tikkun*, social justice, or the restoration of our society, and so now as an emerging adult, I expected Judaism to actively embrace these ideals. To achieve these goals of social justice, I had both studied and experienced the phenomenon that individuals simply couldn't act alone and hope for things to change. Similarly, in Judaism, I sensed that the emotional, spiritual, and moral force of the tradition was not found primarily in moments of isolation, but in moments of shared experience. For much of my time in college, I was not particularly drawn to the Jewish community, mostly for rather arbitrary and superficial reasons. And even though I still held those same petty judgments, I made a commitment to connect with the local community because I no longer saw it as an option, but an obligation.

To my great delight and surprise, I found that the Jewish community in college was actually much more diverse and dynamic than I had assumed it would be from the outside. It was a motley crew of seekers, *ba'aley teshuvah* ("masters of repentance," or those "returning" to Judaism with an orthodox fervor), social justice activists, progressive and conservative Zionists, and everyone in between. At a typical meal at the Kosher Co-op, Orthodox Zionists and radical Jewish feminists engaged in passionate and exacting debate, an encounter seen rarely on campus. In fact, I understand in retrospect that they probably needed each other—in typical Talmudic fashion, each side needed the other to reinforce its point of view through vigorous disagreement.

It was through the Kosher Co-op crowd that I also began to experience Shabbat, not as an abstract concept or a day, but as a lived and communal experience. Through going to Friday night services week after week, the melodies and rhythms became familiar such that I could soon pick up a random siddur (prayer book) and know how to navigate it. I learned, or rather, re-learned in a new context, the prayers and songs for the Shabbat table, realizing that the sacred space of Shabbat may have begun in the service, but actually encompassed the meal and the interactions beyond. After dinner and singing, I sometimes joined people at the "Jewish students' house" where I would continue conversations late into the evening.

Over time, almost imperceptibly, the consciousness of Shabbat became an integral part of my personal life as I developed my own Shabbat rhythm. Even though I did not spend time with the small group of truly observant students at the Kosher Co-Op, I began to take on some traditional practices as my own. I occasionally avoided certain events or commitments on Friday nights, I sometimes took a break from schoolwork on Saturday (not a sacrifice at all), and fairly often I spent some time with a *chumash* (bound copy of the Torah), reading part of the weekly portion in Hebrew and then checking myself against the English translation. Within a short time, an awkward moment made me realize how much I wanted to live within Jewish sacred time, and how I much I relied on others to do it. One Saturday, my housemates decided it was time to collect our garbage and bring it to the city dump with a car that conveniently appeared. I got hooked into going, when, on our way there, I spotted a couple of the orthodox leaders of Kosher Co-op walking on the sidewalk. "Hide me," I pleaded pathetically as I bent down in the back seat, "It's Shabbat and I don't want them to see me!" My close friend Greg, who knew me as well as anybody, said, "You don't really believe that." But the thing is, I did, or at least I was beginning to.

Renewed Passion

When an alternative to the Hillel community began to form, I participated in that as well. The group, which met for Friday night gatherings off-campus in people's homes, was influenced by the *havurah* movement, which some of the leaders had experienced first hand through their families. In what felt like an expansion of traditional prayer, everyone sat in a circle on the floor, and the leader with a guitar led us in continuous singing that filled the space of the room. Afterwards, we shared a potluck Shabbat dinner that always featured a homemade challah.

I was very much a novice in this group, and I drew my inspiration from some forceful personalities who had already gone far down the path of weaving together a robust, song-filled Judaism with a passion for social justice. There was no formal structure, but there were certainly a number of informal leaders. One was a woman who had written an honors thesis combining feminist theory with an analysis of Israeli mothers raising children who would eventually serve in the Israeli army. She eventually became the director of a human rights organization in Israel. Another, my friend Rachel, grew up in a *havurah* that hosted weekly "services" that are almost completely non-hierarchical and to this day comprise the full participation of everyone singing. Her home was the first I ever visited where the bookshelves were lined with row after row of Jewish books and music. Another friend was leader of our campus Progressive Zionist Caucus and now has a senior position in a major liberal think tank, traveling the country to share her views on the politics of the Middle East.

The open and experimental vibe of these gatherings elicited a passionate and creative relationship to Judaism from within me, drawing now on the best of what I had learned during my time in college. For the first time since I was a teenager, I found myself in a community experiencing once again a new *"hitlahavut,"* or experience of "soul on fire." And while much of my passion stemmed from the feeling of respect of the people around me and how much they had to teach me, I also found myself drawn to the newly accessible and relatable views of God we were generating. Whereas my earlier encounters with spirituality and feminism had focused on the deconstruction of God and religious language, these gatherings brought to life the renewing and transforming impulse behind much of what I had studied.

Feminist Theology—Deconstruction and Revival

During that final semester of college, Judith Plaskow published her groundbreaking book of Jewish feminist thought, *Standing Again at Sinai*. Throughout the book, she asserts the power of community and shared experience to discard the old, moribund conceptions of God while re-envisioning the new.

> As I see it, the goal of a Jewish feminist approach to God-language is to incorporate women's Godwrestling into the fullness of Torah by finding images that can communicate and evoke the experience of the presence of God in a diverse, egalitarian, and empowered community of Israel. The experience of God in community is both the measure of the adequacy of traditional language and the norm in terms of which new images must be fashioned and evaluated. It is in light of this norm that images of God as male and as dominating Other have been judged limited and oppressive. And it is in faithfulness to this norm that a range of new metaphors for God have been elaborated, tried on, and discarded or preserved. A consideration of Jewish images of God from a feminist perspective takes us from criticism of established God-language to efforts to open up the metaphors we use, to attempts to reorient the Jewish conception of deity.[9]

9. Plaskow, *Standing Again at Sinai*, 122.

Plaskow's thoughts provide not merely an analysis of the inadequacy of the "old" concepts of God and the possibility of the new. Rather, she proposes something much more radical: the reinvention and regeneration of norms through "experience" and "community." Why is this radical, even subversive? Judaism has always relied on norms as defined by structures of authority, whether that authority was invested in those understood to safeguard the word of God (prophets), the holy rituals of God (priests), or the received interpretation of Torah (rabbis). As Jewish communities evolved, ever-more sophisticated means evolved to keep those norms in place. Many of these norms were healthy and necessary, such as rules governing charity, protections for workers and those who were most vulnerable, even the insistence on a consistency in ritual practice. But at the same time, the structures that kept these norms most often excluded the moral agency and experiences of women, and were even further isolated from the bulk of the community. To abandon the notion of norms altogether may be liberating, but that is not what Plaskow proposes. To do that would be to essentially allow the old, sexist, and otherwise oppressive norms to stay in place, even while pursuing an alternative. Instead, Plaskow proposes a new mechanism for communal, ritual, spiritual, and ethical norms, and one that is bound to change them. Instead of relying on fixed methods of interpretation, or the judgments of a communal or rabbinic elite, Plaskow puts future norms in the hands of the "experience" of the "community." That "community" is not an exclusive one, but rather comprises the voices of those who have traditionally been marginalized. When those voices that have been shut out are given the freedom to bring their experiences and collective wisdom from margin to center, everything is bound to change: who gets counted in a *minyan* of course, but also moral priorities, ritual expression, and, perhaps most fundamentally, who God is.

We were consciously trying to put into practice Plaskow's goal of a completely revitalized Jewishness, beginning with the dethroning of the "domineering" God. Plaskow's words captured what we were looking for, "images that can communicate and evoke the experience of the presence of God in a diverse, egalitarian, and empowered community . . . ." We embraced a creative spirit, but there was an unspoken understanding that we wanted to work from within the tradition and not only in opposition to it. We drew upon what we had learned from a diverse array of sources so as to fashion a collective spiritual experience that closely articulated our own moral aspirations. The services we had were immediate and emotional. For me, their power was driven by our imminent graduation and the question of what kind of community, inner life, and values I wanted to take on to nurture my emerging self. Leaving the vibrant and ever-creative bubble of college, I knew I would never go back to the pallid and vapid suburb in which I grew up. Instead, I would seek out revitalized Judaism that would be a touchstone, moral anchor, and spiritual inspiration. But first I had to know it and create it for myself.

In our prayers we often substituted the inherently hierarchical formula of traditional Jewish prayer with Hebrew modeled on a more reciprocal relationship between God and humanity. Traditionally, a Jewish blessing, whether over food, a ritual act or at the beginning or end of a longer prayer invokes God's "name and dominion," or as the rabbis of the Talmud say it in Hebrew, *"shem v'malkhut."* Already, there is a sense in which God cannot be known except by the ways in which God "rules" over all creation, and we see how that plays out in the specific words of each traditional blessing. The "name" of God is, of course, *"Adonai,"* spelled with the Hebrew letters *"yod, hey, vav, hey"* (יהוה) and rendered in transliteration as YHWH. The name itself has an almost mystical and elusive quality, as the actual pronunciation of the name was expressed only by the high priest, who recited it on Yom Kippur in the temple in Jerusalem. Since the destruction of the temple in 70 CE, the pronunciation was discontinued, and the name of God came to be known ironically as the *"shem ha-meforash,"* or the "pronounced name," which, of course, was never uttered. Absent the knowledge of the actual name of God, the Hebrew of YHWH became known by its popular translation of *Adonai*, which means "my supreme master" and is commonly translated as "Lord." Hebrew is a gendered language, so inasmuch as the unknown and untranslatable name of God becomes "Lord," all language of prayer is rendered as masculine, even though there are female images of God throughout the Bible, such as those of lover, wife, and birthing mother.

To diversify our relationship to God in prayer, we followed the example of the scholar and liturgist Marcia Falk. In much of her work, Marcia Falk reverse engineers the traditional prayers by drawing on metaphors of God that are rooted in the Bible and rabbinic literature. Following much of Jewish feminist thought, Falk's changes accomplish two broad goals: facilitating a more diverse and authentic experience of prayer and drawing on the language of divine-human partnership to facilitate the "diverse, egalitarian, and empowered" communities Judith Plaskow and others envision. And so, the traditional motif of "King of the Universe" becomes the "Wellspring of all Creation" or the "Source of all life." Thinking of God in this way means that we, the community of Jews, must also address the divine in a new way. No longer is the male-inflected, hierarchical, one-way *"Barukh ata, Adonai,* Blessed are You, Lord," even possible. To approach a relationship with the "Wellspring of all Creation," Falk proposes saying, "We come to bless You." The "we" of this blessing, *"n'varekh"* instead of *"Barukh,"* implies that the community joins together in the invocation of God, opening ourselves as we invite the divine presence into our midst. As an additional benefit, the language re-vivifies God from an image or an idea into a living force. The traditional *"Barukh"* is a passive form—past tense, set down, dead. But *"n'varekh"* is a future form, implying process, becoming, and an evolving sense of closeness to God through our collective experience and growth in understanding.

The reinvented language of prayer facilitated a powerful new relationship to each other, to Jewish tradition, and our understanding of what Jewish tradition demanded of us. A sampling of how renewed words of prayer can recast the totality of what Judaism and God mean finds expression in a prayer by Marcia Falk quoted in Plaskow's book:

> Let us acknowledge the source of life
> for the earth and for nourishment.
> May we conserve the earth
> that it may sustain us
> and let us seek sustenance
> for all who inhabit the world.
> Let us distinguish
> parts within the whole
> and bless their differences.
> Like Sabbath and the six days of creation
> may our lives be made whole
> through relation.[10]

For Plaskow, the language and outward metaphors of God were just the beginning. More significantly, the relationship to human beings these words implied were much more significant. While the domineering male God was "Other" and remote, an approach based on experiences of women (though not exclusively) in community would yield a God who speaks to our yearning for connection and relationships. One example could be an expansion of the Kabbalistic concept of the *Shekhinah*, the indwelling presence of God, whose nature is to draw close to humanity.

Some of us had learned about the concept through courses in Jewish mysticism with Professor Ginsburg. The *Shekhinah* is originally a rabbinic concept from the first few centuries CE, referring to the "presence" of God who remained attached to the Jewish people in exile. For a community who lost their sacred center, the temple in Jerusalem, the *Shekhinah* provided comfort in the expectation that God was not restricted to a single place,

10. Ibid., 1423.

but dwelled everywhere. About 1,000 years later, Kabbalah broadened the concept into an aspect of God that human beings could encounter directly.

For the medieval teachers of Kabbalah, the *Shekhinah* is the aspect of God that transmits all divine blessing to human beings, and so is associated with the qualities of God that are loving and generous. At the highest realm of being, God is *"Ayin,"* or "nothing," and this realm is extremely difficult to access for most people. Below this highest realm are eight other mediating aspects of God, each of which has different qualities as they exist in tension with each other. But the potency, or *sefirah* of *Shekhinah*, is the aspect of God most accessible to human beings, and the divine quality with which human beings commune in prayer. Accordingly, the *Shekhinah* is the component of God most robustly imbued with symbolism and imagery. For the rabbis of the Kabbalah, *Shekhinah* is uniquely feminine, expansive in feeling and erotic.

> While the image of the *Shekhinah* was an important constituent of Kabbalism that gained widespread popularity, it was never incorporated into the liturgy as an accepted counter-weight to the masculinity of God. Feminists have tried to use it precisely in this way. . . . (Feminists address) God as Shekhinah in more fluid ways, naming variously the "feminine presence/ She-Who-Dwells-Within."
>
> Shechinah
> calling us
> from exile
> inside us exiled
> calling us
>   home
> home.[11]

For those of us seeking new outlets for Jewish expression, the connotations of the Shekhinah as non-hierarchical, generous, and feminine, was a way for all of us to collectively entertain a different kind of relationship to God, or at least to the way we thought about God. If the father God was dead, then the Shekhinah could at least live in our imaginations, individually and collectively. At our gatherings, even though I am sure we were all skeptical and questioning, the idea of the Shekhinah gave us a feeling that we were reclaiming a silent voice from within the sources of Jewish tradition. From the old books, we uncovered something that perhaps could be part of a living and renewed Jewish spirituality. For me, it touched on the inner exile of the soul, the part of myself that yearned to be nurtured but

11. Ibid., 139.

was neglected, but was finding new attention from the adult I was becoming. In listening to and following the path of my soul, whatever it or who it was connected to, I felt myself being "called home."

Ultimately, though, it was the ways in which my experiences had yet to be named that would yield new views about God, my ongoing spiritual belonging, and my moral commitments. Here is how Plaskow speaks of "The Emerging God of Feminist Spirituality":

> As Jewish feminists seek to name God out of our own experiences, transforming traditional conceptions of God in a deep and far-reaching way, our efforts become part of a wider movement to rename and reconceptualize God that is taking place among women of different faiths all over the country.

Speaking of one example of this process in action, Plaskow continues,

> They began to call out words that meant God to them, putting their designations on a large newsprint board. One of the fascinating aspects of the resulting list was its large number of "ing" words—changing, creating, enabling, nurturing, pushing, calling into question, suffering, touching, breaking through. The God of their experience was not an immutable being "out there," but a process of which they were part. Feeling themselves newly empowered through participation in feminist community, they knew God as the dynamic source and context of that empowerment—a power to be named through rhythm and movement as much as through words.[12]

This is a God not of the past, of remoteness and abandonment, but of the present and future, evolving and waiting to be discovered. It was a God who could actually exist—not just as a concept, but in time and in my experience. And so I came to treasure the many Jewish "firsts" this rogue group provided me—not only because these experiences were fun or even inspiring, but because they pointed a way to a new spiritual engagement, simultaneously both within and outside myself, with people and what potentially lay beyond human community. It was for one of these gatherings that I made my first *challah*. The services gave me my first opportunity to lead something as part of communal worship, even if it was just a short reading. It was through this group that I networked for my first real job interview at a non-profit promoting peace between Israelis and Palestinians. And perhaps most importantly, when this group decided to produce its own alternative

12. Ibid., 1434.

newspaper, I contributed my first-ever public writing, discovering a new manifestation of my inner voice.

An Emerging Voice

At the end of four years being intimidated by the brilliant and forceful people around me, with just a few weeks of college left, I decided to publish an essay as a reflection on the power, promise, and inevitable failure of Jewish community. I described a recent Jewish communal service job fair, at the end of which I hoped to find my first step into the real world. Everyone was lovely and welcoming, but it yielded no job for me. I wove that into a line of poetry by Adrienne Rich, the great feminist poet, in which she distinguishes between that which is "falsely given" and "truly given." I juxtaposed my unsuccessful venture at the Jewish communal job fair with my varied experiences in Jewish life on campus. I observed how there were times when the established community offered promises it couldn't deliver, and others when a newly created community offered real and surprising opportunities for self-discovery amid spiritual companionship.

As I was approaching my connection to Judaism with fresh eyes, I felt a new curiosity to connect with my father. As we had several years before, we agreed on a time and place to spend dinner together in New York. But upon seeing him again, there really wasn't much to feel or experience. I had spent my college years happily living without my father, pretending as if his existence didn't matter. Classes, friends, love filled my life, and so I had no need to reach out to him. There was no way, emotionally or materially, in which he played a role in my life, so it was easy and convenient for me not to give him a second thought. Except, there was always the question expressed by my friends: how could my father's absence not be painful? During my early college years, when I had kept a distance from Judaism and Jewish community, I felt no curiosity or need to see my father. But as I discovered a newfound sense of self through exploring Judaism in all its forms, I wondered if I should look again at this relationship that constituted a central part of my life, albeit one that was shattered and seemingly inert.

I remember little of substance from our meeting, as I asked no question, posed no challenge, and demanded no revelation. There was nothing I really wanted from him, or that I was conscious of needing from him, and so there was no great drama, or insight, or disappointment from that dinner. Perhaps I was doing what Rabbi Kalonymus Kalman Shapira, Scholem, and Buber say we all do—reaching into the nothingness across an existential gulf of loneliness for some reassurance that my father was still there. That does make some sense.

Except, in the wake of nothingness created by my father, I had begun to build relationships to new sources of wholeness, inspiration, and purpose. I had begun to understand more about what Hasidic tradition described as *Devekut*, a complete and total attachment of the soul to God. I was drawn to thinking about *devekut*, not only as an abstract idea I had encountered in a book, but as something real, because I now knew what that love felt like on a human level. And in the face of real love, relationships, and my maturing passions, there was little my father could provide.

And yet, even though my father was basically a nonentity in my life, I don't know if I was yet ready to let him go completely. Thinking about becoming a rabbi, I was interested in bringing together the best from within myself and from whatever I would discover around me. Perhaps I felt that my emerging self would be incomplete without at least trying to engage with my father, if only to rule out the possibility that he had something to give.

Like both the biblical and rabbinic Elishas, I saw myself as ready to dedicate myself to a life of relationship and service, and I wanted to know more about what was on the other side of the gulf of ultimate loneliness. Just as their lives were driven by the irony of a God who was both a dominating presence and a mysterious absence, so my spiritual life was fueled by the contradiction between my father's absence as well as the hope of a renascent Jewish connection.

As I graduated college and looked out toward my future, I knew that the life I envisioned was one that, while providing its own version of community, was out of step with the times and the culture. At a time in life when most Western adults feel that God and religion are dead to them, I was passionately curious to know more about the Jewish God and Jewish practice, perhaps with the goal of dedicating my life to their study and teaching. At the moment that people find their idiosyncratic paths among varied and competing cultural mores, I was choosing a specific set of cultural and behavioral norms. As the path of Jewish life, in any form, requires that one live among symbols, rituals, and practices that do not conform to the rhythms and references of modern secular society, I knew that I was choosing a life of separateness. This did not deter me. The inner reality of isolation and abandonment was familiar to me from my experience with my father, and as a counterpoint, the prospect of living within the realm of Jewish spirituality and community offered a promising alternative. Here, the gulf between me and the traditional notions of God was animating and inspiring, an awareness that revealed my yearnings for connection, yearnings that could be met week after week, day after day, in moments of prayer, study, and contemplation. I knew as I left college that I would face two ongo-ing existential questions. How would I know when it would finally be time to fully cut off from my father? And how would I find a healing connection, whether human or divine or both, in the increasingly marginal Judaism I was growing to love?

Part 3

Tikkun/Integration

Elisha, Prophet of Justice and Healing

2 Kings 4

(1)A woman, the wife of one of the disciples of the prophets, cried out to Elisha, "Your servant, my husband has died. You know how your servant was one who feared God. But now the creditor is coming to take away my two sons as bonded servants!" (2)Elisha said to her, "What shall I do for you?" Tell me, what do you have in your house?" She said, "Your servant has nothing at all in the house, except for only one jug of oil." (3)He said, "Go, borrow vessels from outside from all of your neighbors—empty vessels, and do not scrimp. (4)Then go in and shut the door behind you and behind your sons, and then you shall pour oil into all of those vessels, removing each when it is full."

(5) She left him and closed the door behind her and behind her sons. They continued to bring vessels to her and she continued to pour oil. (6)As the vessels were full she said to her son, "Bring me another vessel," and he said, "There are no more vessels." And the oil ceased. (7)She came and told the man of God and he said, "Go, sell the oil and pay your creditor, and you and your sons shall live on the rest."

(8)One day Elisha visited Shunem, and there lived a wealthy woman, who urged him to eat bread with her; whenever he would pass by, he would have a meal with her. (9)She said to her husband, "Surely, I know that this is a holy man of God who visits us regularly. (10)Let us make a small loft for him, and we will place in there for him a bed, table, a chair, and a lamp so that he may stay there whenever he comes to us.

(11)One day he came there, went into the loft and slept there. (12)He said to Gehazi, his servant, "Call the Shunammite woman." And he called her, and she stood before him. (13)He said to him, "Tell her, you have gone through this trouble for you. What shall we do for you? Is there a matter for which you wish to speak to the king, or to the army commander?" She said, "I dwell among my own people." (14)"What can be done for her?" he asked. "The fact is," said Gehazi, "she has no son, and her husband is old." (15)"Call her" he said. He called her, and she stood in the entrance. (16)And Elisha said to her, "At this moment next year, you shall embrace a son." And she said, "Please, my Lord, man of God, do not deceive your maidservant."

(17)She became pregnant and bore a son at the same season the following year, just as Elisha had told her. (18)The boy grew up. One day, he went out with his father to the reapers. (19)He cried to his father, "My head, my head!" He said to a servant,

"Carry him to his mother." (20)He carried him and brought him to his mother, sat on his mother's knees until noon, and then died. (21)She brought him up and lay him down on the bed of the man of God, closed the door behind him, and went out. (22) She called to her husband and said, "Please send me one of the servants and one of the she-asses, and I shall hurry to the man of God and then I shall return." (23)But he said, "Why do you go to him today? It is neither the New Moon nor the Sabbath." And she answered, "All will be well."

(24)She had the ass saddled and said to her servant, "Drive on, and do not slow down unless I tell you." (25)She journeyed and came to the man of God on Mount Carmel. When the man of God saw her from afar, he said to Gehazi his servant, "Here is the Shunammite woman. (26)Go, hurry toward her and ask her, 'Is all well with you? Is all well with your husband? Is all well with the boy?'" And she replied, "All is well."

(27)But when she came to the man of God on the mountain, she held his feet. Gehazi approached her to push her away, but the man of God said, "Let her be, for she is bitter of heart; God has hidden this from me and did not tell me." (28)Then she said, "Did I ask my Lord for a son? Did I not say, "Do not mislead me?"

(29)He said to Gehazi, "Gird your loins, take my staff in your hand and go. If you meet someone, do not greet him, and if he greets you, do not answer him. And place my staff on the face of the boy." (30)But the mother of the boy said to him, "As God lives and as you live, I will not leave you." So he arose and followed her.

(31)Gehazi had gone on before them, placing his staff on the face of the boy, but there was no sound or response. He turned back to meet him and told him, "The boy has not awakened." (32)Elisha entered the house, and there was the boy, dead, lying on his bed. (33)He entered and shut the door behind the two of them and prayed to God. (34)He rose over and lay down on the boy, placed his mouth on the boy's and his eyes on the boy's eyes, and his hands on the boy's hands, and bent over him. And the boy's flesh became warm. (35)He got up and walked about the room, one way and then the other, and then rose over the boy and bent over him. The boy then sneezed seven times, and then the boy opened his eyes. (36)He called to Gehazi and said, "Call the Shunammite woman," and he called her and she came to him. He said, "Pick up your son." (37)And she came and fell at his feet, bowing to the ground, and then she picked up her son and left.

Chapter 7

Finding Self and Community

Becoming a Grownup

On a warm Friday evening in September 1991, I breathed in sweet autumnal air during my walk to synagogue. In one sense I had nothing—it was over a year since I had graduated from college and I had no job, no admission to graduate school, and only a few concrete leads. But I was hopeful and satisfied. I was living in Baltimore with my love, Judy, after four years of living apart and carrying on our relationship long distance. I was working hard each day to generate job leads and follow up on them. And although Judy and I had been living in Baltimore for only six weeks, we were enjoying a newfound sense of community, both through her friends in graduate school and the tiny synagogue we discovered on one of the tree-lined streets in our neighborhood. On this particular walk to *shul*, I had in mind that it was the Hebrew month of Elul, the month before Rosh Hashanah, a time of taking stock. And so, I took note of a strange, new, and contradictory awareness: the unsettling sense of my "adult" life being unformed while at the same time feeling buoyed by the unknown possibilities of my new independence.

In the language of Kabbalah, I was feeling, and perhaps enacting, a bit of *tikkun*. In Kabbalah, *tikkun* is the final stage in the epic process of creation. Given how widely American Jews have been using the term for the past forty years, *tikkun* is probably the aspect of the threefold view of kabbalistic creation we're most familiar with. Although nothing is simple in Kabbalah, the concept of *tikkun* is fairly straightforward. After the shattering of the vessels of divine light, the shards produced by that cataclysmic event came to constitute the stuff of creation. Everything in creation, from our own bodies to the world of nature and beyond, is comprised of material "husks" that harbor an inner divine essence. In this sense, creation is fragmented, and its true nature is hidden. Our role as human beings is to restore life back to the cosmos by weaving a new wholeness from the created world. Through performing *mitzvot*, by engaging in prayer and moments of spiritual contemplation, and by performing acts of kindness, we release the divine sparks embedded in creation and reunite them with their source. Over time, our collective efforts will result in a universal *tikkun*. In the interim, each of us strives to effect some kind of restoration within the microcosm of our experience, as we each bring some kind of healing to ourselves and the world around us, each of us in our own way.

On that walk, I was thinking of *tikkun* as I considered the ways I was trying to put my life on track as a young adult. Mostly, I was carrying the hopeful sense that my ability to realize my aspirations would win out over some recent disappointments. During that first year after college, nothing worked out the way I had envisioned. Plans for jobs, travel, and ongoing study all failed to materialize or fell through. But then things changed. Judy got into grad school. A new window for travel opened up. Soon we were taking trips from New York to Baltimore to scout out apartments and potential jobs. And though I landed in Baltimore with only a gig to teach Sunday school, I trusted that more would come. By the time of that walk, I had applied to and been rejected from a number of jobs. But in getting to know myself through the process, in part by seeing how others responded to me, I learned to trust that my ongoing effort would eventually yield something worthwhile.

In building my life with Judy in this new city, I sought to build a web of relationships. I found the synagogue I walked to on our first visit to Baltimore. It was a charming brownstone two blocks from our home. I wanted it to be a place where we belonged, where we would have community, where I could find a rabbi, and where I could have moments of prayer and solitude. It's not that I was lonely—living with Judy was a dream and a delight. But I was conscious of wanting something more, without ever really being able to account for what that "more" actually was. At the end of the first season of Jewish holidays, I was beginning to get an idea.

The year before, I had a galvanizing experience celebrating *Simchat Torah* at the Jewish Theological Seminary in New York. *Simchat Torah*, which celebrates the completion of the annual cycle of reading the Torah, is the very last day of the 3+ week string of Jewish holidays beginning with Rosh

Hashanah. At its best, a celebration of *Simchat Torah* entails scores of people singing and dancing with numerous Torah scrolls for hours on end. At the Jewish Theological Seminary in 1990, this was especially true, as the 100+ young people gathered there produced a celebratory intensity, a kind of *hit-lahavut* that I had never experienced in a Jewish setting. I had never experienced people my age doing all the things that made the celebration possible: chanting expertly from the Torah scrolls, generating song after song without exhausting the repertoire, leading a complex service that had its own logic. In all, I took in how everyone around me was able to give voice to an inner joy and sense of belonging through this celebration, and I wanted to be able to do the same. The evening and following morning inspired me to dedicate myself to acquiring the skills and familiarity with the tradition that clearly gave what seemed like hundreds of my peers so much of a sense of place in the world. I knew that it would mean acquiring more Hebrew, familiarizing myself with the intricacies of the prayer book and services, and learning all the songs that seemed to fuel this and other gatherings. While daunting in retrospect, the mountain I had to climb seemed perfectly accessible to me at the time, no doubt because I was fueled by a hunger for the sense of home that I believed Judaism and Jewish community could provide.

By the time *Simchat Torah* came around that first year in Baltimore, I was immersed in the cyclical slog of trying to launch an adult life. I often rode a wave of confidence as I would get called for interviews and disappointment when I wasn't offered the particular job. I was glad for the break of the holidays and of *Simchat Torah*, if only to get a respite from this exhausting pattern of hope and failure. While I knew I wouldn't be able to replicate what I'd experienced the year before, I found a small synagogue in the city with a modest but dedicated crowd for the morning service. When it was over, I walked outside a little after noon, and felt alone for the first time since I had moved to Baltimore two months before. Without the rituals, the people, and the sense of community that had accompanied me over the previous three weeks, I let it sink in that I was not yet where I wanted to be, a bit adrift. But along with this thought was a sense that these experiences of ritual in community could buffer me against the feeling of being utterly alone. It was one of a handful of newly adult moments in which I felt the disappointment of unfulfilled expectations alongside moments of real joy. The sense of both/and was healing. I had always believed that achieving my aspirations, whether by succeeding in school, finding love and now meaningful work, would launch me over the vault of the abandonment and loss I experienced in my family. Now, seeing that my future was a work in progress, I began to experience Jewish life as its own existential grounding, especially as my life was working itself out more slowly than I had envisioned.

And while my curiosity about God continued to grow deeper and wider in scope, it was really the experience of developing relationships in community that provided me with the more immediate avenue for *tikkun*.

Elisha—Prophet of *Tikkun*

In the context of the Hebrew Bible, Elisha emerges as the prophet of *tikkun*. Unlike all other prophets who prescribe the world's remedies by channeling the words of God, Elisha singularly acts in the space of God's silence to relieve the world of pain and suffering. Instead of confirming his authority by speaking the divine word, Elisha delivers the divine life-source through his interactions with other people. Through Elisha's story, we see how relationships among human beings, and not momentary revelations of God, are the primary vehicles of *tikkun*.

Perhaps the most well-known story of Elisha's person-to-person devotion is his encounter with the woman of Shunem, from 2 Kings 4. Initially, Elisha and his servant Gehazi were shown generous hospitality by this woman and her husband, who set aside a special room for the "man of God."

> (8) One day Elisha visited Shunem, and there lived a wealthy woman, who urged him to eat bread with her; whenever he would pass by, he would have a meal with her. (9) She said to her husband, "Surely, I know that this is a holy man of God who visits us regularly. (10) Let us make a small loft for him, and we will place in there for him a bed, table, a chair and a lamp so that he may stay there whenever he comes to us."

This story, with its parallel in the lives of Abraham and Sarah, demonstrates how hospitality to a stranger is a precursor to the fulfillment of a divine promise. Of course, only a few characters in the Bible have this privileged opportunity to be visited by a person, or an angel, who can deliver. But the deeper point is that such an interaction is really a microcosm of the relationship between human beings and God in general. All is predicated upon the sincere desire for relationship, and perhaps more importantly, the everyday gestures that nurture it. In this story, it is not a gesture towards God that prompts Elisha's unusual promise to the Shunammite woman. Rather, it is her display of generosity and kindness, which Elisha did not ask for. True, the Shunammite woman realized that Elisha was a "man of God," but Elisha did not impress this upon her explicitly. She came to this realization, and the acts of hospitality that followed, from her own ability to recognize the unique humanity of her guest.

Presumably as a consequence of his host's generosity, Elisha offers the Shunammite woman the gift of his intervention. When she declines, her humility and decency prompt Elisha to fulfill her unspoken yearning to bear a child.

> (11) One day he came there, went into the loft and slept there. (12) He said to Gehazi, his servant, "Call the Shunnamite woman." And he called her, and she stood before him. (13) He said to him, "Tell her, you have gone through this trouble for us What shall we do for you? Is there a matter for which you wish to speak to the king, or to the army commander?" She said, "I dwell among my own people." (14) What then can be done for her? he asked. "The fact is," said Gehazi, "she has no son, and her husband is old." (15) "Call her," he said. He called her, and she stood in the doorway. (16) And he said to her, "At this moment next year, you shall embrace a son." And she said, "Please, my Lord, man of God, do not deceive your maidservant."

The interaction between Elisha and the Shunammite woman seems to be a test of her fidelity to Elisha as a human being, and not as someone who can secure some kind of advantage in addition to the wealth she already possesses. It is hard to imagine Elisha sincerely offering the Shunammite woman access to power and privilege, since it is precisely those things that Elisha scorns. When she refuses, Elisha understands that her generosity and kindness are sincere, and so he proclaims that she will bear a child. The skepticism of the Shunammite woman only confirms her dedication to Elisha, that she was hosting him out of a sense of honor and respect, not to fulfill any existential needs.

But a miracle wrought by God proves to be a fragile thing as the boy suddenly dies. Perhaps the boy's sudden death is its own implicit warning not to depend upon divine miracles from a God who is unseen and removed from human affairs. It certainly seems that the Shunammite woman understands that even if there is to be some kind of supernatural intervention to save her son, doing so ultimately rests on her initiative.

> (17) She became pregnant and bore a son at the same season the following year, just as Elisha had told her. (18)The boy grew up. One day, he went out with his father to the reapers. (19) He cried to his father, "My head, my head!" He said to a servant, "Carry him to his mother." (20) He carried him and brought him to his mother, sat on his mother's knees until noon, and then died. (21) She brought him up and lay him down on the bed of the man of God, closed the door behind him, and went out.

Through the mother's initiative, Elisha is called to the scene and re-
vives the boy. And although he prays to God, the scene seems much more
preoccupied with the role of human rather than divine intervention.

> (31) Gehazi had gone on before them, placing his staff on the
> face of the boy, but there was no sound or response. He turned
> back to meet him and told him, "The boy has not awakened."
> (32) Elisha entered the house, and there was the boy, dead, lying
> on his bed. (33) He entered and shut the door behind the two
> of them and prayed to God. (34) He rose over and lay down on
> the boy, placed his mouth on the boy's and his eyes on the boy's
> eyes, and his hands on the boy's hands, and bent over him. And
> the boy's flesh became warm. (35) He got up and walked about
> the room, one way and then the other, and then rose over the
> boy and bent over him. The boy then sneezed seven times, and
> then the boy opened his eyes. (36) He called to Gehazi and said,
> "Call the Shunammite woman," and he called her and she came
> to him. He said, "Pick up your son." (37) And she came and fell
> at his feet, bowing to the ground, and then she picked up her
> son and left.

The scene appears to be one in which Elisha realizes that an act of
personal devotion, rather than divine intercession, is the only means to revive the boy. Sending Gehazi with his magic staff fails. Prayer fails. And so,
Elisha learns that no other intervention except direct contact will bring the
boy back to life. As if to emphasize the intimacy between them, Elisha shuts
the door to isolate himself with the boy. True, Elisha facilitates a miracle in
drawing down the divine power to save the boy. But rather than standing
apart, Elisha cloaks that same power in the immediacy of his physical connection. Elisha realizes that the divine power must flow through him. All
depends upon Elisha's ability to establish a deep and urgent contact with
this boy.

The Revolution of Elisha's Healing Power

Elisha's ability to bring healing through a personal connection, rather than
by appealing to God as a third party, constitutes a revolution in understanding. In the depictions of Sinai and the wanderings in the desert, the
ultra-domineering nature of God is so overwhelming that both God and
humanity depend upon a gulf to sustain their relationship to each other.
If God reveals too much of God's being within creation, everything will be
obliterated. In place of direct contact, Exodus proposes a number measures

to keep the people safe while also making possible at least some connection to God. Moses serves as an intermediary, the *mishkan* (tabernacle) becomes a safe point of meeting between God and humanity, and the divine presence is safely contained as a cloud by day and a pillar of fire by night during the forty years of wandering. This gulf between God and humanity stands as an imperfect compromise, as God can never fully and directly communicate with human beings so that they might perform the divine will, and the people will never be absolutely sure that God is present to protect and defend them when they are vulnerable. In the stories of Exodus, both God and humanity accept their distance as necessary, despite the cost of their mutual alienation from each other.

But Elisha's stories propose an alternative solution to the seemingly unbridgeable gulf between human beings and God. Elisha demonstrates that we do not necessarily require greater intimacy with the source of creation, but rather greater empathy among each other. Compassion, kindness, and dedication to each other's welfare renews the bond between God and humanity and permits the divine power of healing to become manifest in the world. While God's overwhelming power was necessary to bring about the national revolution of Exodus, the theological revolution of Elisha shows how God's ability to heal everyday pain—poverty, oppression, sickness—depends on human intention and moral agency.

Elisha's stories provide us then with a fresh way to actually affirm God's remoteness from the day-to-day lives of human beings. These stories advance the novel argument that, in the absence of the divine presence, people themselves must become channels for the healing forces that originate in God but come to exist as part of the created world. Hence the child of the Shunamite woman is brought back to life not simply to make the point that God can do anything, but rather, that the renewal of life is found within nature itself, with human beings as the conduit by means of relationships bound by trust and intimacy. In this way, God's remoteness from our world and our experiences is not a tragic consequence of our inability to understand God or act in a manner deserving of God's proximity. Rather, God's absence is necessary for our world, and our humanity, to function. As the sun's distance from the earth insures that plants and animals will be able to absorb and benefit from its energy, so the feeling of God's remoteness fosters a sense of mutual dependence among human beings to insure that we will attend to each other's material and spiritual vulnerability. God's silence is the existential condition that allows for *tikkun*.

Loneliness as Source of *Tikkun*

The necessity of God's absence serves as the foundation of Rabbi Isaac Luria's classic understanding of *tikkun*. In the words of the great scholar Gershom Scholem, *tikkun* is both the end and the beginning of God's own creation and self-evolution. Therefore, if God's distance from creation is part of the plan, then it is also a part of how we as human beings find relief, restoration, or *tikkun*, from this existential loneliness.

In the Lurianic story of creation, all that originally existed was God's being as light and nothing else. At the moment of creation, according to the Lurianic book *Etz Chaim*, "When it arose in the mind of the Exalted Creator to fashion a universe," God contracted within God's self, as it were, creating space for all creation to come into being. According to Luria, the original divine intention was to have closeness between God and creation, "so as to lavish goodness on creatures so that they would know God's grandeur." But God also understood, from the very beginning, that the divine light could only be contained by means of distance, by some kind of separation between Godself, the pure light, and the manifestation of divine energy that would constitute the created universe.

And so, God attempted to exist both close to the created universe and separate from it at the same time, taking the undifferentiated divine energy and channeling it into vessels. Nevertheless, the energy of the Creator was too powerful to contain in these vessels, and so they shattered under the strain. After this initial, unforeseen flaw in God's creation, the broken vessels would assume a new function, continuing to hold at least some of the divine light, but certainly not all of God's being. Creation could exist, but on the condition of a compromise. The universe would contain a fraction of Godself, separated into shards, and now mixed with non-sacred, created stuff, some of which was even destructive to creation itself. This state of things is potentially tragic, as all of creation could self-destruct without the unity of God holding everything together. However, the inherent quality of God in all manner of things, even aspects of creation that are themselves destructive, holds out the promise that all is redeemable, all can be restored to its original wholeness.

This fragmentation of God and non-God, creation and destruction, inheres in all created things, including people, animals, and even inanimate objects. In this sense, God is in everything, but at the same time, God is nowhere. From a mystical perspective, God may be the One that pervades all of creation. But from a human perspective, God is known only in whispers, if that, and mostly hidden behind the seemingly endless veils of ordinary life. Here is a brief description of the state of the world requiring *tikkun*, one that emphasizes the distance of creation from the Creator:

> Behold, since the Supreme Creator saw that the vessels were shattered because divine light was so great and they were unable to withstand it, it arose in His mind to restore (bring *tikkun*) to all of the worlds in a manner that the vessels could hold the light. This would occur through a devolution of the light and its distancing from the Supreme Creator, such that the lights would become more concealed, and in this manner would all the worlds continue to exist.[1]

From this state of separation from God, *tikkun* speaks to our inevitable loneliness by proposing that the way back to closeness with God is not by transcending or negating creation, but seeking its restoration from within. The gulf between people and God, exacerbated by the notion of God being "broken" into fragments, seems infinite, but is actually overcome by turning to the brokenness of the world. While God brings about *tikkun* by constantly creating and re-creating Godself, making the vessels that hold all of God's light in creation more resilient and strong, there is a small but essential aspect of *tikkun* left to humanity.

Our Role in *Tikkun*

This charge to restore the created world as well as God becomes our existential and spiritual task, expressed with great brevity and power in *Etz Hayyim*:

> . . . as the divine light (from creation) escaped toward its source in heaven, nevertheless a small remnant of the sparks of holiness still remained and fell into these "shattered garments" below, and from them the husks of creation were constituted. And so, even though the "food has been sorted from the garbage," and has risen upward, there are still sparks of holiness within them. And this is what is left for us, to repair, by means of prayer and acts of loving kindness toward each other.[2]

In this one sentence, we see how Luria confronts the inevitable loss and pain of the world, but within that brokenness finds the conditions of

1. Vital, *Etz Chayim*, 1:2.
2. Ibid., 1:1.

that bring healing. In a world that is literally broken, even comprised of "garbage," we fragile and limited human beings wield enormous power. Each prayer, each ritual, and every anonymous kindness weaves anew the "shattered garments" of creation. In this way, as small as we are, we assume center stage in the restoration of the world.

Each person is a microcosm of a greater spiritual process, and so *tikkun* also entails the aspiration of bringing one's isolated soul toward something greater. Conversely, one person's journey towards wholeness through righteous acts is part of God's ongoing evolution. Again, the *Etz Hayyim* says it simply and powerfully. He anticipates a student, pondering Luria's story of creation, asking the question of why God created the universe with its inherent flaws of God's distance, fragmentation, and mutual isolation. Luria imagines the student wondering why God couldn't create the universe in such a way that it would have space for its creatures, yet without the distance between God and humanity. The *Etz Chaim* responds,

> One might say, "Why did the Supreme Creator not fashion the world . . . so that there would not be shards that would be shattered? For surely, it is revealed and known before God that these fragments could never have withstood the divine light." The answer is that the intention of the Supreme Creator was to give choice and will to human beings, so that there would be good and evil in the world. For the root of evil springs from the broken vessels of creation, and the good comes from the great light. And if this were not the case, then there would only be good in the world, and there would not be reward and punishment. But now, there is good and evil, just as there is reward and punishment—there is reward for the righteous and punishment for the wicked. The reward for the righteous occurs by means of their good deeds in which the holy sparks that descended are raised from their shells. And the punishment of the wicked occurs because of the manner in which they cause the descent of the holy sparks into their shells from the great light. The shells themselves are the instrument of punishment to chastise the wicked. . . . Therefore, there is power, by means of our prayer and our good actions, to raise the Divine Presence to her place where she was originally.[3]

Ultimately, Luria emphasizes the extraordinary capacity we have to effect *tikkun*, to mend a world of brokenness, pain, and alienation. Luria evokes for us a world marked by the fearful prospect of suffering, but also characterized by the hope of repair. The pain of the world exists simply as

3. Ibid., 1:2.

a by-product of creation. The original wholeness of God could not be sustained if God was to be known by creation; the Great Light was too great for any vessel to hold it. And so the vessels shattered, eventually comprising our created universe. But within these shards, these "shells," were also remnants of the divine light. Through our righteous deeds, prayers, and acts of kindness, the light is released and returned to its source. Most dramatically, we can raise the *Shekhinah*, the aspect of God closest and most accessible to humanity, to Her original source. Therefore, without any supernatural intervention, we are given extraordinary power. In the absence of God, the power of *tikkun* is entrusted to our fragile hands. And perhaps the restoration we can effect would be more whole than God's original wholeness before the dawn of creation.

And so, this is our experience of the world according to Luria: we are separated from the benevolent, all-powerful God, and yet we have almost limitless opportunity to engage in acts of kindness and devotion so as to heal the brokenness of the universe and restore God to the divine, original self. In the act of *tikkun*, our feelings of alienation and our yearnings for connection constitute the fuel to engage in these acts of healing. From my vantage point simply observing how people act, I believe that many of us are either engaging in acts of *tikkun* or yearning to without even realizing it. Perhaps we do simple things like contact a friend, sign a petition, join a class or group, or call our parents simply to do something that takes us beyond ourselves. Perhaps we do these things simply to feel less lonely, or because it feels as if we have no other choice.

Love and *Tikkun*

As a young adult, cut off from my father and finding my way in a world that could be profoundly mundane, I found the most fundamental *tikkun* in love. But as essential as that love was to me, I found that I had to draw from sources of a different kind of love found in the rituals and communal spaces that were becoming the basis of my mature Jewish life. Every Friday night, Judy and I made Shabbat dinner at home. Doing so became our anchor, our way to connect with each other, with old friends, and with new people we wanted to bring into our lives. We joined our small neighborhood synagogue, which we attended regularly. I paid close attention to the cantor so that I could learn how to pray from the inside out, and within a year, I led Friday night services when he was on vacation.

We lingered over the *oneg Shabbat* after services, and to my great surprise I found myself becoming friends with people at different stages of life.

There was one man in particular, a sixty-something gentleman who had been a teacher and educational administrator. He was charismatic, progressive, and funny, and I loved hearing him offer his beliefs of what students could do if just given the chance. There was Saul, the ninety-something powerhouse who was born in Poland and fought in Israel's War of Independence. He would hold forth on his views on sociology and anthropology, and on multiple Shabbat mornings Saul convinced me to join him at a small Orthodox *shul* to help make the *minyan*. Gila inspired us all—she was a thirty-something lawyer confined to a wheelchair since she was a child, and she was fierce, having taken on the role as the conscience of the community.

Our time together at services, at meals in each other's homes, and on walks on Shabbat became essential to my growth in learning about the world and the people who inhabit it, as well as to my feeling of having a Jewish story among people at different stages of life. Together, we celebrated conversions to Judaism, professional milestones, and the occasional wedding. Eventually, I would become a part of the communities of Jews who were exceedingly knowledgeable and seemed to know every obscure song and custom. But it was this small, motley, and largely unknown community that showed me the qualities of Jewish community at its very best: companionship, loyalty, and the generosity of sharing our journeys.

At the same time, away from community, I was cultivating my own sense of a Jewish self. While Friday evening was a time for the experience of a shared and public Judaism—Shabbat dinner with Judy and friends, time in synagogue—Saturday was a time I could devote to my inner connection to the tradition and its sources. I would often walk a mile or so to the synagogue where I celebrated *Simchat Torah*, and once there, I would pay close attention to the service, noting how it worked and how it was structured. I observed the rabbi with a keen eye, and deeply appreciated his short, insightful summaries of the Torah portion, always framed by a compelling intellectual slant. At home afterwards, I would study. One ritual was taking out a *chumash*, a bound copy of the Torah with Hebrew and English side by side, with a biblical dictionary next to me. I would read the Hebrew, look up the words I didn't know (which were many), and then check myself against the English.

When I grew tired of the Torah portion, I would take out the Talmud volume I had bought in Israel during the trip I took with Judy, the volume I bought in the bookstore in Me'ah Sha'arim. My progress was mind-numbingly slow, and I went for percentages. I would read a sentence in the original Aramaic/Hebrew mixture, and I would turn to a Talmudic dictionary to look up the unfamiliar words, often four or five in a sentence. Periodically, I would check myself by seeing if I could understand the Hebrew commentary by the great scholar Adin Steinsaltz printed alongside the traditional text. If I could understand half of it, I knew I was onto something. If I could get 75 percent, I felt as if I'd really learned. I could have made things easier on myself by simply buying an English translation. But there was something about wrestling with the Hebrew that made me feel more connected. While foreign and at times impenetrable, the Talmudic Hebrew was my key to being on the inside of something greater, and so I wanted to be immersed in it.

Tikkun without the Presence of God

While I see my adult embrace of Jewish life as part of Luria's mystical *tikkun*, I was not drawn in by a personal or immediate way of experiencing God in my day-to-day life. Even as I pursued a greater devotion to Jewish observance, study, and ritual, I did so with the sense that Judaism was a this-worldly pursuit, all within the realm of the natural rather than the supernatural. God was important to me, but as an idea, a way to articulate the highest and loftiest projections of the self, and a vehicle to encapsulate the collective spiritual strivings of the Jewish people. God was not a presence in my life, or a being, or some thing to which I looked. This might strike some as irreligious, but it never seemed strange to me to be drawn to the beauty of Jewish life and community while remaining skeptical about a supernatural God.

Fittingly, I was drawn to the work and thought of the great rabbi and scholar Mordecai Kaplan, who developed the radical thesis that Judaism did not grow from a direct encounter between the Jewish people and God. Rather, Kaplan believed that Jewish civilization appeared first, and from within that historical experience, the Jewish people gave birth to the Jewish God. Kaplan was born in Lithuania in 1881 and moved to the United States as a young boy. Though raised in an Orthodox home with a thoroughgoing knowledge of Jewish texts, he studied at Columbia University as well as the Conservative Jewish Theological Seminary in New York. At the time, there was little practical difference between being a Conservative or Orthodox rabbi, with one crucial exception. The Jewish Theological Seminary established itself as a center for the "scientific" study of Judaism. Originating in Europe as a means to achieve a modern and revived understanding of Jewish tradition, the scientific approach subjected the entire corpus of Jewish tradition to historical analysis without interference from traditional beliefs.

Such an approach became, and remains, controversial when applied to the Torah. From a traditional perspective, the text of the Torah is inherently sacred, the word of God, and the mountains of commentary exist to help us discern the divine essence sometimes obscured by human language. But from a historical-critical perspective, the Torah is a document created by human beings. If it is a work of genius, or a record of humanity's encounter with God, then such methods as comparing the Torah to other documents from the ancient Near East, or discerning the Torah's different authors and their concerns, should elicit a greater appreciation of its message. A traditionalist will be wary of or even shun a scientific approach, as it divests the Torah of any kind of divine authority and reduces the Torah to being another historical document. But the historically minded scholar will contend that Jewish tradition has always recognized the Torah's internal inconsistencies, and the scientific approach takes the further step to enlighten readers rather than indoctrinate them into any kind of restrictive religious belief.

Mordecai Kaplan, though he began his rabbinic career as the Rabbi of an Orthodox synagogue, fully embraced the historical critical method. On these twin foundations of loving tradition and embracing historical criticism, Kaplan became an innovator of Jewish ideas and practice up until his death at 102. Even among his fellow faculty at the Jewish Theological Seminary, he was often sidelined and marginalized as one who took the freedom of innovation too far in both his philosophical ideas and his liturgical explorations. Kaplan's most dramatic statement came in 1945, when he published a prayer book that introduced a number of changes to the traditional liturgy, replacing the time-honored theme of Jewish "chosenness" with more egalitarian language. This and other innovations earned Kaplan the rare distinction of being placed in *"herem,"* or excommunicated, by the Union of Orthodox Rabbis, who demonstrated their disgust by holding a rally at which they burned Kaplan's book in a birdcage.

Kaplan elaborated upon his groundbreaking approach in a philosophical tome proposing a "reconstruction" of Jewish life. His radical new book, *Judaism as a Civilization* (1934), was a thorough re-evaluation of Judaism, its foundations, current practice, and future. It was built almost entirely upon the notion that Judaism and its spirituality springs from human experience, and not from a collective encounter with God or any kind of divine message. But even though God was, in Kaplan's view, a human creation, Kaplan retained the idea of God as indispensable to the vitality of Jewish thought and practice.

Kaplan and a "Natural" God

Three central themes animate much of Kaplan's discussions about God. The most important, already mentioned, is that God is not a supernatural being, independent of nature. Instead, human civilization created the notion of God to express a sense of ultimacy, moral authority, and universalism, and the Jewish civilization created the Jewish God through the prism of its own unique experience. For Kaplan, the "invention" of God does not make the Jewish God any less real or compelling, but rather shifts the philosophical ground on which we think about and even experience what we call "God." It follows that if God is the product of human civilization, then God's so-called commandments in the Torah are not obligatory, as they were not truly "revealed" by God. Kaplan instead refers to the traditional *mitzvot*, or commandments, as "folkways," devised by the Jewish people to concretize our sense of morality and ethics so as to remind us of what is most meaningful day to day. And finally, Judaism lives not because of any special protection from God or by dint of any special virtue that other civilizations lack. Rather, Kaplan believed that Judaism owed its survival to its embrace of progress and change, adapting and evolving in response to new historical circumstances. Going forward, it would be the living and changing community of Jews, as opposed to strict fidelity to traditional law, that would propel and renew the ongoing spiritual vitality of Jewish life.

As a young man figuring out my Jewish self, I read Mordecai Kaplan's *Judaism as a Civilization* and found it to be a page-turner. With every new idea, expressed in a tone both clear and urgent, I felt as if Kaplan was speaking directly to me. I found so much compelling in Kaplan, but most of all the sense of a rational, honest, and mature foundation for religious life—one that was willing to dispense with fairy tales and false pieties and embrace the vitality of experiences that I was seeking out in solitude, partnership, and community.

Newly independent, launching my adulthood and unsure about the road ahead, I was particularly drawn to Kaplan's view that what we call God is rooted in the perennial human quest for knowledge of ourselves and our relationship to everyone and everything around us. Through the "unity" of one's "person," Kaplan says, we become "intuitively aware of that phase of reality" that human beings have "gropingly and blunderingly tried to reckon in . . . various religions." In other words, all religious life springs from an intimately personal experience in which we see ourselves as part of a seemingly infinite reality. Religion—through its rituals, rhythms, and, most of all, communities—seeks to help us understand this dazzling but otherwise incomprehensible series of relationships between ourselves and all that exists.

Interdependence: Our Experience of "God"

Many people disparage religious life and spiritual contemplation as "navel gazing," and yes, one can become lost or overly self-involved. But Kaplan understood, rightly I believe, that an earnest seeking out the depths of self brings one to a consciousness beyond the self. He speaks of this going through the self and outward as an awareness of "inter-relatedness." For Kaplan, human beings derived the idea of God from their experience of being connected to each other and all reality. And once this view of divinity was established, people no longer had a need to ponder the self, but rather, articulated the idea of God as a way to encapsulate all reality, as well as everything within reality.

> In the past . . . man always imagined himself as standing outside reality conceived as a whole. When, therefore, he sensed the inter-relatedness which gave to reality that meaning out of which he derived his various notions of godhood, it did not occur to him to look for that same type of meaning in his own personality.[4]

But for Kaplan, it is still not enough to contemplate God within reality as an abstraction. The unfinished work lies in finding what we call "God" within *ourselves*. Ultimately, our task is to discover for ourselves that the divinity we project onto the universe actually lies within, thereby beholding the grandeur of our inherent humanity:

> Only an occasional gleam of the truth that the human being possesses more of godhood than anything else in his environment flashed across man's mind, as, for instance, when he achieved the notion that he was created in the image of God. But that gleam was only for a moment. It has to be recaptured by increased self-knowledge for man to realize that he belongs within reality, the whole of which determines his life.[5]

For those of us who have experienced the moment of internal bliss, that "occasional gleam" where we may feel something like being created in the image of God, Kaplan would say that is only the first step. Whether in the afterglow of a baby being born, or consummating love, or simply feeling the rush and thrill of our own vitality, Kaplan would say that we need to understand that our moment of transcendence is not from beyond, but entirely *from within*. We live entirely "within reality," and not as the beneficiaries of

4. Kaplan, *Judaism as a Civilization*, 315.
5. Ibid., 316.

something that graces us from outside the day-to-day realms of the self and the natural world. Even though the Bible speaks of God in the third person, as when Genesis 1:26 states, "in the image of God He created them (the first man and woman)," the Bible, prayer, and all forms of externalized God-language are really articulating the grandeur we see in ourselves. When we say "God created human beings in the divine image," we are really saying, "we have discovered this unifying, transcendent, life-giving, and moral force within ourselves."

Even with this insight, hard as it may be to achieve, Kaplan asks us to go a step further. For Kaplan, the ideal way of seeing things is to view ourselves, and our inherent grandeur, not only through the lens of our own experience, but in the universal context, the web of life and humanity, of which we are a part.

> Man has come to understand that the act of contemplating reality in its wholeness does not place him outside reality. He now realizes that the inter-relatedness which is the source of his awareness of godhood operates within him, no less than outside him. Thus is eliminated the very need of making any dichotomy either between the universe of man and the universe of God, or between the natural and the supernatural. There is only one universe within which both man and God exist.[6]

This formulation represents the end of religion as a purveyor of false promises. Instead, to be religious or spiritual is to discover "godhood" in the world as it is. God is found not outside oneself, and not in miracles, but within, and within the laws of nature. There is no "natural vs. supernatural," because there is no supernatural realm, except in works of fiction. In order for Judaism to be a truthful system of thought, we must re-read it as speaking of God *within* everything, not *above* everything. There is no "universe of God" and "universe of humanity," because it is all one, and our task as human beings, and as religious people, is not to escape from reality or denigrate it, especially by turning away from a scientific understanding of how our world works. Instead, we are to understand and embrace this world as it is, in all of its contradiction and brilliance, and by doing so discern the godhood within ourselves and all reality.

Here, Kaplan expresses himself most clearly:

> The so-called laws of nature represent the manner of God's immanent functioning. The element of creativity, which is not accounted for by the so-called laws of nature, and which points

6. Ibid.

to the organic character of the universe or its life as a whole, gives us a clue to God's transcendent functioning. God is not an identifiable being who stands outside the universe. God is the life of the universe, immanent insofar as each part acts upon every other, and transcendent insofar as the whole acts upon each part.[7]

Kaplan isn't so popular these days, in part because he is often seen as a spiritual spoiler, as one who rains on our moments of bliss by saying, "It's all made up." But such an assessment misses the point. I have heard from students of Kaplan, a few of whom were beloved teachers of mine, that he loved Jewish observance, and understood that the even the most humble of ritual acts, such as wearing *tzitzit*, were powerful reminders of our connections to each other and the all-encompassing reality we call God. Far from diminishing our experiences of the sacred, these passages show Kaplan giving us language to see the holy in everyday experiences, in the world and with other people.

When we go about our lives, subject to the immutable laws of nature, we are experiencing "God's immanent functioning," in other words, God working through things we can't control. There is, in fact, very traditional Jewish language for this. When we hear of a moment that strikes us as filled with goodness and hope, such as the birth of a child, we say, "*Barukh ha-tov v'ma-metiv*," Blessed be the good and the bestower of goodness. Alternatively, when we hear the news of a death, our tradition counsels us to say the blessing, "*Barukh dayan ha-emet*," Blessed be the Judge of truth. Both the rabbis of the Talmud and Kaplan would agree (remarkably!) that these moments reflect natural and divine forces at work.

Some people claim that Kaplan, in demythologizing the supernatural God, took God out of the equation for modern Jews. In my opinion, that is simply not the case. If anything, Kaplan made it possible for rational people, unconvinced of the existence of any kind of a personal God so popular in our culture, to name the world we know as a manifestation of God's presence:

When the modern man studies reality scientifically, he abstracts from it certain specific aspects, such as the physical, the chemical, the biological, the psychological. When, in addition, he tries to grasp the significance of the parts of reality in their relation to the whole, and of the whole in its relation to the parts, there emerges that entire universe of values in which are reflected his

7. Ibid.

yearnings to be at one with life at its best. To recognize this is to sense the divine aspect of reality.[8]

Once again, we do not find God by seeking refuge or retreating from our lives. Instead, we "recognize" the "divine aspect of reality" when we see ourselves as part of the whole, and use every tool we have to understand this inordinately complex world in which we live.

Most forcefully, though, Kaplan invested human relationships with an inherent sacred quality that did not require any kind of leap of faith. If God is found in our experiences of this world and our "inter-relatedness," then the heights of our spirituality are those moments when we experience that connectedness most strongly with other people, in this world, as part of our day-to-day relationships. As I began to come into my own, I knew that Jewish life was built upon these moments of connection, in the forms of people gathering to share a Shabbes meal, to study and debate with, to work at a soup kitchen, to share joy and provide comfort.

Becoming Ourselves

Facing the burgeoning blessings of adulthood along with the prospect of never having a father, I sought out these experiences as moments with special urgency because I saw them as invested with the kind of sacred quality Kaplan saw. It is not that I was looking for these experiences to "transport" me to a transcendent state of spiritual consciousness. Rather, I found that these very ordinary moments of shared experience in community were inherently healing and powerful, and so fit what I was yearning for in my life. The cast of characters at my local synagogue became my gateway to a number of formative experiences that would not have been possible without them. Saul, the ninety-something raconteur, persuaded me on a number occasions to make the *minyan* at a dying *shul*, where not only did I have my first exposure to Orthodox Judaism, but I read the *Haftara*, the section of the Prophets that accompanies each Torah portion, for the first time since my bar mitzvah. The two women who lived down the street from me became part of my Shabbat *chevra*, sharing conversation, meals, and study together. After a year or so, while the cantor was away, I volunteered to lead services, and all of these friends showed up to cheer me on.

Over time, I recognized how these experiences both satisfied and fed my yearnings, and began to recognize how and why Jewish tradition has always called these moments "holy." As I embarked on an adult journey of

8. Ibid.

tikkun, I did not expect or even believe that my new wholeness would come from some being outside my experience. Rather, I expected whatever healing I could find to emerge from within the expressions of love, earnestness, skepticism, and seeking that I witnessed in moments of Jewish gathering.

While I admired Kaplan's daring, it was his rootedness in the sources of Jewish tradition that helped me see myself in his words. I was looking for a sense of belonging more than I was an abstract rational spirituality. Through his devotion to Jewish sources and teachings, Kaplan showed me that Jewish engagement through skepticism, curiosity, and human connection was not only an acceptable modern path, but also a deeply traditional one. Reading him, I felt myself encouraged to think in ways that questioned convention and tradition, with the promise that by doing so, I would find a spiritual home.

By demonstrating that the forms of religious life were merely the channel for a deeper impulse, Kaplan reassured me that my lack of a learned and traditional Jewish upbringing would not be an impediment to drawing closer to the fruits of a Jewish life. If I wanted to partake of these experiences, I could study them and assimilate them into my life, independent from my father, my family, and my past, all along knowing that my spiritual core was a desire to be a part of the web of connection we call "God." To deepen my sense of Jewish belonging, I could continue to live as I had been living, as myself, in the reality I knew and was shaping. To be a fully realized Jew and a spiritually connected man, perhaps some day a rabbi, I could simply continue to be me.

Chapter 8

Toward the Other

But learn one thing, impress it upon your mind which is still so malleable: man has a horror for aloneness. And of all kinds of aloneness, moral aloneness is the most terrible. The first hermits lived with God, they inhabited the world which is most populated, the world of the spirits. The first thought of man, be he a leper or a prisoner, a sinner or an invalid, is: to have a companion of his fate. In order to satisfy this drive which is life itself, he applies all his strength, all his power, the energy of his whole live.

—From Balzac, The Inventor's Suffering, epigram to *Escape From Freedom* by Erich Fromm

Returning to Rabbi Eliezer and the Sages —Moral Experience as Religious Experience

The story cited earlier, the famous argument between Rabbi Eliezer and the Sages about the Oven of Achnai, and their ultimate rejection of God's voice, is often seen as a cornerstone of modern Judaism. In an age of skepticism and doubt, even cynicism, the story is seen as a validation of reason and the democratic spirit of rabbinic Judaism. As I have emphasized, it is also a validation of living with the absence of God by embracing it, even going so far as to take the active step putting God into eclipse so as to allow our own voices to develop. If the space between ourselves and God is, after all, part of the structure of creation, then we have an obligation to grow those capacities as much as we can, without resort to crutches or quick fixes.

But the story, as compelling as it is, remains incomplete without its second half. That second half describes the tragic cost of sidelining Rabbi Eliezer. And it also demonstrates how the rabbis do not advocate a total eclipse of God, their treatment of the divine voice notwithstanding. If anything, the story lands on a note that emphasizes the urgency of our ethical obligations to other human beings. This, in the end, may even be more important than, or perhaps identical with, our connection to God.

As resolute as the rabbis appeared to be in banishing the opinion of Rabbi Eliezer, they immediately realize the potentially devastating consequences of their actions.

> That same day, they brought all the things that Rabbi Eliezer had declared "pure" and burned them, and they took a vote and excommunicated him. But then they asked, "Who will go and inform him?" Rabbi Akiva said, "I will go lest someone else who is not fit will go and inform him, and we will find that the whole world has been destroyed."[1]

Rabbi Akiva's admission is remarkable. True, the rabbis have gained a measure of, say, intellectual security in knowing they followed the path of reason. But at what cost? Rabbi Akiva's warning, I believe, prompts us to wonder if the rabbis missed something in their absolute rejection of God's voice and their marginalization of Rabbi Eliezer. In the end, was their decision about the oven all that important? Certainly, the rabbis' intellectual victory should not have been more important than forestalling the grievous outcomes of hurting Rabbi Eliezer so emphatically. The Talmud continues to describe the heartbreaking scene in which Rabbi Akiva gives the bad news to his friend:

> Rabbi Akiva wore black and wrapped himself in a black cloak and sat in front of Rabbi Eliezer at a distance of four cubits. Rabbi Eliezer said to him, "Akiva, what is happening today?" He said to him, "My teacher, it appears that the friends are separating themselves from you." And then he as well rent his garments, took off his sandals, and lay on the ground. As tears fell from his eyes, the world was afflicted: a third of the olive crop, a third of the wheat crop, and a third of the barley crop. There are those who say that even the dough in women's hands became sour.[2]

Whatever the Rabbis had been arguing about now takes a back seat to the pathos in the relationship between Rabbi Akiva and Rabbi Eliezer. Note

---

1. Babylonian Talmud, Tractate *Hagigah*, 15a.
2. Ibid.

that Rabbi Akiva calls Rabbi Eliezer "My teacher." Note also how he spares him the details of their rabbinic compatriots burning everything Rabbi Eliezer declared to be "pure." It seems that if Rabbi Akiva could prevent Rabbi Eliezer's pain, he would. Of course this news is absolutely devastating to Rabbi Eliezer, despite how gently Rabbi Akiva delivers it. And any of us who has experienced loss or especially rejection can identify vicariously with the destruction that ensues. Who among us has never felt this way?

Eventually Rabban Gamliel, the head of the Sanhedrin who would have approved the excommunication of Rabbi Eliezer, is caught up in the cataclysmic reverberations of Rabbi Eliezer's pain. But then we see something interesting. Despite the rabbis' earlier dismissal of the divine voice, Rabban Gamliel appeals to God to explain their treatment of Rabbi Eliezer.

> It is taught—he was fearsome on that day. For every place upon Rabbi Eliezer lay his eyes was consumed by fire. Even Rabban Gamliel (the brother-in-law of Rabbi Eliezer and upon whose authority the excommunication went forth) when he was on a boat as it was about to capsize. He said, "It appears to me that the only reason for this is on account of Rabbi Eliezer ben Hyrcanus." He stood up and said, "Master of the Universe, it is revealed and known to you that I did not do this for my own honor, and not for the honor of my father's house, but rather for Your honor, so that we would not proliferate arguments among Israel." The sea calmed from its roiling.[3]

Rabban Gamliel's response is a highly imperfect one. Just as Rabbi Eliezer appealed directly to God to justify his view of *halakhah*, so Rabban Gamliel makes a direct plea to explain his actions and save his life. True, one can quibble and say that the rabbis banished the divine voice in matters of *halakhah*, Jewish law, and that prayer is different. But Rabban Gamliel's excommunication of Rabbi Eliezer was also a matter of *halakhah*, in fact, it is perhaps among the most weighty and consequential of decisions. Yes, prayer and legal decision-making are different, but both ultimately are vehicles to draw close to the same God. Rabban Gamliel, it appears, wants distance in the legal realm, but closeness when his neck is on the line.

Ultimately, it takes Imma Shalom, whose name literally means "Mother of Peace," to suggest how this complex interplay of real world and divine presence are linked. Imma Shalom is both the wife of Rabbi Eliezer and the sister of Rabban Gamliel and so in the context of this story weaves together the seemingly conflicting modes of approaching the divine presence. The

3. Ibid.

question she must resolve is one of obligation, and where the sacredness of obligation to God becomes most urgent.

> Imma Shalom was the wife of Rabbi Eliezer and the sister of Rabban Gamliel. From the moment of this episode she did not allow Rabbi Eliezer to bow low to the ground (for fear of the destruction that would follow). That particular day was the New Moon and she was mistaken that it was the end of one month and not the beginning of another (and thus it would not be customary to lay prostrate in prayer). Others say a poor man came to the door and she went to get him a loaf of bread. She left him, and he prostrated himself on the ground. She said to him, "Get up, for you have killed my brother." At that moment an announcement went out from the home of Rabban Gamliel that he had died. "How did you know?" he asked her. She told him, "So have I received as a tradition from my grandfather, 'All the gates are closed, except the gates of wounded feelings.'"[4]

The Talmud gives Imma Shalom one of its most evocative and heroic lines, "All the gates are closed, except the gates of wounded feelings." It is a statement of both recognition and obligation. On the one hand, she is shedding insight on a previously unresolved question raised earlier in the Talmud's discussion, "Which ways to the divine are open and which are closed?" Acting on behalf of those with wounded feelings, for Imma Shalom, is the only channel open. Whatever we do—whether it is our own *teshuvah* or attending to the needs of those rendered vulnerable by isolation and rejection—we should expect some kind of spiritual response.

But Imma Shalom is not only sentimental. She is the daughter and granddaughter of the foundational Sages of rabbinic Judaism, and so she understands their effort to articulate the nature of our obligations to a God who has always been invisible and remote, and now even more so with the destruction of the temple in Jerusalem. In these circumstances, she asserts that the primary obligation to God is itself the obligation to those with "wounded feelings." Other *halakhic* obligations, whether having to do with ritual, food, prayer, or anything else, are certainly important, but they are all part of the realm of "locked gates." We may get these obligations right or we may not, but God is essentially indifferent to them. However, this one gate remaining open is itself a statement about what our moral aspirations should be. God may be remote from most of our affairs, but not in how we treat those who are vulnerable. In this realm, the realm of "open gates," God

---

4. Ibid.

is most present, and so our most pressing religious obligation is to attend to those with "wounded feelings."

A Growing Obligation

Not having grown up in a traditional Jewish household, I may have felt compelled by Jewishness, but I never felt obligated to pursue Jewish ritual in the rabbinic sense as an obligation before God. As a fifteen-year-old, I felt compelled by my connection to friends, to my rabbi, and to the Jewish people to explore this God given to me by Jewish tradition. Several years later, when I sought out the organized Jewish community in college, I realized that living a Jewish life with others was a requirement, and not an option, if I wanted to deepen my overall sense of Jewish connection. This realization brewed slowly, but crystallized when I read Judith Plaskow's Acknowledgements section to her book of Jewish feminism, *Standing Again at Sinai*. The simple words of thanks to a group called *"B'not Esh* (Daughters of Fire)" were a reminder that Jewish ideas and practice live most forcefully as a collective rather than individual pursuit. And eventually, as my involvement in Jewish practice deepened, I took on not only the obligation to engage with community, but to live with a personal obligation to Jewish tradition and God through *halakhah*, or Jewish law.

Without a doubt, my impulse to delve deeply into Jewish life was and continues to be driven by a desire for a *tikkun neshama*, a healing of the soul. The more I see and feel of the brokenness of this world, and the more I study Jewish tradition, the more I feel that Judaism, Jewish life, and Jewish teachings have to contribute. In this way, I have come to see and experience the whole of Jewish living as an existential obligation—not just an optional priority. However, I do not pursue this sense of obligation because I feel that there is a personal and immediately present God taking account of my actions and intentions. Rather, I experience the space of this world, of my life, as distant from God's presence. But within that space I sense a need to discern some of the things I must do for the sake of my own humanity. Occasionally, I pursue acts on behalf of others, and at times even for the sake of some inchoate sense that transcends us all. And while I do not necessarily feel or expect the presence of God in moments of study, of connection, and of service, neither do I feel God's abandonment in these moments. My attraction to the humanity-focused philosophy of Mordecai Kaplan notwithstanding, I sense God to be greater than a human construct, albeit a collective one. Beyond the normative instructions of Jewish law, I sense a broader Jewish and universal obligation, whose force comes through the workings of this world, but whose source lies in an origin that I am completely unable to express.

This jumble of thoughts is not so different from the beliefs about God and Judaism I brought with me to rabbinical school in 1993. Growing up Reform, and spending college in an academic and social environment that challenged everything, the Conservative Jewish Theological Seminary was not necessarily a natural choice. If I were looking for a more comfortable political and personal fit, I would have chosen the Reconstructionist Rabbinical College, whose expansive curriculum and outlook fostered the kind of inclusive diversity in which I felt at home. But JTS offered the gifts of a Jewish university, and its rabbinical school curriculum was just what I wanted: a steady march over six years through the canon of Jewish thought. On an informal level, I wanted to be immersed in the thoroughgoing traditional Jewish life that was unavailable to me growing up, and exceedingly rare in non-Orthodox circles. I wanted to feel the rhythm of Shabbat, live and study in a community whose days were shaped by times for daily prayer, and develop relationships with colleagues similarly shaping our lives through the integration of tradition and egalitarian modernity.

All rabbinical programs strive for this same mix, but the way in which JTS did it was uniquely helpful to me. Recognizing that their students came from worlds that were largely non-observant, JTS vetted its candidates by making sure that they were, in fact, keeping kosher, observing Shabbat, and praying each day. To an outsider, such a requirement may seem overbearing and intrusive. But it was an effective way to cultivate of group of self-selected learners, diverse in belief and thought, but united in practice. Once on the inside, many of us thought the litmus test was absurd, but at the same time, we worked very hard to answer the question of who really was compelling us to lead traditional Jewish lives.

For me, it certainly wasn't God. I did not believe that the Holy One particularly cared what I did on Friday night, or in any other aspect of my ritual life. Apart from ritual practice, there was a more consequential dimension to my growing sense of obligation and a deeper question about who had the right, and the power, to define that obligation. At the time, the rabbinical school at the Seminary was debating whether to admit students who were openly gay or lesbian, and no one even thought about trans folk at the time. The status quo was that openly gay or lesbian candidates would not be welcome at JTS, and if they came out while they were rabbinical students, they could be asked to leave. It is almost impossible to conceive, but gay friends who were at JTS in those years stayed closeted, at least to all but a handful of close and trusted friends.

I couldn't fathom accepting an opportunity denied to someone else, no matter how great the JTS faculty or curriculum. A friend supplied me with a binder of essays that were presented as part of the debate. Some of the essays were awful in their outdated notions of homosexuality, and frankly so long and turgid I didn't bother reading past the introductions. But there were two, forcefully argued and infused with reason and deep compassion for those who felt themselves to be on the margins. One of those papers was by Rabbi Elliot Dorff, a well known figure in the Conservative Movement. His essay helped me to see that Judaism's vision of obligation transcended the narrow tendencies of halakhah, or Jewish law. K'vod ha-briyot, a fundamental decency toward all humanity, was not a sentiment or an ideal, but itself the root of all obligation. Where that fundamental decency and the practice of Jewish tradition appeared to conflict, a thoughtful rabbi would have to go back to the sources to find an inner rationale for why decency would win out. Jewish tradition would have to rise to the occasion of serving humanity, and not the other way around. I wanted to be that kind of rabbi, to know enough so that I could reach back through 2,000 years of scholars and sages and texts to find the roots of what should compel us every day.

A Rabbinic Mentor

By the time of my admissions interview at JTS, I was clear in my own incoherence: my obligation to observe the ritual practices of Jewish tradition came from within, even if the goal of these practices was to take me outside myself. However, the Jewish sense of obligation to humanity was absolute, transcending anything that human beings could devise. Rabbi Elliot Dorff, whose essay affirmed the validity of this basic approach, was in my interview and clearly supported me. When I answered a question about my essays on my philosophical influences, he added a gloss to them that made me sound much more learned and insightful than I actually was. At the very end of the interview, Rabbi Dorff asked me to wait and speak with him afterwards. I didn't expect it, but after waiting for about fifteen minutes I was told that I had been accepted, and Rabbi Dorff spent about half an hour encouraging me to begin my studies where he taught at the University of Judaism, at the time the affiliate of JTS in Los Angeles. When Judy and I arrived in LA, Rabbi Dorff invited us over a number of times for Shabbat meals. In the first week of rabbinical school, Rabbi Dorff announced a mentoring program, in which we would pick a rabbi somewhere in the community to meet and talk with once a month. I approached Rabbi Dorff and he immediately agreed, almost expecting that I would ask him.

Beyond his immense erudition, his accomplishments, and his standing in our community, Rabbi Dorff taught me most simply by letting me in, and giving me the chance to see what a thoroughly Jewish life looks like up close. In our talks, we certainly talked through theological questions and picked apart various intellectual issues, but most of all, I was taken by Rabbi Dorff's unfailing kindness. With Rabbi Dorff, it felt as if everything he studied and thought, everything he participated in, every cause he advocated for, both flowed from and served this fundamental aspect of his being. It almost seems trite to laud Rabbi Dorff for something so simple, but in my experience, it is actually incredibly difficult to be fully engaged in the world while also being thoroughly compassionate. To work hard at a job, to read and study consistently, to write books, to promote oneself as a teacher, to devote oneself to community projects—all things that are part of a normal rabbi's life and which Rabbi Dorff accomplished on a singular scale—require the self-involvement to spend a lot of time alone. It is often necessary to believe that the project of the moment, whether an article, a class, or a meeting, is the most important thing in the world, and sometimes it is. And so, to pursue that life of constantly sharing oneself, while also letting others in with gentleness, humility, and humor, is truly rare.

A God Cloaked in Human Responsibility

Several months into my first year of rabbinical school, Rabbi Dorff introduced an idea about the obligations between self and other in a way I had never heard it before: that merely by being human, we are obligated to pursue the welfare of another human being. Interestingly, he did not refer to any particular Jewish source or teaching about God to express this idea. Reading it off the page, it may seem intuitive, or perhaps obvious, but to me in my early 20s, it was not. Throughout my college education, I encountered thinkers who puzzled over why we have ethical obligations in the first place. Given that we can be so selfish and cruel, these thinkers wondered how it was that we can also be good, as if basic goodness were an exception to human behavior, not its normal state. But Rabbi Dorff was drawn to the exact opposite way of thinking—not that human beings are inherently good, but that within the context of human society, if we can get the conditions right, we will see that we are compelled to serve each other rather than competing for every little scrap.

This, in essence, was Rabbi Dorff's introduction to the towering modern French Jewish philosopher Emmanuel Levinas. Born in Kovno in

1906, Levinas came to live in France in 1930 after pursuing his university education in philosophy at Strasburg and Freiburg. When France declared war against Germany, Levinas was ordered to serve, but was captured in 1940 when Germany invaded France. He spent the remainder of the war as a prisoner near Hannover in Germany, in a special barrack for Jewish prisoners where he was prevented from any kind of worship and had to perform menial tasks. His wife and daughter were hidden in a monastery and survived the war, but his mother-in-law was deported and disappeared while the SS murdered his father and brothers in Lithuania. After the war, Levinas sought out university teaching positions in philosophy, eventually serving on the faculty at the Sorbonne. But he was also deeply committed to Jewish education, studying Talmud with a mysterious teacher named "Chouchani" who also taught Elie Wiesel, and serving as the director of a Jewish high school, the *Ecole Normale Israelite Orientale*. It was in this latter context that Levinas gave a number of lectures on the Talmud, known to enthusiasts as *Nine Talmudic Readings*. He never wrote a memoir that shared his own sense of personal loss and the ways it shaped his thinking. Instead, he concentrated on a philosophy of self and other that envisions God as the key to the moral potential of humanity.

To begin with, God for Levinas is not the deity of our popular cynical imagination, who makes false promises, grants reward, or executes punishment. God is being itself, and in particular, represents a moral way of being that Jewish tradition calls "holiness." As Levinas himself observed, the Talmud gives God the name, "Holy One, Blessed be He (sic)," which is to say, that the quality of holiness between people is itself the most convincing manifestation of God.

> God—whatever his ultimate and, in some sense, naked meaning—appears to human consciousness (and especially in Jewish experience) "clothed" in values; and this clothing is not foreign to his nature or to his supra-nature. The ideal, the rational, the universal, the eternal, the very high, the trans-subjective, etc., nothing accessible to the intellect are his moral clothing. I therefore think that whatever the ultimate experience of the Divine and its ultimate religious and philosophical meaning might be, these cannot be separated from penultimate experiences and meanings. They cannot but include the values through which the Divine shines forth. Religious experience, at least for the Talmud, can only be primarily a moral experience.[5]

5. Levinas, *Nine Talmudic Readings*, 14-15.

Don't be intimidated by the circular prose and the strange terms. Just imagine you are listening to a deeply intelligent and feeling man whose thoughts are hard to follow, but whose essential beliefs come across. Notice, first, how Levinas admits his inability to define or even to know God. Yet, there is much in the approximate meaning of God, in the "values" in which God is "clothed." In fact, all moral considerations are God's "moral clothing." That's our field, our arena for experiencing and understanding God. "Religious experience . . . can only be . . . a moral experience." While much of God remains hidden, moral experience is enough for Levinas. In fact, it's more than enough. For human beings, it's everything, and for Levinas, it is the way in which the "Divine shines forth." Moral experience is all we need to live and contains all we need to know.

The Sanctity of Engaging the Other

This basic concept—that God is "clothed" or "found" primarily in moral experience—has powerful implications for how we understand ourselves as we try to bring healing to the world. The first of the essays in *Nine Talmudic Readings*, "Toward the Other," is a reflection on a famous passage from the Talmud about Yom Kippur. This essay is an extended meditation on the conviction that all religious experience serves the obligation to treat other human beings with kindness and justice.

For Levinas, it all begins with a Mishnah, a deceptively straightforward rabbinic teaching about the ritual of atonement on Yom Kippur.

> One who says, "I will sin and then repent, I will sin and then repent," has not acted sufficiently to atone on Yom Kippur. "I will sin and Yom Kippur will atone for me"—Yom Kippur does not effect atonement. The transgressions of human beings toward God are forgiven by Yom Kippur, the Day of Atonement; the transgressions against other people are not forgiven by Yom Kippur, the Day of Atonement, if one has not first appeased the other person.[6]

There may be a natural tendency to interpret this Mishnah as speaking to the way in which a sense of personal integrity is a prerequisite to a religious life. Building backwards from the end of this Mishnah, we should feel that it is the height of hypocrisy to pray fervently while treating other people badly. And so, the Mishnah comes to teach us that a life of God can only be built upon a life of honesty and humility before other human beings. If one

6. Babylonian Talmud, Tractate *Yoma*, 85a.

can live like this, then Yom Kippur can be a time of renewed wholeness and transparency before human beings and, ultimately, God.

This is certainly one compelling way to read the Mishnah, but for Levinas, it's not enough. In Levinas' moral universe, there is no separation between treating other human beings well and worshipping God. For if God is "cloaked" in the moral workings of humanity, then a transgression against human beings *is* a transgression against God. Human relationships are not only the sphere in which we meet God, but they are the most essential, the most determinative of our moral and spiritual integrity.

> My faults towards God are forgiven without my depending on his good will! God is, in a sense, the *other, par excellence*, the other as other, the absolutely other—and nonetheless my standing with God depends only my myself. The instrument of forgiveness in my hands. On the other hand, my neighbor, my brother, man, infinitely less other than the absolutely other, is in a certain way more other than God: to obtain his forgiveness on the Day of Atonement I must first succeed in appeasing him. What if he refuses? As soon as two are involved, everything is in danger. The other can refuse forgiveness and leave me unpardoned. This must hide some interesting teachings on the essence of the Divine![7]

To live in a religious way is to live with a profound irony. In one sense, God is above all. And yet, it is human beings who really have power over us—other people truly hold the keys to our sense of whether or not we are living righteously. We depend upon others to know that we are living in a way that benefits human beings. Therefore, in Levinas' understanding, human beings are more "absolute" than God. Whereas God will freely "forgive," other people will not. God will forgive us simply if we ask for it, for God is all compassion. But we cannot rely on such ready forgiveness from another human being. The moral demands then, of human beings, are even more onerous than those of God. To be human is to live and adjust one's life to the absolute moral demands of the other, which is to say human beings, not God.

At Yom Kippur services, we may hear a rabbi teach that offenses against human beings are offenses against God. In such moments, perhaps it feels to us as if such a rabbi is making an analogy: wronging another human being is "as if" we are doing something ultimately really destructive, "as if" it were an affront to God. But when Levinas says it, there is no "as if." Levinas reminds us that "It is well understood that faults toward one's neighbor are

---

7. Levinas, *Nine Talmudic Readings*, 16.

ipso facto offenses toward God." It seems as if he is saying that these offenses toward people *and* toward the source of all moral being are happening at the same time, whether we see it or not. Traditional Judaism believes that human beings exist to serve the Creator out of a sense of obligation. For Levinas, the starting point of that obligation is the interaction with another human being.

But that is not all, says Levinas. The kind of healing that we need to do with other people is actually part of a deeper repair that requires the elements of a completely internal spiritual life. Reflecting on the natural distinction in the Mishnah between moral offenses against people vs. ritual offenses against God, Levinas shows how they are, in fact, intertwined.

> But does calling these ritual transgressions "transgressions against God" diminish the gravity of the illness that the Soul has contracted as a result of these transgressions? Perhaps the ills that must heal inside the Soul without the help of others are precisely the most profound ills, and that even where our social faults are concerned, once our neighbor has been appeased, the most difficult part remains to be done. In doing wrong toward God, have we not undermined the moral conscience as moral conscience? The ritual transgression that I want to erase without resorting to the help of others would be precisely the one that demands all my personality; it is the work of Teshuvah, of Return, for which no one can take my place.[8]

"To be before God would be equivalent then to this total mobilization of oneself"

While moral experience is religious experience for Levinas, he understands that we need to pay attention to our internal lives in order to shape our moral experience. To this end, Judaism provides us with the ritual well that helps us attend to the "illness that the Soul has contracted" and bring about its "healing." Furthermore, inasmuch as a ritual misstep is, within the confines of Jewish tradition, a transgression against God, it certainly exists on a continuum with the moral transgressions we enact against others, which for Levinas is of course a sin against God. To take care of one is to take care of the other. One could easily go down a rabbit hole of obsessing over ritual commandments and certainly lose sight of our everyday obligations. Examples abound of this phenomenon unfortunately. But that is not, I believe,

8. Ibid., 17.

where Levinas wishes to lead us. Instead, he wants us to envision life as the "total mobilization of oneself." In such a life, we cultivate a rich inner life built upon prayer, study, and celebration that necessarily infuses our moral life, the distinction between so-called "religious experience" and "moral experience" being totally false. They are one and the same, and each one leads to the other. Both lead to an awareness of our relationship with God, which finds its pinnacle in service to the other.

Levinas, God, and the "Other" in the Real World

In a world that conspires to silence the "other," there is no denying the appeal of Levinas' God, who exists most palpably through our acts of justice and kindness. In one notable example, I read an article in the *New York Times* in 2009 about a young Israeli radiologist, Dr. Yehonatan Turner, who had a hunch that if he could attach a photograph of a patient's face to the scans of their bones and organs, he could "relate to each patient in a deeper way." Dr. Turner's hypothesis became a study that yielded dramatic results. Predictably, the change resulted in better care and better outcomes. According to the *Times*, "The researchers found that the radiologists' reports were significantly more thorough in all cases when a photograph was attached to a patient's scan. Reports were longer, more recommendations made, summaries usually included, and more incidental findings recorded." But not only did the patients receive better care, the doctors also felt better about themselves and their work. In questionnaires, doctors "felt more like physicians" when they could see the faces attached to the scans. Not surprisingly, Dr. Turner drew explicitly on the sense of mutuality and obligation found in the work of Levinas. In presenting his study and findings to American colleagues, he quoted Levinas directly: "In front of the face of the other, silence is impossible."[9]

This same sense of obligation before the "face" of the other also underlies much of the impetus behind the advocacy in the Jewish social justice world. When the phrase *Tikkun Olam* began to gain traction in the late '80s and early '90s, the term tended to connote a direct service approach to social problems as synagogues and other Jewish groups took on the work of forming and staffing soup kitchens, clothing drives, tutoring programs, and other initiatives that help people in a direct and personal way. The immediate need of another, particularly one who is vulnerable and in need, is undeniable. But what about the imperative to work and advocate for change at its roots?

9. *New York Times*, "Radiologist Adds a Human Touch: Photos," April 6, 2009.

In his book *Justice in the City*, Aryeh Cohen explicitly draws on the work of Levinas to show us how living among others, particularly in an urban environment, imposes upon each of us an obligation to care for the silent "others" we do not yet know and to act on their behalf. Cohen speaks of an obligation that is not explicitly cited in classical Jewish law, or *halakhah*, but is no less "normative" in prescribing our engagement to attend to those who are vulnerable. Drawing on Talmudic precedent, Cohen speaks of citizenship in a city as a "privilege" which makes it incumbent upon us to attend to the various "others," particularly those whom we do not see. The "face of the other" need not be directly in front of us, and is always in relationship to us. And in the spirit of "silence" being "impossible" before the other, we should see ourselves not has helping from our position of privilege, but rather "serving" the other, whose needs necessarily come before our own.

In a personal illustration of his moral and philosophical sense of inescapable responsibility, Cohen draws a stark contrast between events in a single day of his life and the life of a man named Stanley Barger, who was jailed for being homeless. Cohen evokes a birthday celebration with his partner and friends at a local club. They walk back home, past apartments and single family homes:

> We entered the house, walking past the lawn, the trikes and toys and plastic furniture on our patio, paid the babysitter, checked on our kids, and went to sleep. . . . I was just back from an academic conference and thought I would get some grading done. The only thing on my calendar was a three o'clock meeting with a friend at Delice, a cafe on Pico.
>
> Nine miles away, in downtown Los Angeles, life was very different for Stanley Barger. Stanley Barger suffered a brain injury in a car accident in 1998 and subsequently lost his Social Security Disability Insurance. His total monthly income consisted of food stamps and $221 in welfare payments. On the night of the twenty-third of December, Barger, who could rarely afford a place even in a single-room occupancy hotel, bedded down on the sidewalk on the corner of East Sixth Street and Towne Avenue. At 5:00 a.m., December 24, Los Angeles Police Department officers roused Barger from sleep and arrested him. . . . As I woke up on the morning of the twenty-fourth to the sounds of a raucously peaceful household, Stanley Barger was jailed—perhaps the first time that the county had provided him with shelter.

The coincidence in time of these two events provokes me to ask about my connection with Stanley Barger.[10]

Toward the Other: Urgency Without Ego

Reflecting on these ideas in the early days of a Trump presidency, I see around me a new kind of urgency to act on behalf of the "other" who is threatened with violence, dehumanization, and silence. And remarkably, I see many people who have never spoken out before attending rallies and demonstrations and expressing themselves publicly about justice for people of color, Muslims, refugees, and undocumented immigrants. In this new context of concern and activism, I had the privilege of participating in an act of civil disobedience that evoked a new experience of myself in relationship to other people and my deepest spiritual core.

As part of a demonstration of 200 rabbis in New York City protesting the presidential executive order barring refugees and immigrants from seven predominantly Muslim countries, I was asked to be part of a smaller group of twenty rabbis who would risk arrest. The organization, *T'ruah*: The Rabbinic Call to Human Rights, wanted to seize the moment and make a visible statement to a Jewish community that in some powerful corners was turning a blind eye to this odious travel ban. After speaking with Rabbi Jill Jacobs, the visionary director of *T'ruah*, I believed in the rationale for this act of civil disobedience, but I was still hesitant. The prospect of being part of an action like this easily conjures up an image of myself as a hero or as a martyr, both of which are enormously self-aggrandizing, and neither of which I wanted in my head.

The next day was Shabbat, and as part of introducing the Torah reading in synagogue, I shared my ambivalent feelings: this travel ban was shameful and struck at the core of what it means to be a Jew, and yet, was I fit for the task? As I went the synagogue around with the Torah, people there said encouraging things like, "I'll pay your bail money," "We've got your back," or "See you in jail." I knew then that I had to do this, precisely because doing so wasn't at all about me, but about the collective moral aspirations of our community, our shared collective history, and a reflexive yearning to prevent others from suffering in ways our ancestors could have, might have or actually did.

I spent the next week thinking about and preparing myself for the action. I met with a friend of mine, a local minister who trains people to do

10. Cohen, *Justice in the City*, 66–67.

civil disobedience and had been arrested herself dozens of times. She gave the "extremely watered-down" version of her training, which included all sorts of practical advice, but most importantly, the charge to "be a conduit, make your behavior consistent, and be a friend to everybody." I took this piece of advice quite seriously, as I had done a lot of reading about non-violent protest of African Americans in the civil rights era, and how the extraordinarily brave men and women who sat at lunch counters, or rode the "white" sections of buses or registered to vote were trained in carrying themselves in a spirit of love. By comparison, what I was about to engage in was an almost risk-free situation, what one of my sons called "an inconvenient day" rather than a real arrest. But still, I wanted to approach this moment in the appropriate frame of mind.

The evening of the action, we all prepared for this moment of risking arrest by the New York City Police. One of our group, Rabbi Sharon Kleinbaum, was a veteran of civil disobedience protests over decades. She emphasized to us the Ghandhian principles at stake here. Our intention was to have no enemies. The police were our friends, and they were there to do their jobs, jobs for which they are most likely overworked and underpaid. We were advised to avoid distractions and treat the officers respectfully. Sharon urged us to see this moment as a spiritual moment, joining with other people in a holy act. As we went around the group, some people were afraid, some people were moved. I passed on the advice of a local attorney I consulted: if you're carrying weed or any other illegal drugs, get rid of them.

The procession down to the site where we were going to risk arrest was quite exciting, though I repeated my mantra of "being nothingness," to focus on the work I had to do. We were 200 rabbis walking down Broadway with protest signs, singing songs to the accompaniment of drums and tambourines and the help of megaphones. We had a police escort and occasionally stopped traffic. Local passersby gave us the thumbs up and cheered while some joined us. People working in local shops and restaurants danced and cheered us on. And while I normally sing as loudly as I can, tonight I was subdued, focusing instead on the people who encouraged me to be here, my Muslim friends with whom I have had the privilege to collaborate, and all the people I didn't know at the airport protest a week earlier who spoke of their families' journeys to this country, and their revulsion toward this travel ban.

By the time we reached the site where we were to risk arrest, I felt like I had a job to do, and that's all I was focused on. My rabbinic colleagues who did not risk arrest cheered us as they moved to the opposite side of an iron barricade. I reminded myself that without them, there would be no action. Each person here had a vital role to play. I observed the street, the time, and the presence of about twenty police officers and a few squad cars. I focused on Jill, waiting for her to tell us what to do. After a brief huddle, she said, "OK, let's walk," and we walked into the middle of Central Park West, and as the others sat down, I sat down. We began to sing, and at that point I noticed I was short of breath. "Interesting," I thought, as I chose not to get caught up in the spectacle of the moment. Instead, I felt the presence of those around me and sang. After a minute, we heard "Please disperse, you are about to be arrested," but by concentrating on the moment and what I was supposed to do, the message left no impression on me. After a few minutes more, the police broadcast, "You are now under arrest." As the police came to arrest us, I and others around me stood up calmly and let them cuff our wrists behind our backs. I heard myself saying "yes sir/ma'am," and "thank you, officer," and found the officers to be very businesslike and professional. It was all very humdrum.

The whole series of events became surreal only after we were released. In truth, aside from an hour and half in handcuffs, the whole experience was actually quite moving. On the bus, we followed our friend Sharon's lead and shared Torah insights and chanted songs. Once in cells at the police station, we talked more about Jewish issues, our rabbinic lives, and sang some more. At one point, we had an almost hour-long debate on Jewish law and intermarriage.

At 1:30 in the morning, after we were released, I called Judy. "There's a picture in the *New York Times*," she said. It turns out that media had posted the story within just a couple of hours after we were arrested and it went viral. Muslim friends congratulated me and shared it. Friends I had growing up who never did anything political sent me messages of congratulations. People whom I hadn't thought paid much attention to me were now telling their friends about me, how proud they were of "their" rabbi. This was all a complete surprise to me. With the preparation I had done, I didn't even think of how individual people would respond. I simply felt that they were there with me.

The next day was the final day of the conference, and some of the people who were arrested with me came back. But for people who were all of a sudden front-page news in the Jewish world, we were doing remarkably pedestrian things. One friend had meetings with lay leaders to plan programs. Another had to teach a class. Another had to meet a boy who was becoming bar mitzvah. The whole experience was a kind of mini revelation. In my own eyes, I had done so little: I had shown up because I was asked and because my community wanted me to. But by doing that, I understood, mostly from other people's reactions, that showing up to make a statement moved people. A local news reporter cried on the phone as I told her the simple details of the action. I felt like I was living as a Jew—doing something because I had to, without real regard for what it demanded of me. In fact, just the opposite—I felt an enormous sense of privilege that I was called to act, and that I could in this moment. The embrace I felt was the embrace of humanity at its most transcendent when we join together in a common moral aspiration.

I hesitate to cast anything I experience as any kind of ideal, but this experience was one that shares attributes with the moral vision of Levinas. While we were all rabbis, we were not invoking the power of God. Rather, we were promoting the realistic hope that we, against the evidence of human history, are capable of attuning each other to our common humanity. Like Levinas, we acknowledged a world broken by human dehumanization and cynicism. But just as we create those gulfs, so may we be able to find our bridge over them again.

I leave it to my colleagues to express whether they felt or drew on a feeling of closeness to God, or the *Shekhinah*, the presence of God in humanity's suffering. But I would say that the feeling of God's closeness is not in and of itself a prerequisite toward just action, and was not an essential part of this action. Perhaps it may have been a by-product of striving for a sense of "nothingness," or being a conduit for love and justice. Reflecting on the experience, I certainly felt something I had never felt before and I treasure that experience. Maybe I felt a sense of closeness to something transcendent I would call God, maybe not.

But in general, I believe that a sense of spiritual distance may be instructive, for it engenders our need for and awareness of the other, who is and should be the object of our greatest moral aspirations. The repair we do in this world is made possible by the very distance we seek to redress, whether that distance is between ourselves and God, or between ourselves and other people. Through the "Other," one is always reaching toward the ultimate, toward God, and in doing so one reconciles to the withdrawal of God by overcoming it through the world as it exists.

Re-engaging My Father as the Other

Inevitably, Rabbi Dorff and I talked about my life and my father's absence. He offered no advice or prescription for what should happen, only the sympathetic acknowledgment that I had unfinished business and his affirmation of who I had become without my father. I also knew internally that as much as I appreciated my newfound closeness with Rabbi Dorff, the real work I needed to do was to come to a new understanding about my father and the role he would play in my life, or not. Drawing on my inherent curiosity as well as this new sense of obligation, if only to myself, I resolved to call my father once a month. I did this without any real expectation that our conversations would yield fruit, or any feeling that I was somehow the one responsible for the estrangement between us. In fact, I wasn't even sure that I really wanted a closer relationship with my father. I had initiated all our previous meetings, and while our dinners were always filled with pleasant conversation, I never heard from him afterwards—never a phone call or a letter. In my life, there was nothing lacking. Judy and I were newly married, my studies were fully engaging, and we took great joy and companionship in a robust and lively community in which I found lifelong friends. If anything, there wasn't room for another project, let alone another complicated relationship. Nevertheless, I felt it was something I should do, if only just to see what would happen.

Initially, nothing dramatic took place in our conversations. That wasn't our way. But then I realized that my half-brother Max, whom my father had emphasized when he was born that he was my brother and not just a "half," was now in college. I thought back to when I had been eighteen and a first year student in college and how I saw myself: independent, exploring, defining my own identity. I didn't really have any expectation that my father would draw close to me, or any desire to really draw close to him. But developing a bond with Max seemed like it could be a *tikkun*, a happy restoration of what was lost. I imagined that, were he to receive a letter or a phone call from me, Max would respond as I saw myself at eighteen: open, eager to make a new connection and embrace a new identity as a brother.

My father saw it differently. After several months of talking, I asked my father what he thought of facilitating a meeting with Max. He responded, "Lauren and I have concerns. Your record of reaching out to us over the years has been checkered, off and on. And we don't want to put Max in a position where he could get hurt."

I was not stunned, even though I had every reason to be. When I told my story to Judy and friends at the time, they all reacted with shock that my father would place the burden of our relationship on me. But as with my confronting my father almost ten years earlier when I asked him why he retreated from my life, his words merely confirmed what I had always felt. I can't say there were specific words I expected, but the baldness with which he stated our disconnect ("your contact with us has been checkered") simply confirmed reality. And yet, I did feel that same surge of adrenaline I felt when I was sixteen, born of that same fight-or-flight response. Then, I was carrying the old fear of losing him with the new and surprising one of losing my recently garnered strength if I failed to challenge him. Now something more was fueling the immediate adrenaline rush: a sense of absurdity, anger over our profound brokenness, and the personal injustice of being denied the right to be united with my half brother.

Without much of a pause, I shot back forcefully, "I have nothing to prove." I would have said more, but my father interrupted me, cut me off with a kind of defensive, wordless sputtering on the line. I'm sure he said something, but I don't remember what it was. The die was cast: he expressed his view, designed to foster the distance between us, despite my attempts to draw closer. I held my ground, knowing that there was no one on the other side to hear it. Over the next few months, we would continue to call to each other across the gulf in the form of polite conversations and updates. But I knew that, most probably, our ongoing distance was assured.

Adam's Prayer—*Tikkun* in Our Hands

A crucial aspect of healing, or *tikkun*, is that it occurs amid experiences of isolation, in which we are bereft of the resources we should ideally have. Levinas asserts the moral grandeur of humanity when the history of his century points in the opposite direction. And yet, in embracing this paradox of *tikkun*, we are not that far from the spirit of Rabbi Hayyim Vital, who in the name of his teacher Rabbi Isaac Luria in the sixteenth century, expresses *tikkun* as a vision of restoration in which all rests on the work of our fragile hands, far removed from the source of creation.

Vital explores the extent to which ordinary human beings are responsible for the repair of the world through an unconventional take on the story of Adam in the opening chapters of Genesis. Contemporary readers spend a lot of time trying to figure out who corrupted the Garden of Eden—was it Eve, who took the first bite of the forbidden fruit? The snake, who tricked her? Adam, who heard the warning from God but kept Eve in the dark? Or is God to blame for setting humanity up for the fall? Vital reads the story completely differently in that none of the principal characters are to blame. Instead, the narrative of creation, its idyllic state, and then its fall allude to the dynamic inner life of God.

Adam, the first human being, did not so much fail at his task, but rather played his part in the ebb and flow of divine energy, helping to stabilize the flow of God's primordial emanation.

> Adam, the first human being, came and restored (*tikken*) the worlds by means of his prayer, by the secret of "to work and

protect." See, before Adam, the first human being, there were
the six days of creation by means of the secret of the thirty-nine
labors.... And then there was Shabbat, and therefore the thirty-
nine labors were forbidden.[11]

In its own language, the text speaks of the evolution of God's emanation from being everything to existing alongside the created universe. According to Kabbalah, the created universe came into being as four different
"worlds," and the last one, the world of "creation," by means of Adam, the
first human being. Even without extensive knowledge of the dense symbolism of this brand of Kabbalah, we see that the world of "creation" has its own
quirks: time, labors, things that are permitted and forbidden. As is known
from Genesis, Adam and Eve are given the charge to "work and protect" the
Garden of Eden. Except here, we see that the charge to "work and protect"
the Garden means something else. Instead of literal farming and steward-
ship, Adam is envisioned as praying, and that prayer is a kind of tool by
which to organize and stabilize this new aspect of God's being. Although
it seems to have a supernatural function, Adam's prayer is something that
arises wholly out of his own humanity.

Even though Adam's prayer is something that comes from him and
not from God, it is a potent source of strength to respond to our disorderly
universe. As the sage Elisha Ben Abuyah noted, our world is one of powerful
contradictory forces and we see some of them here: labor and the cessation
of labor, a lower world and an upper world, things that are permitted (at
certain times) and things that are forbidden (at other times). But Adam's
"prayer," his act of "*tikkun*," sets the world on its equilibrium. Vital imagines
that at the moment of this new manifestation of creation,

> ... the judgments descended downward. ... The First Cause
> (God) saw that the shells and the judgments could grow stron-
> ger in their descent and become harsh judgments individually
> in the lower world ... and so Adam, the first human being, came
> and restored (*tikken*) his actions, and by means of this restora-
> tion—fencing in the vineyard, cutting the thorns, and thereby
> cutting away all of the husks from there—restoring them to
> their original place.[12]

For Vital, God's blessing to Adam to "guard and protect" the Garden
of Eden is a metaphor not only for Adam's spiritual labor, but also for our

11. Vital, *Etz Chayim*, 7:7.
12. Ibid.

ongoing pursuit of *tikkun*. Adam's prayer and his actions were not enough to heal all the worlds, but it was the ideal tool with which to repair this one:

> Adam was able to restore only the upper worlds, but this world of creation, which is all husks, he was unable to restore . . . and so this world remained . . . where there are many husks, and great waste on account of food; attachment to external forms . . . and so when Adam, the first human being came, he only was able to restore the emanated worlds above, but the created world remained . . . .[13]

Note that last qualification, that the prayer of Adam could only restore "the emanated worlds above." Adam could do much, but he could not do everything. According to Vital, there were different levels of creation from the most sublime to the most material, and Adam's prayer could only restore balance to that of which were above him. From where, then, would the restoration of this world come? Could we, who have none of the intimacy with God that Adam did, bring about restoration in this world, where Adam could not? For Vital, this is precisely what we can and are supposed to do. In Vital's words on this section, the *tikkun* of our world "is accomplished by our prayers and our actions according to the moment."

Tikkun—whether we understand it as social justice, personal healing, cosmic wholeness, or simply a better relationship—is within our power, and because it is within our power, it naturally becomes our responsibility and our obligation. Both Levinas and here Vital seem to provide us with a vision for living that is at once filled with immediate and ultimate purpose and yet devoid of any expectation that God will be there to help us. And while such a seeming absence of divine presence might leave spiritually inclined people feeling bereft, *tikkun* sees God's apparent absence as an opportunity. Where God cannot act or exist, we human beings are provided the gifts with which we can step into the breach. God may be ever-present—for Levinas in moments of ethical encounter with the "other," and for Vital embedded in the husks of all creation—but God does not reveal Godself unless we take the steps that are in our capacity to take through acts of love, justice, and inwardness. If God can be driven from the world by human hands, we can also restore God's attributes of kindness, love, justice, and generosity to the day-to-day life of the world.

13. Ibid.

Elisha—*Tikkun* by His Own Hands

In this vein, the character of Elisha stands as a powerful example of finding healing amid the brokenness of the day-to-day world by attending to
the pain of others. In the first of the healing narratives after he becomes
a prophet, Elisha miraculously rescues a woman from dire poverty. The
woman, married to a man who was part of the prophetic circle, has fallen
behind in paying her creditors, and so appeals to Elisha as the creditors are
threatening to come and take her children to work as bonded servants. This
story is found in 2 Kings 4:

> (1) A woman, the wife of one of the disciples of the prophets,
> cried out to Elisha, "Your servant, my husband has died. You
> know how your servant was one who feared God. But now the
> creditor is coming to take away my two sons as bonded ser-
> vants!" (2) Elisha said to her, "What shall I do for you?" Tell me,
> what do you have in your house?" She said, "Your servant has
> nothing at all in the house, except for only one jug of oil." (3) He
> said, "Go, borrow vessels from outside from all of your neigh-
> bors—empty vessels, and do not scrimp. (4) Then go in and shut
> the door behind you and behind your sons, and then you shall
> pour oil into all of those vessels, removing each when it is full."

Although a prophet with the ability to effect miracles, Elisha's response
to the woman is very much grounded in the real world, in his simple and human response to her predicament. After the woman draws Elisha's attention
and explains her plight, Elisha asks, "What can I do for you?" The phrase,
as it appears both in Hebrew and English, carries two meanings simultaneously. "What can I do for you?" as in, "I too am a prophet, penniless, with
no access to wealth. I can't help you." But there is another sense, embedded
in the Hebrew especially, of "What shall I do for you?" as if to say, "Although
I am penniless and have nothing to give, there must be something that I
can do." From reading the verse itself, it's hard to know which wins out:
confidence that any human being can do something, or simple resignation
that something has to be done, even if the path is not clear or even seemingly impossible. Indeed, the expectation that all the oil she could ever need
will flow from this one jug seems absurd, and that is the point. Elisha will
effect a miracle, but one that arises from the circumstances of the real world,
transforming the woman's pain into abundance.

> (5) She left him and closed the door behind her and behind her
> sons. They continued to bring vessels to her and she continued
> to pour oil. (6) As the vessels were full she said to her son, "Bring

me another vessel," and he said, "There are no more vessels."
And the oil ceased. (7) She came and told the man of God and
he said, "Go, sell the oil and pay your creditor, and you and your
sons shall live on the rest."

Of course, this story may appear preposterous and out of reach for us
because it rests on a miracle. But the story of Hanukkah rests on a similar
tale of one small canister of oil becoming miraculously abundant, and the
holiday has become among the most widely observed. In the Elisha story,
as in the Hanukkah story, an absurd miracle is the culmination of human
beings imagining the improbable within the realm of what can actually be
achieved. In the case of this destitute woman, it appeared that Elisha could
do nothing for her, for she had convinced herself that she had nothing. But,
in fact, she had something, no matter how meager, and that recognition
prompted Elisha to think of the grand possibilities that could come about
when people bond empathically toward a common and righteous goal, in
this case the fending off of merciless creditors.

Even the ultimate outcome of this story points us back to the trans-
formative possibilities of *tikkun* in the world that we have. As a miracle
worker, Elisha could have given the woman and endless supply of oil or
some other form of wealth. But the oil stops, and the solution is to sell it
off, work through the real world, to hold off the creditors. Ultimately, God's
intervention may have been announced through a miracle, but only because
human beings found ways to be present for each other: Elisha responding to
the woman, the woman taking stock of her own resources, the woman, her
family, and her neighbors all cooperating to amass what was needed. The
haunting question of this story is not whether God is real—that is almost
irrelevant. Instead, we have to ask ourselves about all those who are vulnerable and go ignored. Do we create societal conditions that facilitate poverty
or end it, and what small (or large) part do we play the perpetuation of
oppression or in helping to bring about its end?

Tikkun and Human Agency: Talmudic Thinking

These kinds of day-to-day interactions, in which God seems absent but
becomes manifest through moral action, form the core of the Talmudic
imagination. Perhaps more than any way of thinking, the Talmudic genre
is most unique to Jewish tradition. It is a dialectical way of thinking: rever-
ential yet skeptical, fanciful yet grounded, deferential to order yet allergic
to authoritarianism. In this dialectical mode, Jewish thought was able to
carve out a position vis-à-vis God in which God was real, yet distant, but

in that distance gave human beings space to imagine how reaching toward each other was itself an act of reaching toward the divine. To illustrate the point, here is both an instruction and its following story, warning us to keep in mind the "other" as we go about building our communities. The Talmud passage (*Baba Batra* 7b) begins with the teaching of the Mishnah, the first layer of the Talmud that received its final form at about 200 CE:

> We compel one to build a gate house and door for a courtyard. Rabban Shimon ben Gamliel says, "Not all courtyards require a gatehouse." We compel one to contribute toward building a wall and locking gates for a city. Rabban Shimon ben Gamliel says, "Not all cities require a wall."[14]

So far, we see that the rabbis of the Mishnah are concerned with making sure that everyone in a collective living space, be it a courtyard or a city, participates in contributing to the general welfare. But we also see shadows of ambivalence about the projects to which they apparently must contribute. While the majority of the rabbis believe that one who lives in a courtyard or city has an obligation to contribute to a gate, gatehouse, wall, etc., Rabban Shimon ben Gamliel, a towering sage who eventually became head of the Sanhedrin, does not believe every collective living space requires structures to protect its residents. Although he doesn't say so, we can infer that he knows that walls isolate us from those in need more than they protect us.

This is where the Gemara, compiling the traditions from the third to the sixth century CE commenting upon the Mishnah, picks up:

> Are we to say that a gatehouse is an advantageous thing? See, there was once a pious man who would regularly converse with Elijah the prophet. Then he build a gatehouse and Elijah no longer spoke to him.[15]

Although the Gemara does not tell us why Elijah the prophet stopped speaking with this admittedly pious man who nonetheless built a gatehouse, Rashi, the eleventh-century French commentator, supplies the gloss that has become the standard interpretation: "Elijah stopped speaking with the man because the gatehouse that he built became a barrier for the poor, who would yell for attention but their voices could not be heard."

14. Babylonian Talmud, Tractate *Bava Batra* 7b.
15. Ibid.

Tikkun and Human Agency: Our Contemplative Legacy

As much as *Tikkun* in this chapter is discussed conceptually and in the realm of action, it also very much has a contemplative element, even when our acts of *tikkun* are directed towards ameliorating concrete circumstances. In particular, I am moved by a teaching of a Hasidic teacher from the early eighteenth century, Kalonymus Kalman Epstein, who wrote a book called *Maʾor va-Shemesh*, the Moon and the Sun. It is a collection of thoughts on the Torah portion of the week, and to a unique degree, he is often concerned about the nexus between the inner life and the social/ethical realm.

One particular teaching stands out for me, in part because of its evocative context. Much of the Book of Exodus seems to me a mediation on the conditions of oppression. We are introduced to Pharaoh as the classic demagogue, one who identifies and then demonizes a foreign people living peacefully among the Egyptians. As the Passover *Haggadah* enumerates, Pharaoh becomes a master of humiliation and subjugation, devising ways of not only breaking the bodies of the Israelites but their souls.

As we read about Moses confronting Pharaoh and the growing loyalty between Moses and the Israelites, there is an implied existential question: how do we respond to the conditions of oppression? How do we conduct ourselves, now, as those conditions are still in our midst? And, just as our ancestors were initially so beaten down that they were unable to heed Moses' call to liberation, where do we begin to undo the ways in which we are subtly ground down to a state of inertia?

For Kalonymus, it is all summed up in how we see ourselves in relation to other people, and by implication, in relation to God. His starting point is actually a verse from Deuteronomy 5:5, in which Moses recounts his role of being an intermediary between God and the Israelites. It is a role that could either block access to God or facilitate it, and for Kalonymus, the verse alludes to a perennial choice we have in our attitude towards others at all times.

> "I (*Anochi*) stand between God and you . . . ." When one assumes for oneself a position of stature over others (*bar maʾalah*), one creates through this an obstructing veil. And this is the meaning of "I" (*Anochi*), as a sign of arrogance to say, "I (*Anochi*) am a person of stature and impressive qualities." Such a person is one who "stands between God and you," for in assuming this role he establishes an obstructing veil.[16]

---

16. Epstein, *Maʾor va-Shemesh, Parashat Bo.*

I imagine we are all familiar with this problem. It is easy to get caught up in our own ego, in the ways in which we feel that we are impressive people. We might even readily admit that our culture encourages us to find those unique and impressive qualities within ourselves so that we may acquire a bit of power we wouldn't otherwise have. But, says Kalonymus, such power is really an illusion, an "obstructing veil." Arrogance obfuscates the truth. His answer to this problem, however, is novel and deep.

> Rather, a person should understand the s/he is but nothingness
> (*efes v'ayin*), and it is only the Holy One who provides one with
> life force to do something great or small, for God constitutes all
> that exists (*m'haveh kol ha'havvayot*).[17]

As I have mentioned earlier, to see oneself as "nothingness" is not the same thing as seeing oneself as worthless. In fact, it is quite the opposite. If we follow Kalonymus' logic, it is clear that when we are able to inhabit that contemplative space of "nothingness," we are actually feeling ourselves to be one with all that is, the essential life force. And to feel that essential life force is to feel oneself to be part of the presence of God, who "constitutes all that exists."

To bring this insight back to its original context, Kalonymus is saying something quite radical: that to work against the oppression of the world is first to relinquish any power that one pretends to have over another. It is to go toward the other, and to see oneself simply as part of what the other is a part of.

In this way, we are all enacting the revelation of truth, the unification of all things in the life force of God. And it begins with an inner attitude that makes available all the space necessary for the "other."

17. Ibid.

Chapter 9

God as Ineffable

Rabbi Yitzchak said, "The Torah could have begun with the verse, 'This month shall be for you . . . ' (Exodus 12:1)," then why did God reveal to them the work of creation? Because the Israelites said (at Mount Sinai), 'We will do and we will listen . . . .' In this manner, our Sages of Blessed Memory said, 'Israel arose in the mind of God (before creation); . . . this primordial will was to insure that Israel would be righteous in every generation.' So God constricted, as it were, God's brilliance, in the manner of a father who conceals his intellect and speaks childish words for the sake of his small child. And in this manner, all of the traits of being childlike become manifest in the father, who loves to act with childlike playfulness so that the child will have delight, and the child's delight is a wonder for the father.

And so with God, the past and the future are the same from the divine perspective. And the Holy One delighted in the deeds of the righteous, and so contracted Godself. 'Contraction' is called 'Wisdom,' and 'Wisdom' springs from 'Nothingness,' for 'Wisdom is found in Nothingness' (Job 28:12). And the contraction is for Israel, as love was the impetus for this contraction . . . ."

—Rabbi Dov Baer of Mezritsch, *Maggid Devarav l'Ya'akov*, 1

This teaching, which is the beginning of the signature book by Rabbi Dov Baer of Mezritsch, encapsulates much of what I have tried to convey in my reflections here about longing and the eventual liberation of accepting the imperfections of this world. This teaching springs from a child's experience. From a child's perspective, she or he knows a father whose principal delight is to play together, and that the child's laughter is the parent's greatest joy. How blessed is the child who has this as her spiritual *beresheet*, her spiritual beginning. But as the child grows to maturity, and perhaps becomes a parent, she realizes that while the playfulness of her father is an act of great generosity and kindness, it is not the same thing as a full sharing of himself. For an adult consciousness is one that often must turn to things other than play, sometimes out of necessity and sometimes to pursue other pleasures. And so, the child who has become an adult realizes that her father's love entailed a "concealment" of at least part of his whole self, even as he was fully present in caring for his child.

The adult child who has come to understand the adult consciousness of a playful parent now experiences a new kind of longing. Possessed of a searching mind herself, the adult child wants to encounter the parent on an equal intellectual/emotional/spiritual plane, to know the parent as a full human being, not merely as a playful father or mother. Depending on the parent, such a meeting may be possible. But we can also imagine scenarios in which such meetings are often quite partial. The parent of the adult child may be gone. The adult child may have developed interests or passions that diverge from those of her parent. The parent may have grown in a direction quite different from the child, or perhaps the parent did not grow at all. And so, even if the parent to an adult child is present, even lovingly present, there may be a way in which both experience a kind of estrangement. For a child who has grown, the work of *tikkun* is to live with the presence and absence of one's parent simultaneously.

In the language of the above passage, the same is true of God. The search for an understanding of God, or the quest to encounter God's presence may or may not spring from one's relationship to one's parents. Reaching out to God may be a vicarious gesture in place of reaching out to a parent who is unreachable; it may also be patterned on early experiences in which parents were loving and available. Or, the inner feeling to reach toward something or someone may reside deep within us, perhaps shaped by our experiences of family but ultimately independent from them. But wherever this desire to encounter the most inward source of intimacy and most grand sense of transcendence comes from, it is sure to be met only partially. The sense of incompleteness in wanting to approach the presence of God is sure to produce longing, which fuels the ongoing questioning.

The impossibility of fully meeting God is presented to us as "*tzimtzum*," divine constriction, the true *Beresheet*, or beginning of everything. Of course, it is a great contradiction—in order for God to be fully Godself and become known and delight in God's creatures, God had to be hidden and concealed. The constriction is, ironically, the way in which God bridges the gulf between Godself and humanity, much in the same way a parent bridges the gulf with a child.

But as with forming a mature relationship with one's parent, so a full sense of spirituality requires much of us. To overcome God's withdrawal through *tzimtzum*, and the ensuing hiddenness and fragmentation of the Divine Presence, one must find a way to understand and experience both God's presence and absence. For Dov Baer, this entails finding one's way to experiencing the Divine "Nothingness." The idea may strike us as absurd, but as I have reflected throughout, it is a "Nothingness" that ultimately reveals dimensions of being we can eventually put into words. For Dov Baer, that "Nothingness" is characterized by wisdom and love. It was love that brought about God's withdrawal or constriction in the first place so as to draw close to humanity. And if we can allow ourselves to entertain and name those experiences of God's "Nothingness," perhaps we will absorb a sense of the "wisdom" that partakes of them, separate from our usual reactions to absence that evoke indifference or despair.

The "Nothingness," initially confounding or painful, reveals itself as a relief and a liberation, maybe even a revelation. Once we encounter this "Nothingness," the love and wisdom flow as a matter of course, by-products of reconciling our spiritual yearnings to the counterintuitive manifestation of God as both immediate and infinitely remote.

Ultimately, the depth of Nothing nourishes our longing for something.

God beyond Reason

Much of the thinking in this book has been rational. Even though I freely admit that much of Jewish tradition says that God eludes understanding, I have tried to give expression to a variety of concepts that clarify rather than obscure. This is the exercise of the mind and heart, as limited and flawed as it is.

But in my experience, reason only gets us so far. The paradox offered by the above text may appear intellectually interesting and can occupy hours of thought and conversation, like a Zen koan. But its power does not come from its conceptual gymnastics. Rather, whatever truth it has derives from the degree to which is flows from human experience. And in the spiritual life, while there is much that needs to be processed and thought through, perhaps the most illuminating moments are those that defy our ability to think and understand.

For example, I am, perhaps to a fault, attracted to scientific or psychological explanations for the kinds of intense experiences that people will describe as "spiritual." I know a few things about religion and very little about brain chemistry, but I would be willing to bet that quirks in the flow of neurotransmitters account for much of what we see outwardly as ecstasy or religious passion. But, there are moments, probably many more than I am consciously aware, when I yearn to feel or experience the abiding presence of another—not another person specifically, but just another, the "Other," without any sense of boundary or limitation. Over time, I have come to understand that my yearning itself may be a confirmation that the "Other" whom I seek is really there. Perhaps this is what we might call "mystery."

After two years of rabbinical school when I was in my mid-twenties, I began to take my own minute steps toward thinking about this sense of mystery. For me, rabbinical school was an immersive experience in texts—in Talmud mostly, but also in the Bible and its commentaries, rabbinic stories, philosophy, modern Hebrew literature, and Jewish law—but with little time devoted to the ways in which these teachings change our views of the world, of God, or ourselves. At times, thoughtful teachers helped me see how the texts expressed overarching values and aspirations, things that can be conceptualized outside of the murkiness of one's inner life. But as I arrived in Israel for a year of study, I realized that my religious life drew its real strength from inchoate desires and yearnings that had little to do with reason. It struck me as ironic and also limiting that, while the whole reality of God ultimately challenged and even defied reason, my studies prized the predictable workings of the mind above all else. It wasn't so much that I was rebelling against my program, but I began to recognize that I needed to engage with sources and conversations whose ultimate goal was to present me with unanswerable questions.

Soon after getting settled in Jerusalem, I became friends with Jonah, a rabbinical student in my program from New York. Jonah and I clicked, and I saw in him a version of myself, but a few more years down the path. Whereas I had studied with Professor Ginsburg, Jonah had become close to Professor Ginsburg's teacher. This was my first time studying for a year in Israel; Jonah had done the same thing twice before. When I brought up my interest in Scholem and scholarship around Jewish mysticism, Jonah could talk about the scholars who criticized Scholem and why and put it all into context. My Hebrew was good; Jonah spoke Hebrew with an ease that seemed lyrical.

When I shared my thoughts with Jonah about wanting to study something that transcended the rationality that dominated our program, I suggested we meet to study the Zohar, the thirteenth-century text from Spain that is the foundation of Kabbalah, Jewish mysticism. Jonah had done some study of the Zohar, but felt that we would be rewarded more if we looked at some of the classic Hasidic teachers, mostly from the eighteenth and nineteenth century. These great thinkers often latched onto the core of mystical teachings, but then often wove them into the spiritual and psychological dimensions of everyday life. Jonah suggested that we study the book *Kedushat Levi* by the great nineteenth-century master Levi Yitzchak of Berditchev.

I had been drawn to Jewish mysticism and the Hasidic masters since my college classes with Professor Ginsburg. But as I began my textual study in earnest in rabbinical school, I felt it necessary to gain familiarity with the classical teachings of the rabbis, mainly Talmud and Midrash, the stories that often respond to gaps in the Torah. One of my final classes in college was a seminar on the history and thought of Hasidism. Although the reasons for the rise of Hasidism are many and subject to vigorous debate, the classic opinion is that the movement arose to fill a need for an emotional and seeking approach to daily life and to Jewish ritual life. For the early Hasidic masters, such as the iconic Rabbi Israel Ba'al Shem Tov and his disciples, the dynamism of the God of the Zohar was not to be limited to the initiated, but made relevant to ordinary people. While the highest levels of spiritual consciousness were achieved by the most pious and dedicated teachers, every person could experience closeness to God through their daily life.

In the modern period, the great philosopher Martin Buber emphasized certain qualities of the spiritual life of Hasidism as essential to a cultural revival of modern Judaism. At a time of great discovery for me, Buber's emphasis on the virtues of *hitlahavut*, passion, and *devekut*, closeness to God, rang true as personal spiritual aspirations. As I made my way through my first two years of rabbinical school, wrestling with basic rabbinic texts, I kept looking for the sense of spiritual immediacy that Professor Ginsburg showed me through the Hasidic masters. There is a popular rap on rabbinic texts that they are "rational," whereas Hasidic texts are "spiritual." I think this is an oversimplification. However, I would say that the classic Talmudic texts—whether *aggadah* (stories) or *halakhah* (law)—tend to speak to the mind before the heart. Hasidic texts, while intellectually demanding, address our deepest senses of belonging and healing much more directly.

The World of Levi Yitzchak of Berditchev

A distinctive feature of studying Hasidic texts is that each author not only has his own style and method, but his own spiritual world. Books by these individual masters are not just collections of different ideas, but ways of living and thinking in which the reader becomes absorbed for a time to gain a glimpse into a unique and rarefied way of living.

Levi Yitzchak of Berditchev was one of these truly towering Hasidic masters. Born in 1740 in Galicia, in Poland, he was married at seventeen, already with a reputation as a brilliant young scholar. Near the home of his father-in-law was Rabbi Shmelke Horowitz (later to gain fame as Rebbe Shmelke of Nikolsberg), who was a disciple of Rabbi Dov Baer of Mesritsch, a disciple of the Ba'al Shem Tov, the father of Hasidim. The legend goes that Levi Yitzchak was drawn to the teachings of Reb Shmelke, but his father-in-law would not permit Levi Yitzchak to devote himself to learning with Reb Shmelke. Levi Yitzchak fasted in protest of his father-in-law's restriction, and eventually he was able to leave his home and immerse himself in the ways of this new movement. It appears that Levi Yitzchak had a natural sense of the ways of the spirit. It is said that Reb Shmelke referred to Levi Yitzchak as his "student" in the ways of *"nigleh,"* things that were revealed. But in matter of *"nistar,"* things that are hidden, Reb Shmelke was the student and Levi Yitzchak the teacher.

Levi Yitzchak's passion for the inner life and his protest against his father-in-law may have been a foreshadowing of his unique ability to level protests against God. Of all the great Hasidic masters, Levi Yitzchak was unique in his reputation for protesting to God against the suffering of humanity. Many of these stories are the products of oral tradition rather than being found explicitly in his great Torah commentary, Kedushat Levi. One typical story is of Levi Yitzchak crying out to God on Rosh Hashanah: "For many centuries, thousands and thousands of Jews have sounded a hundred blasts on the shofar each Rosh Hashanah for You, asking for just *one* from You for our freedom. Still, You have not sounded the Shofar!" These famous stories were given a grand voice by the great African American bass singer Paul Robeson in a song called Levi Isaac of Berditchev. Recalling the suffering of the Jews, he sings before God, "And I, Levi Yitchak, son of Sarah of Berditchev, say,/From my stand I will not waver,/And from my place I shall not move/Until there be an end to all this . . . ." The song reaches its climax as Robeson booms the opening words of the Mourner's Kaddish ("*Yisgadal, v'Yiskadash, shmei rabbah!*) like thunder.

Studying the Inner Life

Jonah and I began to meet each week to study the great Levi Yitzchak of Berditchev, focusing on a small selection from his commentary on the Torah portion of the week. Studying together meant primarily reading and translating the text and trying to figure out what exactly Levi Yitzchak was saying as we sorted out the language of the text, new terms and concepts, and novel ways of thinking. From our study of rabbinic texts, we had come to expect how a teaching could take a verse, make a fanciful or wide-ranging inference from it, but always root it back in the logic of its grammar or its commonly understood range of meanings. But with Levi Yitzchak, every quotation from the Torah seemed to point to something else—beyond the text, beyond the story of the Torah, even beyond day-to-day life. Instead of focusing on the six days of creation, Levi Yitzchak turned his attention to the unfolding internal dynamic within God, and how that mirrors an unfolding spiritual dynamic within ourselves.

For example, Levi Yitzchak opens his book with the following reflection on the first words of the Torah:

> *Beresheet bara Elohim*—when God began to create the universe.
> . . . A principle: that the Creator, Blessed be God, created everything, for God is everything, and God's influence never ceases. For in every moment God showers the divine sustenance upon all of God's creation, in all the worlds, in all the palaces, among all the angels and heavenly beings . . . for all is from God, for God is complete, and God is comprised from everything. Therefore, when a human being arrives in a spiritual state of nothingness, and knows that one is insubstantial, God gives that person strength . . . .[1]

It was enough to spend an hour or so reading the text and trying to figure out what it meant. The few lines above, rendered in a facile translation, would have easily occupied a good forty-five minutes of study. On a deeper level, studying a text—its words, its concepts, its patterns of thought, its inner life—is a way to transform one's thinking and consciousness.

In the lines above, it's clear that Levi Yitzchak is not asking us merely to understand the meaning of the opening words of the Torah. Rather, he is engaging us in a fundamental reorientation about the nature of reality. "All" is God. We are completely insubstantial. And yet, through seeing and knowing the essence of our being ephemeral, we are "strengthened." That is to say, we feel ourselves to be part of everything, or actually part of the "all" which is God. In our supposed "nothingness," we are, in fact, part of everything, and everything is a part of us. But understanding even these new conceptual moves of the text, the way in which it holds up a very different mirror onto our existence, is itself only the first part of a first step. Ultimately, the object of this text is not merely to understand it, but to see oneself, the world, and

---

1. Levi Yitzchak of Berditchev, *Kedushat Levi*, *Beresheet*.

God differently because of it. Instead of "getting" the text, the text changes you.

As I looked at these new teachings with Jonah, I was certainly learning the new language of Levi Yitzchak and Hasidic thought. But our learning together brought about a change on a deeper level, one not even addressed explicitly by Levi Yitzchak's words. In the language of Jewish tradition, we had a *chevruta*, and with a *chevruta* it's impossible to separate the relationship with one's partner from the text itself. Ideally, your *chevruta* is both your teacher and your friend, with roles both hierarchical and reciprocal. To keep those roles alive in the process of study involves an unspoken agreement by both parties to inhabit these roles for each other. Being a *chevruta*, a teacher and a friend simultaneously, entails listening and asserting, pressing your point but adopting, if only for a moment, your partner's alternative or even polar opposite reading as your own. Studying in *chevruta* entails not only understanding your partner's unique interpretation of words on a page, but having a feeling and sympathy for his questions, obstacles, and yearnings.

At its deepest, *chevruta* is an exercise in empathy—not merely in the emotional sense of feeling what another person is experiencing, but of seeing through the eyes of the other. It is an affirmation of hope and connection over loneliness. Levinas said, "the ills that must heal inside the Soul without the help of the other are precisely the most profound ills."[2] *Chevruta* reminds one, on a deep unspoken level, that we are not alone in our longings or our spiritual seeking. The holistic sense of learning in *chevruta* extends beyond us, though, because in the collaboration, both partners reach through each other to the source of the teaching, and when there is a common sense of the sacredness of the text, then *chevruta* is a means to draw close to the divine presence. As the rabbis say in *Pirke Avot*, whenever two sit and study Torah, the *Shekhinah* (divine presence) resides with them. In a more contemporary vein, Levinas said about these moments with the "other," "To be before God would be equivalent then to this total mobilization of oneself."[3] Through study, and through study of these mystical texts, I was searching for this kind of total engagement in the spiritual and intellectual search. When I needed him, Jonah was a great *chevruta* and became a close friend.

2. Levinas, *Nine Talmudic Readings*, 17.
3. Ibid.

From Inner Life to Transcendent Life:
Abraham Joshua Heschel

When speaking of the inner life of longings, of wrestling with the callousness and absence of human beings, and ultimately of openness to wonder
and mystery, one must speak about Abraham Joshua Heschel. For someone
who has never read Heschel before, his writing may appear overly supernatural, personal, and pious, not to mention occasionally opaque. This was
my reaction when I first read Heschel in college with Professor Ginsburg.
It took another half dozen years of living and learning before I was able
to feel as if he was speaking to me. These years were a time of some of the
most important and triumphant events in my life such as marrying, beginning rabbinical school, and forging mature lifelong friendships, but they
were also years when I experienced the loss of my grandfather who raised
me, the fear of losing everything, and the adult realization that my father
would never be a meaningful part of my life. Heschel meditates copiously
on wonder, but I needed to struggle with the fruits of being and the fear of
nothingness before I could appreciate how hard won that wonder can be.

Heschel was born into a Hasidic family in Warsaw with an auspicious
lineage, though his own immediate family was of modest means. His father was himself a rabbi, living on community donations, and I imagine
his home was not unlike the scenes that Isaac Bashevis Singer recounts in
his memoir of Warsaw, *In My Father's Court*. Though cloistered, Heschel
was not completely sheltered. In fact, Warsaw was a cauldron of every sort
of Jewish expression: traditional, Hasidic, secularist, Yiddishist, and everything in between, with the Jews who inhabited all of these movements living
in close proximity to each other. In fact, as a young teenager Heschel was
counseled by a psychologist and Yiddish novelist, Fischel Schneerson, who
had a specialty in helping orthodox boys negotiate the pull between tradition and modernity.

Heschel was recognized as special within his own family and community, and so was given wide latitude to explore his diverse intellectual
and spiritual interests. Around the time he graduated from gymnasium, he
published a volume of Yiddish love poetry, studied for his BA at the University of Berlin and rabbinical ordination through the Reform *Hochschule*
in Breslau, and eventually toward his PhD. After the Nazis invaded Poland,
Hebrew Union College, the Reform rabbinical seminary, rescued Heschel
along with other Jewish scholars, and set him up with a teaching position
at their school in Cincinnati. He then moved over to the Jewish Theological Seminary in New York after a few years, in part to be closer to Hasidic

cousins who had also escaped and were living in Brooklyn, and he remained there until his death in 1972.

Driven perhaps by his internal struggles as well as his prodigious gifts, Heschel expanded his world beyond the Jewish Theological Seminary in the '50s and '60s. Most famously, he forged a friendship with Dr. Martin Luther King, with whom he shared not only a passion for activism, but also a love of the Hebrew prophets. Among Jews, the picture of Heschel marching with King on the road from Birmingham to Selma is part of the iconography of our moral aspirations. But even when King declined in popularity as he advocated for an end to the Vietnam war and economic inequality, Heschel remained loyal both to King and his goals as he strayed even further from the Jewish mainstream. Before the end of his life, Heschel appeared publicly with the draft resister and priest Daniel Berrigan upon his release from prison and campaigned for the new left Presidential long-shot George McGovern, much to the chagrin of his Seminary colleagues.

Among Jewish scholars and writers in the twentieth century, Heschel's literary legacy is arguably without peer in both output and scope. His published works, written originally in one of three languages, include a three-volume investigation of rabbinic thought (Hebrew), his own philosophy of Judaism (English), a meditation on hasidism and moral philosophy (Yiddish and English), and volumes of essays that continue to be fresh and relevant today. The experience of reading Heschel is akin to listening to a beautiful but dense piece of music: enveloping, unquestionably great and beautiful, difficult to parse into easily delineated chunks, and eventually too much. Heschel is also famously dialectical in his thinking. Even though readers are often at a loss to trace his arguments from point A to point B, there is never any doubt that all of his thoughts, wide ranging, elevated, and shot through with references to all periods of Jewish history, circle around a central point. Often, that central point is the conundrum of how we see only the most limited contours of what we experience day to day when, in fact, everyday reality constantly borders on the infinite.

Heschel in Broad Strokes

There appear to be at least three themes that animate Heschel's prodigious work and his singular achievements. His biographers relate how, upon moving to Cincinnati, Heschel was immediately disturbed by the racism he witnessed, offending his belief in the universal divinity inherent in all people, a conviction engendered by his knowledge of the Prophets and confirmed by the destruction of the Nazis. Although he found a refuge in America, Heschel was decidedly unimpressed with postwar American society. As the United States enjoyed prosperity and productivity unequaled in human history, Heschel saw the society as hollow and conformist, and willingly disengaged with what really mattered: care of the soul and the resulting obligation to attend to the voiceless. Finally, Heschel found himself at the center of the effort to infuse an animating spirit into what he saw as a spiritually moribund Jewish world. American Jewish society reflected the "dull and insipid" American culture, and Heschel saw himself as restoring a measure of depth and meaning to a Jewish world that had lost so much in the Holocaust, but that also appeared willing to give up the rest to assimilation.

Heschel is eminently quotable, and it's easy to get lost in the beauty of his language and forget how his ideas challenge us to experience the world in a way radically different than what we have become accustomed to. There was, Heschel believed, a category of experience called the "sublime." The "sublime" exists perpetually, but locked within the walls of an apathetic society beaten down by political oppression and self-satisfaction, we fail to see it. Our ability to see greater forces at work in our everyday lives is a path toward the "sublime" experience, but it is only a path. More accurately, to encounter the sublime is to face an existential conundrum: we glimpse something, beyond and much bigger than ourselves, that encompasses all, but we do so as we are grounded within the contours of our lives and our understanding, which are always limited. For Heschel, an encounter with the "sublime" takes us both beyond and through the everyday, leaving us with a sense of wonder and mystery that constitute the "grand premise" of religious life, better expressed as a series of questions than as declarative statements.

> How does one find the way to an awareness of God through the beholding the world here and now? To understand the Biblical answer, we must try to ascertain what the world means and to comprehend the categories in which the Bible sees the world: the sublime, wonder, mystery, awe, and glory.[4]

Heschel's "philosophy" is really a challenge to live each day by seeking out "wonder, mystery, awe, and glory." Again, this is not a simple prescription, but rather, an invitation to another series of existential questions.

> *Lift up your eyes and see* (Isaiah 40:26). How does a man lift up his eyes to see a little higher than himself? . . . How does one rise

---

4. Heschel, *God in Search of Man*, 33.

above the horizon of the mind? How does one free oneself from the perspectives of ego, group, earth, and age? How does one find a way in this world that would lead to an awareness of Him who is beyond this world?[5]

To partially answer these questions, Heschel defined the ideal frame of mind as one he called "radical amazement." Heschel took the "radical" part seriously. It wasn't just that he was advocating that we experience what we already find to be "amazing" with greater intensity. Rather, we need to face how we have habituated ourselves to see the world in the most pedestrian way, and then we need to break with those habits of mind and soul in order to be open to a sense of surprise. Here is a classic statement of Heschel,

> The greatest hindrance to knowledge is our adjustment to conventional notions, to mental cliches. Wonder or radical amazement, the state of maladjustment to words and notions, is, therefore, a prerequisite for an authentic awareness of that which is.[6]

In ironically, and perhaps humorously, praising a state of "maladjustment," we can hear Heschel's revulsion for the world of 1950s American conformity. But Heschel was also challenging a universal habit of mind through which we harmonize our experiences so as to make them orderly, when in fact we will learn much more by seeing things as they are, in all their contradiction and messiness.

> Standing eye to eye with being as being, we realize that we are able to look at the world with two faculties—with reason and with wonder. Through the first we try to explain or to adapt the world to our concepts, through the second we seek to adapt our minds to the world.[7]

To avoid getting lost in Heschel's rhapsody of language, we should take a moment to pay attention to what he is saying about how we experience the world. When Heschel proposes that we approach the world with "wonder," I imagine most of us think, "of course." Wonder seems like such a benevolent attitude; it connotes the innocence of a small child beholding something in nature for the first time, and we all want to live with that sense of freshness and curiosity. But actually, wonder for Heschel is the province of a mature soul. It takes the fortitude of one who is able to set aside his or her

5. Ibid.
6. Heschel, *Man Is Not Alone*, 11.
7. Ibid.

assumptions about how the world works and how things should be. Wonder entails busting cliches and de-mythologizing. Wonder means holding no illusions—about anything—as we "adapt our minds to the world."

Heschel writes about how jettisoning our learned assumptions takes us beyond things, beyond our minds, and to the surprise of pure being.

> Inquire of your soul what does it know, what does it take for granted. It will tell you only no-thing is taken for granted; each thing is a surprise, *being is unbelievable*. We are amazed at seeing anything at all; amazed not only at particular values and things but *at the unexpectedness of being as such*, at the fact that there is being at all.[8]

The Ineffable

Heschel devised a term for this special knowledge that comes from a posture of radical amazement, wonder, and pure being that gives the lie to our conventions of mind and heart. It is not even knowledge in the conventional sense, but rather an experience of the "ineffable," a mystery at the core Jewish tradition and the universal striving for God. "Holiness" may be a more familiar and usable term, but "ineffable" conveys Heschel's conviction that true spirituality does not consist of any certainty, but rather the willingness to face ongoing questions.

Perhaps most simply, God being "ineffable" means that God is present and absent at the same time, at once fully present but hidden in everything:

> The ineffable inhabits the magnificent and the common, the grandiose and the tiny facts of reality alike. Some people sense this quality at distant intervals in extraordinary events; others sense it in the ordinary events, in every gold, in every nook; day after day, hour after hour. To them things are bereft of triteness; to them being does not mate with non-sense. They hear the stillness that crowds the world in spite of our noise, in spite of our greed. Slight and simple as things may be—a piece of paper, a morsel of bread, a word, a sigh—they hide and guard a never-ending secret: A glimpse of God? Kinship with the spirit of being? An eternal flash of a will?[9]

Notice here how Heschel doesn't rush to piety to convince us how, where and in what form we can discover God's presence. He resists naming

8. Ibid., 12.
9. Ibid., 5.

an experience definitively as a manifestation of God, or God's being at work through X, Y, or Z. But he is naming what I believe is a universal experience—the kind of everyday occurrence in which the conventional notions of language and understanding fail us. While being unquestionably devoted to the Jewish people and Jewish observance, maybe even the Jewish establishment, Heschel's goal is first to evoke for us the almost primal human experiences of awe and wonder, and then show us the language from within Jewish tradition that may serve as both translation and vehicle for return.

In fact, it seems that, more important than knowing and naming "what" we have discovered in moments of awe and openness is the radical awareness that there is always something more to experience and understand. For Heschel, "The ineffable . . . is a synonym for hidden meaning rather than for absence of meaning." Our goal, then, is to approach the world assuming that there is always something more to discover.

However, the veil should not be too thick. For Heschel, the experiences and insights that lead to an awareness of pure being, and of God, are not impossibly remote. While Heschel believes that our daily experiences are only "allusions" to a greater reality that we do not currently understand, that greater reality is not concealed forever.

> The answer to the ultimate question is not found in the notion that the foundations of the world lie amid impenetrable fog. Fog is no substitute for light, and the totally unknown God is not a god but a name for the cosmic darkness. The God whose presence in the world we sense is anonymous, mysterious. We may sense that He is, not what He is. What is His name, His will, His hope for me? How should I serve Him, how should I worship Him? The sense of wonder, awe, and mystery is necessary, but not sufficient to find the way from wonder to worship, from willingness to realization, from awe to action.[10]

Accepting the Ineffable

Having arrived at a time in my adulthood when I am better able to live with the composite of joy and pain in my life, I find that Heschel speaks to the ways I feel, seek, and yearn. Heschel speaks to the doubter and the skeptic in me by reminding me that the God of words and ideas is just a shadow, and cautions me against formulaic and hackneyed expressions of religion and spirituality. Heschel reflects the continually youthful and awakening part

10. Ibid.

of me who wants to rediscover grandeur and love for the first time. Heschel engages me as a mature and inquisitive adult who researches things, who ponders and explores them, but who realizes that conventional conclusions won't adequately capture what I have learned. As I see cherished myths and life-ordering narratives come undone, Heschel comforts me by reminding me that the mix of surprise and disappointment, awe and fear, freedom and regret that accompanies seeing things as they really are is a necessary part of learning and growing as a human being.

It is impossible for me to think of Heschel's idea of the ineffability of God without considering how it was that I finally I accepted that my father had abandoned me long ago, and that there was nothing I could do to restore the lost wholeness I would have had with him. The final confrontation with my father came after my year in Israel, when Judy and I returned to New York to continue my rabbinical studies. During my year in Israel I had stopped calling my father each month, and during that time, he didn't call me either. I had always planned that when I settled in New York, I would try to see him in person and try to jump-start some kind of relationship, hopefully one in which I would grow closer to his sons, my half brothers. It was a dream of a new and recovered wholeness, and I was more compelled by the dream than by my father himself. At the same time, Judy and I were envisioning our own wholeness as we anticipated the joy of raising children.

One evening, Judy and I met my father and Lauren, my father's wife, for dinner in Manhattan. I felt good, strong, proud of where I was in my life, grateful to have Judy with me in every way. It had been several years since I had seen my father, and nearly eighteen since I had seen Lauren. They looked older, but still had the same mannerisms and ways about them that I remembered from when I was a boy. I did have an agenda—to explore the possibility to seeing them more regularly, the main reason being to get to know my half brothers. I wasn't particularly nervous or afraid, but I wasn't particularly angry either. I was not intending to confront them or do battle, but rather I was looking forward to a reunion, a reconnection, and initiating a new conversation.

The evening was pleasant for a time, as both my father and Lauren were smart and skilled conversationalists. As when I was sixteen, it was almost disarming. Speaking so pleasantly about interesting topics with nice, engaged people was certainly more attractive than inviting a discussion about healing old wounds. But it was my role to raise the topic of a future that in many ways was conditioned by the past. However, I quickly discovered that whereas I was prepared to open a new chapter, my father and Lauren were not. I calmly but directly expressed my desire to see Max, and to develop my relationship with him and his younger brother. At this point, Lauren took up the reins of the conversation, and countered with reservations that my father expressed earlier. Lauren shared her concern that, since I hadn't followed through when I was a teenager and reached out inconsistently over the years, I would similarly maintain an on-again, off-again relationship with them and my half-brothers. I countered, as I had previously with my father, that I had nothing to prove, that it wasn't my role to keep the relationship going, and that I actually had called regularly without much of a response.

This thrust and parry continued between me and Lauren for some time. I was certainly agitated internally, but did everything I could to keep completely cool on the outside. Lauren's argument reached its peak when she said, "Justin, we don't want to have to deal with your anger." "I'm not angry," I replied, something that was both true and an impossibility. How could I not be angry? And yet, I kept the anger at bay, engaging with her calmly and with kindness. I don't believe I convinced Lauren or my father of anything, because they weren't there to be persuaded of anything. They came to the meal to reiterate their sacred myth that they had given me an open door that I refused to walk through, and now, too much had passed to change anything, to bring the healing that I was seeking. But perhaps I had made some headway, because Lauren's intensity subsided, and we were able to end the meal by agreeing to work on things slowly. We talked about meeting fairly regularly, where to meet, and that we would see how things worked out. I left feeling hopeful and eager to begin a connection with my father and Lauren as adults unburdened by the past, and to initiate a vibrant and reciprocal relationship with my half-brothers.

The feeling lasted less than twenty-four hours. As always, Judy helped me see the broader landscape. As we talked about setting a date on the calendar when we could meet with my father and Lauren again, Judy said, "I don't want to see these people," and I realized I felt the same way and always had. As opposed to the imagined wholeness I envisioned with my father, there were actual relationships all around us that needed our attention. For the first time in ten years, Judy and I were living close to family who were actually delighted to see us and friends with history and deep connections. Why go around chasing an illusion? The real *tikkun*, the real healing was already well on its way. As soon as Judy said that, I knew instantly that I was done trying to connect with my father. The next day, I saw Jonah, an even closer friend and confidante now. I told him of the dinner with my father and Lauren, the tentative agreement we reached, and the subsequent conversation I had with Judy when I realized that I was done. "How does it feel?" He asked. I told him, "I am free."

But that is not entirely true. I will always know that my father abandoned me, and that reality will always have its dark chasm of unanswered questions. I will always have to combat heightened fears of failure, of disappointing others, and feeling alone and isolated. I have no way of knowing if I experience these vulnerabilities more acutely than other people. But amid a life in which everything has gone right—family, health, career, personal satisfaction—I find myself perennially contending with a sense of foreboding, usually against a preponderance of evidence to the contrary. Perhaps many or most of us live similarly, but the only way I can understand these feelings is as a vestige of the fright a small child feels when the worst nightmare has come true: his father has left for no good reason.

I wish my father were now completely absent from my life so that I could fully move on. Instead, I have had to accept that he is ineffable, absent and yet present at the same time. I think about him from time to time, aware that he is aging and that my half-brothers are now men like me. I sometimes compare myself to where he was and what he was like at my age. I contemplate whether when he dies, assuming I learn the news, I will say Kaddish for him. I can imagine foregoing the opportunity because of irreparable distance, but then again, I ask myself if the occasion of his death will give me one last chance to achieve some kind of connection, forged in mourning rather than in life. These thoughts are a variation on what the great Rebbe Kalonymus Kalman Shapira envisioned about the inner spiritual yearning of each of us: that the yearning itself confirms that the One for whom we long is actually there.

And so I turn away from my father and toward Heschel's ineffable God. Though seemingly absent from the day-to-day needs and workings of my small little life, it is hard for me to deny the mystery of a "presence" in wait in every moment, whether I make the effort to sense it or not. In the realm of the past, I wish I had more. For the future, I am more than satisfied yearning for full wholeness, as I listen deeply in silences, seeking and wondering.

This, for me, is walking in the footsteps of the prophet Elisha. Losing, so as to regain by discovering how to call out and cry in hopeful longing. Stepping forward into the world, I face the paradox of being simultaneously alone and yet enveloped. And then, finally, as I live amid the seeming absence, I retain a faith in healing gestures, in *tikkun*, in ways of being that revive connection, justice, and maybe even life itself, against all conventional wisdom and evidence that such things are possible.

Epilogue

God as Everything and Nothing

My New Rabbis

A beautiful July day, surrounded by rabbis who are my colleagues, famous teachers, and rabbinic colleagues who are my teachers. I am alone at a retreat center in rural New York, away from Judy, our two small boys, a precious baby and beautiful toddler, away from my huge synagogue in DC where everyday I contend with constant demands, two senior colleagues, feelings of both superiority and inadequacy, a desire to move up and impatience to move on, confidence and great uncertainty. And so I need this time, part of an eighteen-month program, in which forty or so rabbis meet every six months to study, meditate, think, ponder, connect, and perhaps most of all, be silent. It's not total monastic silence, but Jewish silence—we speak when we pray and study, but for the most part don't speak to each other during meals or breaks. Some people will go off for a walk and a talk, and I have done that, but it's understood that in public space, quiet is the norm. The silence is what is truly amazing—revelatory and liberating. Everyday I spend so much time and energy vigorously engaging with people, trying to be funny, smart, and charming, without even knowing I'm working so hard. So to be around other people, not having to speak, to project, I experience myself just being. It's one thing to just be in solitude, but there is a danger too, for solitude can easily yield to loneliness. But to be silent with others is to be completely myself, with no need to create a facade through speech or gestures, and to feel enveloped in community, and at times, with God.

Our study is dominated by three towering Jewish scholars and teachers: Arthur Green, whose writings I have followed since I first encountered them as an undergrad; and Jonathan Omer-Man, an immensely knowledgeable and creative teacher whose teaching brings me refreshingly out of the mainstream. I am thrilled to listen to their insights and respond to their edgy and challenging questions.

But my real rebbe in this program (my desire for a rebbe in itself is proof that my longings are still alive) is a wise and endearing meditation teacher named Sylvia Boorstein who is becoming known in Jewish circles for her book, *That's Funny, You Don't Look Buddhist.* She is wise, witty, lovable, kind, and generous, and a captivating storyteller. Stories that sound simplistic or trite when I tell them arrive brilliant and profound from her. She is a New York Jewish lady, albeit by way of Northern California, in mannerisms but also in ritual practice. She attends *minyan* everyday, she warmly recalls her childhood shul scenes and the Ashkenazi inflection of her rabbi's Hebrew, she speaks lovingly of her husband, her children, and her grandchildren, but with none of the aggrandizing commentary so common today. Sylvia is also a therapist, and has spent the better part of twenty years studying and practicing what is known as insight meditation, or mindfulness.

Meditation for the Jews

For years, I had wanted to learn about and practice meditation, yearning for a kind of refuge in solitude, where I could sit alone, undisturbed, to get to know the contents of my mind, my mind itself, and through that, the ineffable spiritual reality that I have come to see as an integral part of my life. I wanted and expected this without any understanding about what meditation was about, without reading, or without really talking to anybody. But all the meditation teachers, centers, and seminars were Zen or Vipassana. Was there really a conflict in *halakhah*, Jewish law, that would preclude my going to a Zendo or Vipassana class to learn meditation? I didn't really think so—I would be going not for the "religious" aspect, not to seek out new beliefs, but rather for the techniques, the "how to" of sitting, focusing, concentrating.

Yet I never went, perhaps because underneath it all, I knew that my studies had carried me over a kind of threshold with its own distinct spiritual vocabulary. Not a rigid vocabulary—not that I would ever prohibit myself from learning from the world's religious traditions through their texts, teachers, or practitioners, in fact quite the opposite. I embraced the universality of all religious traditions, but I also deeply respected the specificity and difference of each tradition through the experience of studying my own. Zen meditation, Vipassana meditation, I felt, was meant for people who want to inhabit those traditions. I wasn't afraid that I would "become Buddhist" by being exposed to Zen or Vipassana, or that my Judaism would be diluted. It's that I didn't want to drink the wine half way, taking some things and leaving others. And so, when I learned about this program, it was Sylvia's presence that made me jump to it. Study meditation—not contrived Jewish meditation, but real meditation with a real meditation teacher, who will be teaching to the Jews.

Each day was a day of desserts. Study with Arthur Green and Jonathan Omer-Man was a feast for the mind, time to unwrap presents in the form of new and exciting texts from the Hasidic masters of the eighteenth and nineteenth century. Sylvia's meditation was another kind of dessert—a truffle that promised immediate and great pleasure to the mind, body, and eventually soul. It was gentle, without any kind of uneasy anticipation of what we would encounter or struggle over.

Sylvia's instructions were so simple. Of course, I can't remember them exactly after sixteen years, but they went something like this: "Sit comfortably—in a chair or on the floor, it doesn't matter. Sit in a way that you can be comfortably aware of your posture, of your body and of your breath. Closing your eyes will help you focus on the breath. Just breathe normally, and pay attention just to the breath. Other thoughts will arise—exciting thoughts, titillating thoughts, disturbing thoughts—that's fine. But instead of attaching to those thoughts, latching onto them, let them go. They are a tape. Let them go." And off we went into silence.

My mind was bliss. Focusing only on each breath, there was great beauty, peace, and serenity in just letting go and thinking about nothing. That nothingness was a true gift—luxurious, liberating, and healing. To sit in silence was to be cut off in a precious solitude and yet, at the same time, to be connected to everything. It felt like everything we had been talking about in our study sessions: holiness and closeness to God, the nexus between our individual and fragile breath and the *neshama*, the breath/soul of the universe.

The bliss lasted all of about thirty seconds, because as soon as it arrived, other thoughts began to intrude. All the troubles that I had escaped in this beautiful retreat came right back. I loved being a rabbi but I couldn't stand being with some of the people I had to work with everyday. I wanted to be a teacher to people who would listen and reflect, and I was exiled to work primarily with children and disinterested parents. My senior colleagues seemed to act as if I didn't exist, or that my contributions didn't matter. But if I can be patient and compassionate, perhaps I can learn something from them and grow myself, even if I feel like the things they do and say box me into a corner, limit what I can do, and diminish me. My kindness to them is really a kindness to myself—the anger I feel on a daily basis will destroy me if I don't figure out another way. I wanted to be someplace else, but Judy and I liked our new friends, our network of families, and activities to engage our kids. Not all was going as planned with our son's development. He was all over the place, brilliant in some ways, behind in others, we're taking all the thoughtful steps we should for him, grandparents hovering over us with concern, teachers saying all the nice and right things, but under a pretty thick layer of eggshells. I believe he will be fine, I am frightened that he will be isolated, alone, incompetent. I am mourning not being as present a father as I was when I was a student. I am often away from home from 7:30 in the morning until 9:00 at night. When I share with a senior colleague that I miss giving breakfast to my toddler son and putting him to bed, he basically says, "deal" as I am fighting back tears. I love my job, I hate my job. I love my life, my life is really painful. I discover I am figuring out the meaning of suffering for me. This breathing alleviates the suffering. I want the meditation to end—I want to talk, connect, share, and feel the compassionate presence of others who understand me and will comfort me. I want the meditation to go on forever so that I can dwell in the blissful silence and bask in my retreat in the soul of the universe that I feel caring for me in each breath.

Nothingness

To ground and deepen our meditation, we are given a compelling source for reflection. It is attributed to a Hasidic teacher from the eighteenth century, Rabbi Meshullam Feibush Heller of Zbaracz, but is most probably originally a teaching of Rabbi Dov Baer of Mezritsch, whose teachings have shaped me over time.

> The spiritual intention of the "One," or the "Oneness" of reciting the Sh'ma ("Listen Israel, Adonai is our God, Adonai is One"), is to know that only the Holy One of Blessing exists in all of creation, for "God's glory fills all the earth."
>
> And the essence of this spiritual intention is for a human being to imagine oneself as "Nothingness (*ayin v'efes*)," as one's only essence is the soul within one, which is a part of divinity from above. And so one finds that all that exists in all of creation is the Holy One of Blessing as complete Oneness.[1]

---

1. Heller, *Likkutim Yekarim*, 161.

The Nothingness is a kind of coming home. Back in college, a time of taking myself apart and building myself back up (which I now know can happen at all times), my wonderful Professor Ginsburg introduced us to Judaism's version of mystical Nothingness. He showed us how the Hasidic masters taught that God was *ayin*, nothing. But God's nothingness is not the nothingness we know as human beings. Whereas we experience nothingness as annihilation, frightening loneliness, a void, God's *ayin* is the "nothingness that holds everything."

All of this is familiar, but absolutely perplexing. When I studied with Professor Ginsburg, and began to realize how much there was to learn in Judaism, how much love and companionship there could be just through study, I knew I wanted to immerse myself and become the kind of person who would know different kinds of intimacies: with text, with people, and with community. I committed myself to a path that had a far-off goal of being a rabbi. The path would challenge me, and help me grow into the kind of full person I wanted to become, living a life of obligations to community and humanity, with a personal spiritual life that was intimate yet shared. I would have role models, teachers, and mentors along the way who would provide some of what I yearned for. Most of all, they would understand my yearnings.

But all of this is a "something," not "nothing." And yet, here I find myself, with everything humming in my life: beautiful companionship and family, a great job, space to be a rabbi in a thriving and dynamic community. And yet, within all that is beautiful and wonderful, there is pain. I have to deal with this pain. I can't stay in retreat forever. But the nothingness is profound. I know it is more profound than I will ever be able to put into words over the course of my rabbinic career.

Even the nothingness has a shape and a practice. It has to. We are not a monastic tradition; we live in and embrace the world. And so, all the ways in which I make myself available to people so as to connect in a genuine and sincere way, that is the sharing of a full "nothingness." As with the Hasidic teaching, when I play with my kids, really play with them, as if I'm not just entertaining them when what I really want to do is watch TV, read a book or just veg, that is me doing *tzimtzum*, contracting so as to give them space to enjoy the beauty of being alive in this world. My toddler son sometimes has a hard time figuring out what to do with himself, so play can sometimes be a challenge. Judy and I resolve to work harder to focus on him in those moments. In my work life, which frequently overwhelms and sometimes is a surrogate for my personal life, I want to worry less about being the rabbi of my mind, and respond more to the needs of the moment with the rigor and depth I demand of myself, even if it's the crummy Purim Carnival my colleagues dumped on me. For myself, I read trade books on surviving as "associate clergy" as well as some great work by the Catholic monk and author Thomas Merton. The "survival" book reassures me that checking my ego at the door, making myself a little more "nothing," will be a rewarding, if temporary, practice for its own sake. Merton, with great lyricism, directness, and spiritual force, tells me the same thing, and tears well up as I recognize myself in both books, and the relief and renewed belief in myself that embracing "nothingness" will promise.

Spiritual Practice

So I am very excited to speak with Sylvia at our check-in during the retreat. She is so full of love, and I want nothing more than to please her, to show her how earnest a seeker I am, how I think about everything she says, and how I am truly engaging this practice. I also love being in her company because she gives of her love so easily that I know I don't have to try to please her to be the recipient of her laughter, her wisdom, or her generosity. But I do have something to share. I am working hard at maintaining the focus on the breath, the retreat into the "nothingness" that gives me connection to the compassionate soul of everything. I am not embarrassed or ashamed to admit that, after the first thirty seconds (if that many) I am pulled back to all kinds of afflicting thoughts. That is part of the practice, and Sylvia knows this well.

I tell Sylvia how well the "watching them go by, like a tape" works for me. That instruction is for me the key to maintaining my contact with the nothingness that is fullness, the experience that will give me kindness and compassion, but also strength and wisdom. I tell her how the last meditation session went down. The beginning was all bliss and beauty as I was able to focus on the breath, and that experience occupied my consciousness to the exclusion of everything else. But then I thought about my son, and his therapies. Even though I was in meditation, I saw how my mind went into its familiar routine. I felt the ever-present sense of dread that accompanied the fact that my son needed these therapies. Regrettably, I saw how my mind was inexorably pulled to a series of future disasters: my son would have no friends in kindergarten, he would never do the enjoyable things kids typically do, he would be unable to sustain friendships. I then saw my mind take a comforting and rational turn, which was to acknowledge how those projections are mere fantasies, products of an afflicted mind, as I remind myself how much he has grown and how much he is loved. But the final triumph, which I am very proud to share with Sylvia, is that I *noticed* and *observed* all these patterns of thought as they were happening, and my ability to do that forestalled my usual tendency to get wrapped up in these obsessive mental gymnastics. Instead of being immersed in my own thoughts and ego, I could return to the breath, to the real source of wisdom and compassion, both for me and for everyone I loved. With the confidence born of a first time success, I told Sylvia that the experience showed me that when these thoughts occupy my mind in the future, I will have the ability to hold onto the raging love I have for my kids, yet keep at bay the destructive habits of mind that cause me so much fear and pain.

Sylvia took a thoughtful pause, and with her typical blend of patience and wisdom, responded, "Sometimes." She explained, "When it comes to the health and happiness of your children, you always walk a thin line."

And I knew immediately she was right. Not because I admired her so much, but because her kindness and insight instantly conveyed the truth of what I was trying to do: escape the moment rather than live in it. Our retreat, and the entire eighteen months of the program, had been filled with so many beautiful and meaningful teachings and aspirations: to be present, to be whole, to find the awe in everything, to work for justice after glimpsing that awe. But all of the hoopla around what we were experiencing was truly secondary to the basic work day to day of walking that thin line between great promise and great fear, which for me was a version of feeling the embrace of love along with searing loneliness. No teaching, philosophy of religion, view of God, or meditation practice can take that away from me. In my life, it all goes back to my father leaving me. But what all of the study, community, ritual practice, and everything else about Judaism *has* given me is a series of reminders of how the fear of loneliness does not need to define us. In this way, my experience with Sylvia taught me that the things that trigger my fear of loneliness are the accumulation of stimuli I have acquired over time—they are my baggage, my "things," and I can practice unpacking them through the experience of "Nothingness," which in this instance was accomplished through mindfulness meditation. And sometimes in those moments of meditation, it really works.

Except that I am not really a disciplined meditator, and in response to this Sylvia taught me something else about incorporating this healing "Nothingness" into my life. At our last retreat, I confessed to Sylvia that, while I can say that meditation had become part of my life's repertoire, I was not a "halakhic meditator," meaning that I did not practice with the regularity and discipline that governed my traditional Jewish practice. Frankly, it was enough to keep on track with what Jewish tradition required of me to pray daily, observe Shabbat and holidays (major and minor), keep kosher, and give *tzedakah*, so that adding meditation as if it were an obligation was just too much. Sylvia, generous as always, laughed with me and said, "Meditation isn't my spiritual practice." A master, Sylvia allowed for a pregnant pause wherein I could feel some cognitive dissonance. And then her great teaching: "My *life* is my spiritual practice."

I try to live by Sylvia's words and her example. My life, with all of its joy and the small measure of pain, and with all my longing and skepticism, is one in which I try to live with some sense of spiritual practice. I go through all the modes I have tried to express in this book. There are times when I feel myself yearning, and through that yearning I attach to a source of mystery. I often feel far from any feeling about God, yet take great inspiration, joy, and reassurance from relationships in community. The intimacy I find with my love, Judy, with my children, and the closeness of friends I always experience as sacred, even if that closeness is sometimes elusive. If I were to suddenly lose all spiritual feeling, I hope that I would still cling to a sense of moral obligation to humanity. I am never static, though I have an unfortunate habit of accommodating myself to the outside world in a way that dulls the senses and my capacity for surprise. But then I have my family, my community, a stray teaching or an unexpectedly beautiful or poignant surprise to shake me out of my complacency. However, two things remain constant and have been so since I was fifteen and first awoke to questions about existence and God: my father is absent and I know almost zero about God. To heal and grow, I will have to embrace the nothingness of both.

Bibliography

Baal Shem Tov, Israel. *Tz'va'at Ha Rivash*. Brooklyn, NY: Kehot, 1975.

Babylonian Talmud. Vilna. Reprint. Jerusalem: Tal-Man, 1981.

Bialik, Hayim Nachman, and Yehoshua Hana Ravnitzky, eds. *The Book of Legends, Sefer Ha-Aggadah, Legends from the Talmud and Midrash*. Translated by William G. Braude. New York: Schocken, 1992.

Buber, Martin. *I and Thou*. New York: Scribners, 1970.

Cohen, Aryeh. *Justice in the City*. Brighton, MA: Academic Studies, 2013.

Dov Baer of Mezritsch. *Maggid Devarav L'Ya'akov*. Jerusalem: Yeshivat Tol'dot Aharon, 1976.

Epstein, Kalonymus Kalman. *Ma'or va-Shemesh*. Jerusalem: Mir, 1997.

Heschel, Abraham Joshua. *God in Search of Man: A Philosophy of Judaism*. New York: Farrar, Straus and Giroux, 1986.

———. *Man Is Not Alone: A Philosophy of Religion*. New York: Farrar, Straus and Giroux, 1992.

———. *Torah min Ha-Shamayim b'Aspeklaria shel ha Dorot*. 3 vols. New York: Soncino, 1962.

Kaplan, Mordecai. *Judaism as a Civilization*. New York: Schocken, 1972.

Levinas, Emmanuel. *Nine Talmudic Readings*. Bloomington, IN: Indiana University Press, 1990.

Matt, Daniel. "Ayin: The Concept of Nothing in Jewish Mysticism." In *Essential Papers on Kabbalah*, edited by Lawrence Fine, 67–108. New York: New York University Press, 1995.

Meshullam Feibush Heller of Zbaracz. *Likkutim Yekarim*. Jerusalem: Ma'arechet Divrei Emunah Toldot Aharon, 1974.

Midrash Rabbah. 3 vols. New York: KTAV, n.d.

Miqra'ot Gedolot. Jerusalem: Mesorah, 1975.

Nachman of Bratslav. *Likkutei MoHaRan*. Jerusalem: Chasidei Breslov, 1994.

Plaskow, Judith. *Standing Again at Sinai: Judaism from a Feminist Perspective*. New York: Harper and Row, 1990.

Rubenstein, Richard. *After Auschwitz*. Indianapolis: Bobbs-Merrill, 1981.

Scholem, Gershom. *Major Trends in Jewish Mysticism*. New York: Schocken, 1961.

Shapira, Kalonymus Kalman. *B'nai Machshavah Tovah*. Jerusalem: Va'ad Chassidei Piasetzna, 1979.

Tanakh. JPS Hebrew-English. Philadelphia: Jewish Publication Society, 1999.

Vital, Chayim. *Sefer Etz Chayim*. 1891. Reprint. Jerusalem: Offset Brody-Katz, 1975.

CPSIA information can be obtained
at www.ICGtesting.com
Printed in the USA
LVHW041748041218
599245LV00004B/414/P